MON INTERNATIONAL LIB
of Science, Technology, Engineering
The 1000-volume original pap
industrial training an
Publisher: Rob

Politics and Economic Policy in the UK since 1964

THE JEKYLL AND HYDE YEARS

Politics and Economic Policy in the UK since 1964

THE JEKYLL AND HYDE YEARS

BY

MICHAEL STEWART

PERGAMON PRESS

OXFORD · NEW YORK · TORONTO · SYDNEY · PARIS · FRANKFURT

U.K.	Pergamon Press Ltd., Headington Hill Hall, Oxford OX3 0BW, England
U.S.A.	Pergamon Press Inc., Maxwell House, Fairview Park, Elmsford, New York 10523, U.S.A.
CANADA	Pergamon of Canada Ltd., 75 The East Mall, Toronto, Ontario, Canada
AUSTRALIA	Pergamon Press (Aust.) Pty. Ltd., 19a Boundary Street, Rushcutters Bay, N.S.W. 2011, Australia
FRANCE	Pergamon Press SARL, 24 rue des Ecoles, 75240 Paris, Cedex 05, France
FEDERAL REPUBLIC OF GERMANY	Pergamon Press GmbH, 6242 Kronberg-Taunus, Pferdstrasse 1, Federal Republic of Germany

This edition 1978

First published 1977 under the title: *The Jekyll & Hyde Years: Politics & Economic Policy since 1964* by J. M. Dent & Sons Ltd
For Bibliographic purposes this volume should be cited as: Stewart M *Politics & Economic Policy in the UK since 1964.* Pergamon Press Ltd 1978.

British Library Cataloguing in Publication Data

Stewart, Michael, b.1933
Politics and Economic Policy in the UK Since 1964:
The Jekyll and Hyde years.
1. Great Britain. 2. Economic policy - 1945-
I. Title
330.9'4110856 HC256.5 78-40447

ISBN 0-08-022469-5

Printed in Great Britain by
Cox & Wyman Ltd., London, Fakenham and Reading

CONTENTS

PREFACE

In writing this book I have received assistance from a large number of people, only a few of whom can be mentioned. I am particularly grateful to Brian Lapping and Frances Stewart, each of whom went through the original manuscript with a ruthless eye for lack of logic, relevance and coherence; also to Peter Jay and David Watt, who both found time to make some valuable suggestions. I am much indebted for research assistance to Sally Harrison, whose contribution was immensely helpful; also to Lyn Kemp, Gideon Morris, Stephen Potter and Richard Stanley for digging out a variety of facts and figures. Needless to say, none of these people can be blamed in any way for the final version. The book would probably never have appeared at all but for Margaret Dunphy's indefatigable labours at the typewriter. And I must, finally, record my obvious indebtedness to Jane Austen, Charles Dickens, Thomas Hardy, Rudyard Kipling and Robert Louis Stevenson, the titles of some of whose works seemed so aptly to summarize successive phases of the story, and indeed the story as a whole.

Chapter I
INTRODUCTION

The year 1964 was a significant one in Britain's post-war history. It marked the end of thirteen years of Conservative government. It also marked the end of an era in a wider sense. Until then, the centre of the political stage had been occupied by men whose formative period in politics had been spent before and during the Second World War, and whose interests for the most part lay in the traditional issues of defence and foreign affairs. Of the five post-war Prime Ministers, only Macmillan had any real feel for economic policy, and only Attlee seemed to have come to terms with the fact that Britain was no longer the centre of a great empire. Now a new generation was taking over. The next three Prime Ministers – Wilson, Heath and eventually Callaghan – were all men who had come to politics after the war, who had grappled as Ministers with difficult economic issues, and who had a keen appreciation of the need to improve the performance of the British economy and, in particular, to increase its lagging rate of growth. The year 1964 seemed to mark the beginning of a new era, in which successful economic policies would be the government's main concern.

Whatever the intentions, the results were dismal. In 1963 the Labour Party had attacked the Conservative record since 1951 as 'Twelve Wasted Years'. The same phrase would have been an even more apposite description of 1964–76. Although living standards[1] were higher in 1976 than in 1964, the increase was only about a fifth – compared with a rise of more than a third between 1951 and 1964. Judged by all the other main criteria of economic policy – unemployment, the rate of inflation, the balance of payments position – the situation was far worse in 1976 than in 1964.

By no means all the blame for this sorry state of affairs can be attributed to the economic policies of successive British governments. Britain is dependent on world forces – notably those

[1] Defined as gross domestic product (GDP) per head.

affecting the price of the food and materials it needs to import in large quantities – over which it has little or no control. Similarly, the rules of various international groupings to which Britain belongs, such as the International Monetary Fund (IMF), the General Agreement on Tariffs and Trade (GATT) and in recent years the European Economic Community (EEC), restrict the country's freedom of action, and can sometimes work to its disadvantage. Domestically, too, there are forces in the field – perhaps more than in most comparable countries – which limit the scope for successful economic policies. It is probably not too fanciful to see Britain as still suffering the after-effects of sudden loss of empire, with values, traditions and educational priorities not yet fully adapted to its new role as a second-rank industrial country needing to fight hard to earn its living. It is certainly possible to see it as still suffering from the legacy of the Industrial Revolution, with class divisions and antagonisms which have no close parallel in other countries. These social tensions and anachronistic attitudes may well have played a major role in holding Britain back, by inhibiting new investment, reinforcing resistance to the introduction of new techniques, encouraging sterile argument and self-defeating quarrels, and diverting attention away from the creation and equitable distribution of greater prosperity.

Nevertheless, whatever the constraints, economic policies have to be devised and administered: governments have to do the best job they can in an imperfect world. The main aim of this book is to examine the economic policies which have been pursued by successive governments in Britain since 1964, in the light of the two sets of factors which principally determine these policies. One of these is what might be described as the prevailing economic orthodoxy: the set of beliefs about how the economy works, and what causes have what effects, to which the civil servants and others who formulate, advise on or influence economic policy subscribe. The other set of factors is political, comprehending a spectrum from the values and aspirations of the main political parties to the more mundane need of politicians to retain the allegiance of their supporters and win elections.

The first of these factors – the prevailing economic orthodoxy since 1964 – has been Keynesian demand management. Originally prescribed in Keynes' *General Theory*, and first put into practice in the Kingsley Wood budget of 1941, this really came into its own in the early post-war years. The prime responsibility of government, according to this new approach, was to use fiscal and monetary policy to ensure that there was enough effective demand in the economy to maintain full employment, but not so much as to cause 'demand-pull' inflation. Similarly, it came to be accepted that other policy instruments had to be used to achieve other objectives: notably exchange rate policy to secure a satisfactory balance of payments outcome, incomes policy to prevent trade unions from using the full force of their bargaining power to create and perpetuate 'cost-push' inflation, and selective industrial intervention to strengthen key sectors of the economy. This economic orthodoxy has come under increasing fire in recent years, particularly from the 'monetarist' school of economists, which argues that the main instruments of a satisfactory economic policy are a slow and steady increase in the supply of money and a more or less balanced budget. The extent to which these and other criticisms have influenced the conduct of economic policy has so far been fairly limited: although more attention was being paid to monetary variables and the size of the government's budget deficit in the mid-1970s than the mid-1960s, the guiding spirit of economic policy was still fundamentally Keynesian.

One of the themes running through this book is that this adherence to Keynesian policies was right. There have been many mistakes in the way economic policy has been formulated and implemented, ranging from technical faults in the economic models used for forecasting, to major errors of judgment by politicians or civil servants. But these mistakes reflect human fallibility in an unpredictable world. They may suggest that Keynesian policies should have been pursued with greater care or a greater sense of responsibility. They do not suggest that the whole approach has been wrong.

However, it is not only the prevailing economic orthodoxy which determines the economic policy which a government pursues. Politics influences it as well. Another of the themes running through this book is that since 1964 the way in which the two-party system has been operating in Britain has militated against a coherent economic policy and has had an adverse effect on the country's economic performance. The two main parties, of course, have different political and economic philosophies, and very largely represent different kinds of people. Nevertheless, such differences do not explain or justify the extent to which the essentially consensus policies which each party has eventually come to pursue when in office have been repudiated by it when in opposition.

There is much in the history of economic policy since 1964 that is reminiscent of Robert Louis Stevenson's story *The Strange Case of Dr Jekyll and Mr Hyde.* In that story, the virtuous and amiable Dr Jekyll from time to time administers to himself a drug which brings to the surface all the baser elements in his nature, turning him into the evil and dangerous Mr Hyde. In due course – and sometimes after much damage has been done – Mr Hyde takes a dose of the same drug, and is transformed back into Dr Jekyll. Although the gruesome denouement of the tale – in which the personality of Dr Jekyll becomes permanently submerged by that of Mr Hyde – has so far been mercifully denied us, the switches of personality have not. On each occasion, it is the loss of office which has acted on the governing party like Dr Jekyll's drug. Having pursued, during its last two or three years in office, essentially virtuous and responsible policies, now, in the wilderness of opposition, it becomes a Mr Hyde – irresponsible, wild, savaging what it previously held dear. This Hyde-like phase unfortunately outlasts the party's period in opposition, continuing to influence its actions for the first year or two after it has again become the government. Only then does another dose of the drug lead to the responsible Dr Jekyll reassuming control.

To be sure, the analogy is not a perfect one. In particular, the abandonment of ideas with which it came into office does not always represent a government's conversion from wild rhetoric to sober reality; sometimes – especially in the case of a Labour government – it can represent a feeble surrender to the civil service and the powerful forces in Britain fighting to maintain the status quo. But by and large this has not been the trouble since 1964: as far as economic policy is concerned, the later stages of each government's period of office have been by far the most sensible and successful.

The two basic failures of economic policy since 1964 have been the failure to establish a workable long-term incomes policy and the failure to achieve a high and stable rate of industrial investment. On both counts, the Jekyll and Hyde syndrome has much to answer for. As long ago as the 1944 White Paper on *Employment Policy* it was recognized that if the guarantee of full employment and the practice of free collective bargaining were not to result in inflation it was 'essential that employers and workers should exercise moderation in wages matters' (para. 49). Every post-war government has in the end come to rely on an incomes policy. But the effectiveness of this crucial new instrument of policy has been much diminished by the fact that the party which happens to be in opposition – disregarding what it had itself done when in office, and would do again – has always attacked and attempted to discredit the incomes policy of the day. Much the same is true of policies designed to modernize the industrial sector of the economy and thus achieve a respectable growth in output and exports. The industrial and regional policies which each party has eventually come to pursue when in office have not been so very different from each other; but in opposition, and their early days in office, they have talked and acted in a way which has undone much of the useful work of their predecessor. This charge – like one or two other charges discussed at length in the book – lies particularly heavily against the Conservative government of 1970–74; but Labour has by no means been blameless.

The Jekyll and Hyde theme recurs from time to time throughout the book, and some of its implications are briefly taken up in the concluding chapter. But it is not meant to be unduly obtrusive. No single theme can adequately account for the failures of British economic policy since 1964. The explanations are complex, and the lessons are many.

Chapter 2

THE EBB TIDE

Background to 1964

ECONOMIC PROBLEMS

The most remarkable thing about the British economy in 1964 was that it had enjoyed full employment for nearly a quarter of a century. True, there had been some ups and downs, with unemployment rising once or twice to 3 per cent or so; but over the period as a whole it had averaged less than 2 per cent. This was nothing compared with the 1920s, when it had averaged 11 per cent, or the 1930s, when it had averaged 16 per cent. Although a few economists took the view that post-war full employment had been largely a matter of luck,[1] easily the majority view was that it represented the fruits of the Keynesian revolution. In 1964, the problem of maintaining full employment seemed to have been solved.

Other economic problems, however, had clearly not been solved. One was the problem of rising prices. Since the end of the war retail prices had been rising, on average, by about 4 per cent a year. This contrasted with pre-war experience,[2] and aroused considerable misgivings, particularly in conservative quarters. Inflation, it was contended, had two particular disadvantages. It hit people on fixed incomes, and many such people were among the poorest in the community. And – because it was proceeding faster in Britain than in most other countries – it resulted, under the system of fixed exchange rates negotiated in 1944 at Bretton Woods, in a decline in Britain's international competitiveness: exports became more difficult to sell, imports flooded in. Despite these disadvantages, inflation was regarded as a worrying rather than a critical problem. There were ways of coping with its adverse effects. Those on fixed incomes derived from the state – such as old-age pensioners – could be, and

[1] See pp. 144–5.

[2] Prices rose very little between 1900 and 1914. They more than doubled during and immediately after the First World War, but then fell again. In 1946 prices were still lower than they had been in 1920 (LCES, 1972, Table E).

to a considerable extent were, insulated against inflation by increasing their incomes in line with average earnings. And if inflation led to the exchange rate becoming over-valued then, in the last resort, the exchange rate could be changed: it was for precisely this reason that sterling had been devalued in 1949. As long as the 4 per cent inflation rate showed no signs of speeding up – and there were no such signs in 1964 – it could be regarded as an acceptable price to pay for the maintenance of full employment.

Nevertheless, in the absence of exchange rate changes, Britain's above-average inflation rate was the main cause of a balance of payments problem which, by 1964, had come to seem chronic. From time to time there were surpluses on current account, but more often there were deficits; and as time went on the surpluses grew smaller and the deficits grew bigger. This might not have mattered quite so much but for two unfortunate aspects of Britain's post-war position. One was that sterling continued to be, as it had been since the nineteenth century, an important reserve and trading currency, second only to the dollar in the extent to which it was held by governments and businesses all over the world. Yet in relation to these sterling liabilities – many of them incurred during the war – Britain's own reserves of gold and dollars were small. To a far greater extent than other countries, Britain had to worry about the way that domestic economic developments would be viewed by foreigners. A loss of confidence in Britain by the holders of sterling could lead to a run on the pound – a demand that sterling be changed into gold or dollars – on a scale that Britain simply could not meet. The second unfortunate fact was that the nation – particularly the private sector – continued to invest capital abroad on a scale which might have been appropriate in the nineteenth century, but made little sense in the context of the chronically weak current account of the 1950s and 1960s.

Since the mid-1950s the Conservative Government had always reacted to the periodic balance of payments crises and the periodic worries about inflation by deflating the economy. By increasing taxes and interest rates, and cutting back public expenditure, the Government would reduce the level of demand in the economy. Imports would fall, exports – perhaps – would rise a little, unions and employers would find it a little more difficult to exact wage increases and push up prices. The balance of payments would improve, the rate of inflation would slacken a fraction, foreigners would be reassured and stop taking their money out of London. But the trouble about these periodic bouts of deflation was that by creating excess capacity and unemployment they weakened the incentive to invest and strengthened the resistance of workers to the introduction of new and more productive methods. They thus contributed to what, by 1964, seemed Britain's greatest economic problem: its slow rate of growth.

Between 1950 and 1964 Britain's GDP (at constant prices) grew at an average rate of 3 per cent a year. This was a very respectable performance by reference to the period between the wars, when the growth rate had been well under 2 per cent; and indeed by reference to the first half of the 1970s, when it was only 1½ per cent. Nevertheless, it was disappointing compared with what was being achieved in other countries: during the 1950s and early 1960s France, Germany, Italy and Japan all notched up growth rates of 5 per cent or more.[1]

In 1954 the Chancellor of the Exchequer, Mr Butler, set out as a long-term target the doubling of the standard of living in twenty-five years. Making the heroic assumption – much challenged in recent years – that the standard of living can be defined as GDP per head, this implied an average increase in GDP per head of 2.8 per cent a year for the next twenty-five years; and on the basis of the population projections then available, an annual increase in GDP of about 3¼ per cent. Even though the actual growth rate achieved between 1954 and 1964 fell somewhat below this target figure, it came to be felt that the target was not set high enough. Following the work of the National Economic Development Council (NEDC or 'Neddy'), set up in 1961 by the Chancellor of the Exchequer, Selwyn Lloyd, it became fashionable to talk in terms of a growth rate of 4 per cent. One of the main issues in the 1964 election was which party would be more likely to achieve this faster growth rate.

PARTY OBJECTIVES

Both the main political parties subscribe to the four basic objectives of economic policy – full employment, a reasonably rapid growth rate, stable prices and a satisfactory balance of payments. But this is not to say that they both emphasize the same objectives to the same extent. In two particular ways, one might expect the economic objectives of a Labour government to differ from those of a Conservative government.

[1] Maddison, 1964 and OECD *Main Economic Indicators,* June 1968.

The first difference relates to the 'trade-off' which, many economists would argue, exists between unemployment and inflation. According to this view, the lower the level of unemployment, and hence the more intense the pressure of demand for labour, the faster is likely to be the rate of inflation. The figures given in the previous section, of the very high rate of unemployment and the falling price level between the wars, and the very low rate of unemployment and steady rise in prices after the war, are an indication of this trade-off.[1] The particular trade-off chosen – the relative emphasis put on full employment and price stability – might well be different under a Labour government from under a Conservative government. Some four-fifths of Labour voters are manual workers, almost entirely dependent for their livelihood on having a job.[2] Conservative voters, half or more of whom are middle class, are more likely to have some capital, which will cushion them for a while against some of the effects of unemployment; and many of them have the kind of salaried or professional jobs where unemployment has historically been slow to strike. It is plausible, therefore, to suppose that a Labour government will attach even more importance to full employment than a Conservative government. By the same token, a Conservative government may attach more weight to price stability than a Labour government. It is those fixed incomes derived from private wealth or pension arrangements, rather than those, such as old-age pensions, which are derived from the state and which are regularly uprated, which are hardest hit by inflation. Further, inflation is sometimes associated with a shift in the distribution of the national income away from profits, dividends, rents and interest payments in favour of wages and salaries. Of course, the very fact that Labour may be suspected of favouring full employment at the expense of price stability, and the Conservatives of favouring price stability at the expense of full employment, may itself modify the effect of these considerations on the policy actually adopted. Nevertheless, one might still expect a Conservative government to choose a somewhat different trade-off from a Labour one.

[1] The numerical value of the trade-off, and in particular the question of whether there is any systematic variation in the inflation rate within the range of unemployment that would now be regarded as politically acceptable, are controversial issues. They are discussed more fully in chapter 5.

[2] Any breakdown of voters by class must necessarily be somewhat approximate. Estimates by Abrams, quoted in Blondel, 1963 (revised edn., 1974), p. 55, suggest that about 85 per cent of Labour voters are manual working class, and about 55 per cent of Conservative voters are middle class. Gallup Poll figures, quoted in Rose, 1974, p. 33, imply somewhat lower figures, of approximately 75 per cent and 50 per cent respectively.

The second basic difference one might expect to see between the economic objectives of a Labour and a Conservative government relates to the emphasis put on equality. A Labour objective, to which the Conservative Party does not noticeably subscribe, is the promotion of a greater degree of economic and social equality. For many Labour voters greater economic equality coincides with self-interest; for others, including many of the middle-class Labour voters, it may be more a matter of moral or intellectual conviction: socialism is about equality. Whatever the mixture of motives, a Labour government will be expected by many of its supporters to adopt policies which redistribute income and wealth.

Apart from its intrinsic importance, this egalitarian theme will also have implications for the vigour with which the four main consensus objectives are pursued. For the measures needed to promote greater equality may either coincide or conflict with the measures needed to promote other economic objectives. When there is full employment, for example, the distribution of income is likely to be more equal (or less unequal) than when there is substantial unemployment. This will reinforce the importance Labour attaches to the maintenance of full employment. On the other hand it is often argued that measures which are undoubtedly egalitarian in their effect, such as a highly progressive tax structure, with very fierce marginal rates of tax on high earned and unearned incomes, have a disincentive effect on effort and on saving, and thus make for a sluggish rate of growth. If this argument that there is a trade-off between growth and equality is accepted, then Labour governments should perhaps choose slower growth in the interests of greater equality. (But because the existence of such a trade-off is inconvenient for socialist ideology, in practice the evidence that there is no real conflict between equality and growth, and that to some extent they may be self-reinforcing, will tend to be believed in preference to evidence which demonstrates the opposite.)

Conservative governments are not without similar problems. Conservatives are inclined to believe – or at any rate to claim – that there is a spectrum of economic conditions with equality at one end and freedom at the other, and that it is better to be nearer the freedom end than the equality end. But it is clear that freedom – though a difficult concept to define – may conflict with some of the common economic objectives. In one sense, for example, economic freedom is incompatible with the maintenance of full employment; for the essence of the Keynesian revolution is acceptance of the fact that an economy, left to operate freely and without government intervention, will not tend automatically – as classical economists had supposed – to operate at full employment. More topically, many people would now argue that freedom on the part of trade unions and employers to fix wages and prices on the basis of free collective bargaining and the untrammelled pursuit of profit is incompatible with a reasonable degree of price stability. If the argument is accepted, Conservative governments must settle for either more inflation or less freedom. (But, as with Labour's choice between equality and growth, there will be a strong temptation to disregard evidence that free-market behaviour conflicts with price stability in favour of evidence that they are compatible or even mutually supporting conditions.)

This description of some of the factors which affect the economic policies that Labour and Conservative governments will try to pursue is necessarily brief and over-simplified. It could, for example, be extended to take account of the fact that political parties seeking to obtain or retain office cannot normally rely solely on the votes of their natural supporters; they need to win the floating voter and occupy the middle ground. Nevertheless, it may serve as a reminder that Labour and Conservative governments have overlapping but by no means identical economic objectives, and that their performance should be judged accordingly.

MANIPULATING DEMAND

During the 1950s it became apparent that there was an earthier connection between politics and economic policy than the way in which different political philosophies might be reflected in the trade-off chosen between different economic objectives. Now that Keynesian demand management had become the central feature of economic policy, governments were in a position to manipulate the economic cycle so as to coincide with the electoral cycle. This – said the critics – was exactly what happened. Before an election, demand would be expanded, incomes and consumers' expenditure would rise, unemployment would fall, and a grateful nation would vote the government back in.[1] After the election, as the high pressure of

[1] Later research (Butler and Stokes, 1969) confirmed that although economic recession might slightly strengthen the class polarization of party support, a much more important tendency was for both middle-class and working-class voters to reward or punish the government of the day according to whether the economic situation was good or bad.

demand caused rising prices and mounting balance of payments difficulties, demand would be cut back again, output would fall and unemployment rise. Inflationary pressures would ease, the balance of payments would move back into surplus. In good time for the next election, this 'stop' phase of the cycle would be brought to an end and the 'go' phase would start again.

To what extent this is a valid interpretation of events in the 1950s and early 1960s remains a matter of argument. But the case against the Conservative Governments of the time is a strong one. The first example came in the mid-1950s. The expansion which got under way in 1953 was so strong that by early 1955 it had created acute inflationary pressure, with the rate of unemployment falling to a lower level than in any peacetime year before or since. The Chancellor of the Exchequer, Mr Butler, responded to this by raising Bank Rate and introducing some modest hire purchase controls in February, but then proceeded to make nonsense of that action – and indeed of the whole concept of demand management – by reducing income tax by 6d. (six old pence) in the pound in his Budget in April. Not even the most charitably disposed could fail to observe that in May there was a general election, at which the Conservatives were returned with a much increased majority and that, beginning in July and extending over the next two years, came a series of restrictive measures consisting of tougher hire purchase controls, a credit squeeze, cuts in public investment and increases in taxation.

By 1958 this 'stop' phase had lasted long enough: the balance of payments was in healthy surplus, unemployment had risen to a post-war peak, and the Government was losing by-elections. And so history was repeated. The 1958 Budget was only slightly expansionary, but by July credit controls and restrictions on public expenditure were being relaxed, and this process continued throughout the autumn. The April 1959 Budget was a real bonanza: the standard rate of income tax was reduced by 9d. in the pound, purchase tax was cut, and 2d. a pint was taken off the price of beer. The size of the stimulus was partly to be explained by the fact that the Chancellor's advisers 'had underestimated the delayed-action effect of his earlier measures, and of the head of steam that was now building up in the economy' (Brittan, 1971, p. 225). But it is hard to believe that electoral calculations played no part.[1] By the autumn, consumption was soaring, and unemployment was falling fast. A lot

[1] Brittan (op. cit., p. 224) notes that 'Mr Amory (the Chancellor) was told by his colleagues that he was the one man who could lose the Conservatives the election'.

of people seemed to agree with Mr Macmillan's verdict that the nation had 'never had it so good', for they returned his Government in the October election with an increased majority. But, as in 1955, the days of wine and roses were rapidly succeeded by a day of reckoning. Imports soared, the balance of payments plunged into the red. By the spring of 1960 the Government was already taking steps to squeeze credit and cut consumers' expenditure, and in July 1961 it introduced the fiercest deflationary package yet. The economy soon came off the boil, the balance of payments improved, and unemployment rose to a new post-war peak.

And so history started to repeat itself again. By mid-1962 the Government had started to ease credit, reduce interest rates, and cut purchase tax, and this process was carried further when the new Chancellor, Mr Maudling, introduced an expansionary Budget in 1963. Once again, consumers' expenditure started to rise rapidly and, after a lag, unemployment began to fall. Some Conservatives began to hope that they might, after all, be heading for their fourth successive election victory. More detached observers took the view that an economic policy largely characterized by the manipulation of consumers' expenditure in the interest of winning elections was beginning to look an exceedingly unsatisfactory way of achieving the nation's longer-run economic objectives.

LABOUR AFTER 1959

Labour was shattered by the result of the 1959 general election, in which the Conservatives increased their majority from 58 to 100. This was the third election in a row that Labour had lost and, as Goldfinger observed to James Bond, 'once is happenstance; twice is coincidence; three times is enemy action'. A lot of people began to wonder whether this was not the end of the Labour Party. *Must Labour lose?* asked Mark Abrams and others (Abrams, 1960). *Can Labour win?* asked Anthony Crosland (Crosland, 1960). The answers did their best to be reassuring: in effect Abrams said 'not necessarily, but . . .' and Crosland said 'yes, provided that . . .'. But the answers summed up the mood of the time less accurately than the questions.

Crosland's answer was underpinned by the analysis he had set out a few years earlier in *The Future of Socialism*. In this book – which became the Bible of 'revisionism' – Crosland had argued that Keynesian economics had made the mixed economy a viable, indeed desirable, proposition. By using fiscal and monetary policy, full employment could be maintained and a reasonable rate of growth secured. Nationalization had become largely irrelevant to the achievement of socialism. Much more important was the promotion of greater social equality by reforming the educational system, making the tax structure more re-distributive, and increasing the proportion of the national income spent by the government on social welfare. Crosland now drew the logical conclusion from this analysis: Labour should stop being, or at any rate presenting itself as, a working-class party dedicated to a lot more nationalization, and change its image into that of a progressive, national, social-democratic party, committed to the promotion of greater equality and social justice.

The revisionist thesis of Crosland and other social democrats came under fierce attack from the socialists on the left of the party. Much of this hostility was instinctive and atavistic: the tribal gods were being threatened. But some of it was reasoned. To many on the left, the mixed economy was still capitalism, doomed by its inner contradictions. To others, more prosaically, it appeared that the mixed economy, with its waste and frivolous use of resources, could not compete in the growth of material prosperity with the centrally-planned economies of the Communist bloc: peaceful competition would indeed enable Khrushchev to bury us. Either way, the message was clear: if breakdown and chaos, or Communism or some other form of totalitarianism, were to be avoided, the structure of the Western economies must be radically changed and public ownership and accountability drastically extended. As Richard Crossman put it (Crossman, 1960) the Labour Party must not present itself as 'an alternative board of management for the Affluent Society', but hold itself in reserve – even if this meant its being out of office for much longer periods than the Tories – 'and prepare for the creeping crisis that will confront the West before the end of this decade'

Hugh Gaitskell, who had succeeded Attlee as Leader of the Labour Party in 1955, was in no doubt which side of the argument he was on. Convinced that the Crosland thesis was right, and that Labour would never be elected as long as it was predominantly associated with nationalization, he pursued the point to its logical conclusion: Clause Four of the Labour Party's constitution, which referred among other things to 'the common ownership of the means of production, distribution and exchange' should be amended, to make clear to people that although the party might wish to push the frontiers of public ownership forward a bit here and there, it had no intention of going in for a policy of wholesale nationalization.

It was magnificent, but it was madness. Revise the party's constitution? As soon tamper with the holy scriptures. Hackles rose all over the Labour movement. Four months later Gaitskell conceded defeat. Clause Four stayed as it was. All the same, the public at large had been able to register the fact that at least the Leader of the Labour Party was opposed to any massive new programme of nationalization. And they soon had the chance to observe that as well as being, by the standards of the left of the Labour Party, a moderate, Gaitskell was prepared – in his own words – 'to fight and fight and fight again' to get his views accepted by the party. If Clause Four was no more than a skirmish on the road to 1964, unilateral nuclear disarmament was a battle. Those within the party who thought that nuclear weapons were so hideously dangerous that Britain should unilaterally renounce their manufacture and use had failed to convince the party in 1959; but at the annual conference in Scarborough the following year they won, and the party was committed to unilateral disarmament. To Gaitskell, such a policy was a much surer way to party suicide than possession of the bomb was to national suicide, and after strenuous efforts he succeeded in getting the policy reversed at the annual conference the following year. But the struggle left its mark on the party and, perhaps more fatally, on himself.

Without Gaitskell's tragic death early in 1963 the rest of the decade might have been very different. One view is that the Labour Party would have remained so badly disunited under Gaitskell that it would not have succeeded in gaining its hairs-breadth victory at the next election; in which case it might well have split or disintegrated. A more plausible view, perhaps, is that the personal standing in the nation at large which Gaitskell had attained at the time of his death – attested by the extraordinary emotion which this occasioned – would have secured him a workable majority in 1964; and that the Party's policies in office would have displayed a strategic grip and sense of direction which in the event were sadly lacking.

Labour had lost its Achilles three years earlier, with the death of Aneurin Bevan. Now it had lost its Agamemnon. But at least its next leader turned out to have many of the qualities of an Odysseus. Harold Wilson had first entered the Cabinet in 1947, at the age of thirty-one, but had resigned with Aneurin Bevan in 1951 in protest against the size of the Attlee government's rearmament programme, and the decision of Gaitskell – then Chancellor of the Exchequer – to finance a small part of the programme by imposing charges on false teeth and spectacles. Throughout the 1950s he remained a leading member of the left-wing 'Bevanite' group of MPs, and continued to be regarded by the left wing of the Labour Party as one of their own long after, as Prime Minister, it had become clear that he was far from being on the extreme left of the party. For Wilson was, above all, a pragmatist. What mattered to him was not putting left-wing ideas into practice, but holding the Labour Party together, and turning it into what he called 'the natural party of government'. Where Gaitskell had confronted, Wilson conciliated; where Gaitskell sharpened and defined, Wilson blurred and obfuscated. Gaitskell would surely have been the better Prime Minister; Harold Wilson was indubitably the better party leader. What Wilson set himself to do early in 1963 was to reunite the Labour Party and keep it united, presenting a coherent and acceptable alternative to the Conservatives in the next general election. He did this partly by presenting Labour as the party in favour of growth, change and the application to the nation's problems of the 'white heat of the technological revolution' – a relatively meaningless phrase on which everyone could agree; partly by using his superb powers of invective to draw the nation's attention to the shortcomings of the Conservatives' economic policies; but above all by retaining the allegiance of the Left within the party without alienating the Right. He succeeded brilliantly. By the beginning of 1964, the party had put behind it the quarrels over Clause Four and unilateral disarmament. It was united, in good shape, and looking forward to a fight.

ELECTION YEAR

As 1964 opened, one thing was clear: some time during the year there would have to be a general election. But when? The Prime Minister had the usual lonely problem of deciding the most favourable – or least unfavourable – moment to go to the country. Some considerations – such as the desire to avoid seeming to cling humiliatingly on to office until the last constitutionally-permitted moment – pointed to an election in the spring. But the difficulty about that was that the Conservatives were distinctly unpopular. Many people still remembered the effects of the deflationary package of July 1961, and in particular the accompanying 'pay pause', which covered most workers in the public sector, but did not formally cover either pay in the private sector, or profits and dividends.[1] The

[1] 65 per cent of the population thought the pay pause had been unfair (Butler and King, 1965).

sudden sacking of a third of the Cabinet in July 1962 did nothing to restore the party's image;[1] nor did the Profumo affair of 1963;[2] nor did the semi-feudal way in which, in October 1963, a sick Macmillan engineered the exclusion of Mr Butler as his successor as Prime Minister, and opened the way to the Foreign Secretary, Lord Home – a piece of chicanery bitterly criticised by more modern Conservatives like Iain Macleod (Macleod, 1964). The real trouble, perhaps, was that the Conservatives had now been in office for more than twelve years and were tired, over-exposed and accident-prone.

Nevertheless, hope springs eternal in the politician's breast, and Sir Alec Douglas-Home (as he had now become) decided to wait for the autumn, in the hope that something might turn up. (It seemed a wise decision: on the day he announced it Labour won the elections for the newly-constituted Greater London Council by a landslide majority of 64 to 36.) By the autumn, with incomes and consumption continuing to rise, and unemployment to fall, the Government might hope once again to receive its reward from the electorate.

However, there was a snag. Would things seem so good in the autumn? The expansionary measures of 1963 had done their work only too well, for by early 1964 the economy was growing at an annual rate of over 6 per cent – far faster than could be sustained for very long. Either the Budget would have to restrain demand quite significantly – a far cry from the goodies handed out before the 1955 and 1959 elections – or the economy might badly over-heat, leading to rising prices and a balance of payments crisis. Because of these economic uncertainties the Chancellor, Mr Maudling, wanted a spring election (Howard and West, 1965, p. 124), but may have had to decide on his Budget measures without knowing whether it would be in the spring or not.[3] In the event he chose a very mildly deflationary package, increasing tax on drink and tobacco by about £100 million. This was only half as much deflation as the National Institute of Economic and Social Research (NIESR) had called for in

[1] Macmillan later admitted this had been 'a great error' (Macmillan, 1973).

[2] The resignation of the Secretary of State for War, Mr John Profumo, from both Government and House of Commons opened a Pandora's Box of speculation about security leaks and sex orgies in high places. See Young, 1963.

[3] Sir Alec's announcement that there would be no spring election came on 9 April; the Budget was on the 14th. Sir Alec's decision had probably been taken within the previous few days, whereas the main shape of the Budget is normally decided several weeks before Budget day.

its February *Review*; and was criticized by the OECD in June as insufficient.[1]

It is not necessarily the case that Mr Maudling took less deflationary action than he would have in a non-electoral situation. He was very sensitive to the charge of playing politics with the economy (Brittan, 1971, p. 283); and was undoubtedly anxious to stick to the 4 per cent growth target which had been proposed by the NEDC and adopted by the Government the previous year, and not knock the economy on the head and depress business investment as had happened so often in the past. Moreover, although continued rapid growth was expected to lead to a balance of payments deficit, the deficit did not look as though it would be uncomfortably large. In February the NIESR put the current account deficit for 1964 at about £50 million, and the overall deficit at about £160 million;[2] and even in May, after what it regarded as an insufficiently deflationary Budget, it put the current deficit at no more than £150–200 million, and the overall deficit at £300 million. Given that much of this deficit was expected to reflect temporary stock-building of raw materials, and given the size of the reserves and the IMF credits at Britain's disposal, deficits of this order did not seem too high a price to pay for a policy that at last promised to get the economy on to a path of sustained and rapid growth. Unfortunately, things turned out very differently. Exports rose far less than everyone had expected, and imports – particularly of manufactures – rose far more. The overall balance of payments deficit for 1964 turned out to be about £800 million,[3] of which half was on current account.

Until the summer or autumn of 1964 it was possible to argue that if Britain's growth rate were speeded up first, a satisfactory balance of payments would follow. A faster rate of growth, some economists thought, would mean a more rapid rate of innovation and technological change, which would make British goods more modern and more competitive in export markets – a process which might also be helped by the slower rise in unit costs that could result from a faster rise in output. By the autumn of 1964 this idea – which had perhaps formed part of the framework of thought of Maudling and his advisers – was looking much less plausible, at any rate within the timescale within which the nation could afford to operate. How

[1] According to Brandon, 1966, p. 21, it was also less than the Treasury had been calling for.

[2] i.e. including long-term capital flows.

[3] See footnote 1 on p. 22.

much longer could the economy be allowed to expand at a rate of 4 per cent or so, sucking in extra imports and diverting goods away from export markets, in the hope that one day it would all change? Maudling himself seems to have accepted that something would have to be done, though he hoped to avoid deflation and continue a rapid rate of growth by taking direct action to improve the balance of payments; to this end he asked his officials to work out schemes for restricting the growth of imports, either by quantitative restrictions or by imposing a tariff surcharge. Curiously enough he did not, by his own account, consider devaluation as an option (Brittan, 1971, p. 285) though this would have had the advantage, among others, of encouraging exports as well as restraining imports.

No action to restrain imports was taken, however, and the situation worsened. By the later stages of the election campaign, in October, when it had become apparent that the balance of payments was going badly wrong, Labour started, with considerable effect, to capitalize on the size of the external deficit and the threats it posed for the future. Labour's moral right to do this was not, in fact, very great: James Callaghan, the Shadow Chancellor, had criticized the 1963 Budget as insufficiently expansionist, and had not criticized the 1964 Budget as insufficiently restrictive; and Harold Wilson, addressing the annual Congress of the TUC in September 1964, had criticized the 4 per cent growth target as being, in the long run, too low. One or two lone Labour voices had argued for devaluation on the grounds that sterling was over-valued, and that what was needed was export-led growth, but they were not typical of Labour thinking at this time. Morally right or not, however, Labour made the most of the mess towards which Maudling's dash for growth was inexorably leading, for Labour was worried. True, the campaign seemed to be going well – but so it had in 1959. True, they had been leading in the opinion polls since mid-1961 – but by late September this lead had disappeared. True, Wilson had been running rings round Sir Alec Douglas-Home – but perhaps, in the last resort, the English still loved a lord. With three general election defeats behind them, and an apparent Liberal resurgence taking place around them, many Labour politicians felt that it was now or never.

In the event it was now, but only just. Late on the morning after polling day, Harold Wilson calculated that he had lost by one seat (Howard and West, 1965, p. 225); and it was only when the result from the Meriden constituency came in at 2.45 p.m. that he knew that he had won. The overall majority (excluding the Speaker) turned out to be five. After thirteen years in the wilderness, Labour had ceased to be merely a party of protest, and become once again a party of power. But the question was, what would it do with it?

Chapter 3
GREAT EXPECTATIONS
October 1964-March 1966

There is an innocent enthusiasm about Labour's 1964 Election Manifesto which, in the light of subsequent events, is rather endearing. 'Let's *GO* with Labour for the NEW BRITAIN', it urges. Abroad, this new Britain will be providing dynamic new leads to the United Nations, to the Commonwealth, to NATO. At home, technology will be mobilized, resources harnessed, industries modernized, energized, revitalized. Above all, there will be *purposive planning.* Instead of the Tories' nineteenth-century free enterprise economy and unplanned society, there will be a National Economic Plan which will, among other things, increase investment, expand exports and replace inessential imports. Out of this national planning will come faster growth, and out of the fruits of this faster growth will come higher old-age pensions, better schools, new hospitals.

For Labour candidates and party workers, this was an honourable, exciting, easily communicable vision. For those civil servants assigned to spend the three weeks of the election campaign working out what the Opposition's manifesto meant, in case the Opposition became the Government, it was less satisfactory. For although the Manifesto claimed that Labour was 'poised to swing its plans into instant operation', it was clear that where it really counted – on the balance of payments – no such plans existed. There were a few vague references to 'using the tax system to encourage industries and firms to export more' and to 'encouraging British industry to supply those manufactures which swell our import bill', but nothing to indicate what Labour would actually do in the face of the balance of payments crisis it would inherit.

Too much of the blame for this should not be laid at Labour's door. Although Harold Wilson concentrated his fire on the balance of payments deficit during the later stages of the election campaign, he had no inkling of its true size. On 1 October he talked of the country running into deficit at the rate of a million pounds a day – less than

£400 million a year – and was condemned by the Conservatives for scaremongering (Wilson, 1971, p. 27). And the most up-to-date forecast available to Labour during the campaign was that contained in the August National Institute *Economic Review*, which put the overall deficit for 1964 at some £500 million. It is hardly surprising that Wilson and his Chancellor of the Exchequer, James Callaghan, should have been startled to learn, on reaching their new desks on the evening of Friday 16 October, that the Treasury now expected – correctly, as it turned out – that the deficit would be about £800 million.[1]

Another thing Labour had not expected, at any rate until the last few weeks, was the minuscule size of the majority it obtained. By the standards of the two general elections in 1974, one of which produced no overall majority, and the other an overall majority of three, Wilson's 1964 majority of five (excluding the Speaker) looked almost respectable; but, apart from 1950, it was smaller than anything since 1929, and some authorities regarded it as unworkable.[2] In the event it did prove workable, even after it had been reduced to three by an unfortunate by-election result at Leyton (Wilson had kicked the newly-elected Labour MP upstairs to the House of Lords in order to provide a safe seat for his Foreign Secretary, Patrick Gordon Walker, who had embarrassingly lost his seat to an unpleasantly racialist opponent at Smethwick and then, even more embarrassingly, lost Labour the seat at Leyton). But there was a big disadvantage in operating with such a tiny majority: it put a premium on short-term tactical considerations at the expense of long-term strategic ones. It was difficult to concentrate on formulating new policies for the next four or five years when a nasty accident to a single Westminster-bound taxi could result in the downfall of the government. This, combined on the one hand with the clear need for swift, even emergency, action on the economic front, and on the other with the opportunistic, lightning-witted temperament of Harold Wilson – a man whose best-known saying is that a week is a long time in politics – was not the most favourable setting in which to lay the foundations of a coherent long-term economic strategy.

[1] Subsequent revisions of the figures, partly to allow for some under-recording of exports, have reduced the overall deficit for 1964 to £700 million. But the more relevant figure for understanding the history of the period seems to be the one everyone believed in at the time.

[2] See the view attributed to Lord Attlee (Wilson, 1971, p. 21).

LABOUR'S HANGUPS

Any attempt to predict what Labour might do in this situation would have done well to bear in mind two or three particular features of Labour's predicament – what some of the civil servants trying to interpret its Manifesto must have thought of as Labour's main 'hangups'.

First, there was the fact that this was an exceedingly inexperienced administration. Not a single member of it had ever held one of the great offices of state, and only three of the twenty-three Cabinet Ministers had ever sat in a Cabinet before: Wilson himself, Jim Griffiths (now aged seventy-four) and Gordon Walker (which may explain why Wilson was so anxious to get him back into the Commons). Of the remainder of the Cabinet, half had held no ministerial office of any kind; and this was true of seventy-two of the eighty members of the Government below Cabinet level – two-thirds of whom, indeed, had not even been in Parliament when there had last been a Labour government. However, it was not only, or even mainly, the newness to office of most members of the Government that was responsible for Labour's uncertain touch during the first few critical weeks. It was also the fact that the experience of those who had been Ministers lay so far back in the past. The Prime Minister, in particular, sometimes seemed to inhabit a world rather similar to that of the late 1940s, in which there was rationing, import licensing, allocation of raw materials, and stringent controls over the use of foreign exchange. But such a world no longer existed; results could no longer be obtained simply by pulling certain obvious levers; they had to be obtained by stealth. This lesson took a little time to learn.

The second hangup stemmed from the very nature of the Labour Party – the fact that it is a somewhat uneasy coalition of socialists and social democrats. It has no clear and unambiguous economic philosophy. Some of its leading members want to operate within the framework of the present economic system, making the mixed economy work better; others want to transform the present economic system into a socialist one, with a radically different pattern of ownership and much greater state control over the allocation of resources. The struggle between these two sectors of the party had been somewhat muted since Gaitskell's death just under two years earlier, partly because of the decisive victory Gaitskell had in the end won over the unilateralists, and partly because of the skill with which

Wilson gave the party the semblance – and to a considerable extent the substance – of unity during the run-up to the election. Wilson's skill was well illustrated by the way he defused the nuclear issue itself: the independent British nuclear deterrent of which the Conservatives were so proud was, he declared, neither independent nor British nor a deterrent. Since Britain did not possess an independent nuclear deterrent, there was no need for the Labour Party to agonize over whether, when it formed a government, it ought to get rid of it.

But although the socialists (or, as they sometimes called themselves, the Left) formed only a small minority of both the Government and the Parliamentary Party – much smaller than in the Parliament which convened ten years later – they were not without views and voices. Their actual power, paradoxically, was limited: no Labour MP wanted to risk being responsible for ending the life of the first Labour Government for thirteen years. Nevertheless, Ministers were left in no doubt that many of their supporters, not only on the back benches but also in the trade unions and the constituency parties, thought they should be doing something much more radical than merely tinkering with capitalism.

Closely linked to this ambivalence between socialism and social democracy was – and is – another deep-seated source of tension. Partly because the Labour Party is a largely working-class party with a largely middle-class leadership,[1] and partly because of the much-repeated cautionary tale of Ramsay MacDonald, regarded by many in the Party as a traitor to socialism, the great black fear, hidden deep inside the Party's psyche, is of Betrayal. Either – in the nightmares of many on the left – our middle-class leaders will betray us because, in the last resort, class loyalties are stronger than anything else; or our working-class leaders will betray us, because they will be seduced by the aristocratic embrace. They will have gone over to the other side – ceased to be one of Us, and become one of Them.

Not unnaturally, this anxiety communicates itself to the leadership, or at any rate to the more serious-minded and honourable members of it. *Have* we gone over to the other side? *Have* we become one of Them? For the process of democratic government, even for a basically idealistic party with its own vision of the future, is largely a process of reconciling different interests, of balancing advantages here against disadvantages there, of bargaining, negotiating, and seek-

[1] Of the twenty-three members of Wilson's first Cabinet, no more than seven or eight could have been described as working class, and it could be argued (see Hindess, 1971) that by the end of 1969 working-class membership of the Cabinet had fallen to zero.

ing satisfactory compromises. And how is a Labour Minister, squeezed between the civil servants who bully him with Things As They Are, and the party militants who bombard him with Things As They Ought To Be, to know when he has reached the best available compromise, and when he has sold Us down the river and gone over to Them?

THE BALANCE OF PAYMENTS

The economic situation inherited by the inexperienced and mildly schizophrenic Labour Government in 1964 was grave but not critical; certainly less critical than the situation inherited by the much more experienced but also much more schizophrenic Labour Government of ten years later. The problem lay almost entirely in the balance of payments: unemployment was at the relatively low level of 1.7 per cent, and the rate of inflation, at about 4 per cent, was no faster than it had been for twenty years. Within the balance of payments, the problem lay largely in the current account. Half the £800 million deficit represented an outflow of long-term capital, which increased the value of Britain's overseas assets correspondingly; and although this long-term investment overseas was a foolish policy as long as it had to be financed by short-term borrowing, it would have been a perfectly rational, and indeed responsible, policy to follow had Britain had the sort of surplus on current account that successive governments had said was necessary. But there was the rub: so far from being in surplus, the current account was some £400 million in the red.

Particularly disturbing was the fact that the current account was not merely in deficit, but to a greater extent than at the same point in previous cycles. In 1955 – when the pressure of demand had been particularly high – the deficit had been only £150 million. In 1960 it had been £250 million. Now it was almost £400 million. Naive extrapolation (often as accurate as any other kind of extrapolation) suggested that by 1968 the deficit might be £650 million, and by the early 1970s over £1 billion. These are not large figures by the standard of the oil-dominated deficits of the mid-1970s, but at the time, and in the context of the declared policy of running a substantial surplus, the figures, and still more the trend, looked ominous.

Although it is sometimes argued that a country's balance of payments deteriorates not because some components get worse, but because others fail to get better, it seems safer to stick to statistics than metaphysics, and the statistical picture is clear. While the surplus on invisibles was much the same, at around £150 million, in all three years, the visible deficit worsened, from around £300 million in 1955 to £400 million in 1960 and over £500 million in 1964. It is difficult to blame imports for this. In most industrial countries imports rose faster than GDP during this period; in Britain they rose considerably more slowly. Britain's problem was that exports also rose considerably more slowly.[1]

The reasons generally cited for the slow growth of British exports were various: long – and often unhonoured – delivery dates, feeble salesmanship, products which were outmoded or of poor quality. But much the most important seems to have been lack of competitiveness in terms of price. Since the mid-1950s or before, unit costs in British industry had been rising faster than in most competitor countries – not so much because wages in Britain were rising faster, as because productivity was rising more slowly. Some competitor countries, like France, which also suffered from the British disease, devalued their currency from time to time in order to keep their exports competitive. But Britain did not. As a result British export prices, in terms of foreign currency, rose faster than most other countries.[2] But even this rise in prices was smaller than the rise in British costs, so that profit margins on exports were squeezed – which partly explains why British manufacturers were not especially worried if their delivery dates were too long or too unreliable: the foreign business they were failing to get would not have been very profitable anyway, compared with selling in the home market. It is hardly surprising that Britain's share of world exports of manufactures should have fallen from 20 per cent in the mid-1950s to 14 per cent in the mid-1960s.

The obvious remedy, in this situation, was to devalue the currency, so that the same number of pounds would exchange for fewer dollars or deutschmarks. This would both have reduced the price of British goods to foreign buyers, and raised the profit margin on exports for British manufacturers, so that there would have been a double reason for British exports to rise. The same factors would also have worked on imports of manufactured goods, but in the other direction: imports would have fallen back. From both directions,

[1] OECD, 1966.

[2] Between 1955 and 1964 British export prices rose by 18 per cent – the same as the U.S., but faster than Germany (13 per cent) and France (4 per cent). In Japan export prices fell by 5 per cent, and in Italy by 9 per cent (NIER, November 1966).

forces would have been at work moving the balance of payments out of deficit and into surplus.

NO DEVALUATION

But Labour did not devalue. At the time, this decision seemed to many of those closely involved to be a catastrophic mistake, likely to condemn the Labour Government's economic policies to sterility, and the British economy to yet more years of drift and stagnation. In retrospect, that verdict must still stand.

The decision not to devalue was ostensibly taken two days after the election by Labour's top triumvirate – Harold Wilson, George Brown and James Callaghan – after they had studied Treasury briefs on the economic situation and listened to the advice of their officials (Wilson, 1971). The truth was simpler. Wilson – with all the authority of a newly-appointed Prime Minister who had just led his party to its first victory for more than fourteen years – was implacably opposed to devaluation, and that was that.

A number of considerations underlay Wilson's determination not to devalue. One was his fear that Labour – which had devalued in 1949 – would be branded as 'the party of devaluation'. Just why he thought this would have mattered – even at a time when the small size of his majority might soon force another election – is unclear. It is understandable, if deplorable, that people in the City of London, reluctantly witnessing Britain's decline as a financial and industrial power, should have clung to the pound as a kind of national virility symbol, feeling cheerful or despondent according to whether it was 'strong' or 'weak'. But there is no reason to suppose that the rest of the nation was so irrational, or attached much importance to the preservation of some particular rate of exchange between sterling and other currencies. Of course, devaluation would have been followed by some check to the rise in living standards, but this would have been the result not of devaluation itself, but of the need to eliminate the balance of payments deficit by a once-for-all rise in exports or fall in imports. Any policy to eliminate the deficit – including the obvious alternative, deflation – would have had the same result.

A second reason cited by Wilson for his opposition to devaluation was that it 'might well have started off an orgy of competitive beggar-my-neighbour currency devaluations . . . which would have plunged the world into monetary anarchy'.[1] On the face of it, there

[1] Wilson, 1971, p. 28.

might seem to be some substance in this fear. When devaluation did eventually come, in November 1967,[1] it was soon followed by a period of changes in exchange rates, and in the price of gold, which led to the effective abandonment of the system of fixed exchange rates adopted at Bretton Woods.[2] Nevertheless, although the devaluation of sterling may have been the precipitating factor in all this – and even that is by no means certain – it was not the cause. Sooner or later the absurdity of a regime of fixed exchange rates at a time when different countries were experiencing very different rates of inflation was bound to lead to the abandonment of the Bretton Woods system.

However, the ultimate reason for Wilson's almost pathological opposition to devaluation does not seem to have lain in his fear of the domestic or international consequences, but in his deep distrust of the price mechanism. Although, in the highly-regulated economy of 1948, Wilson had been the President of the Board of Trade who had announced a 'bonfire of controls', he had no faith in the ability of the price mechanism to allocate resources in the efficient way postulated by classical economics. If resources were to flow to where they were most needed – to exports and industrial investment – they had to be pushed or cajoled there by 'direct intervention' – by physical controls or official and unofficial arm-twisting. What was needed, if British industry was to be modernized and to compete in the world, were improvements in management, more industrial training, the development of new techniques and their embodiment in new investment. Compared with these much-needed structural reforms, tinkerings with the price mechanism – such as a change in the exchange rate – were an irrelevance – or, as Wilson kept on calling them, 'an easy way out'. There is much to be said for this 'supply-side' view of Britain's problems, i.e. a view which stresses the constraints on economic performance imposed by inadequate or out-of-date plant and machinery, unimaginative management and perennial shortages of skilled labour. But in the context of the mid-1960s such a view was fatally unbalanced. Getting the demand side right was essential too. Devaluation would have stimulated the demand for British exports, and thus attracted more resources into export markets. With luck, this would not only have closed the balance of payments gap, but also induced an export-oriented increase in industrial investment. But the importance of demand-side

[1] See pp. 82–3.
[2] See pp. 150–3.

factors in a mixed economy – of providing firms and individuals with a financial incentive to produce and sell more – was something that Wilson could never be convinced of.

In the face of Wilson's adamant opposition to devaluation, nothing could be done. Most of the senior economic advisers Labour brought into Whitehall at this time were in favour of devaluation, some vehemently so. But although from time to time during the next two years they sent the Prime Minister Top Secret memoranda urging that the pound be devalued, these were ignored or suppressed; indeed before long Wilson issued an order forbidding anyone in Whitehall to discuss, or even mention, devaluation.[1] It is just possible that things might have been different had a firm stand in favour of devaluation been taken by either the Chancellor of the Exchequer or by the most senior permanent officials in the Treasury. But Callaghan lacked the self-confidence – or the foolhardiness – to challenge Wilson on the issue, and maintained the Wilson line to which he had probably committed himself well before the election.[2] And Sir William Armstrong, the exceedingly able and powerful Permanent Secretary of the Treasury, went to great lengths to maintain a neutral posture on the matter. He was conscious of criticism that in the past the Treasury had bullied governments into adopting its own views,[3] and probably regarded it as improper to try to influence a newly-elected government whose Prime Minister had such a determined view on the subject.

And so the die was cast: the Government was committed to the defence of the $2·80 exchange rate. Fortunately for Wilson, the Americans shared his opposition to the devaluation of sterling, because they feared that this would lead to pressure on the dollar. This was by now clearly overvalued in relation to the stronger European currencies, and in relation to gold, whose dollar price – $35 an ounce – had remained unchanged since 1931. To the U.S.

[1] With the inevitable result, of course, that it was frequently discussed, generally under the codename 'the Unmentionable'. The economic advisers' memoranda are referred to at various points in Crossman, 1975, notably in the entries for 24 November 1964 and 5 August 1965.

[2] According to Brandon, 1966, p. 28, Callaghan had assured the Americans in May 1964 that a Labour government would not devalue sterling. Brandon's book – subtitled *The Struggle for Sterling 1964–66* – conveys the flavour of the time very well, in that he talks of the defence of sterling in 1964 as he might have talked of the defence of Britain in 1940. That the Government might be embarked not on some glorious second Battle of Britain, but simply on a highly irrational and dangerous economic policy, does not seem to have occurred to him.

[3] See Brittan, 1971, p. 272.

Administration – even though, after the November 1964 election, President Johnson was as firmly in the saddle as any cowboy in his native Texas – the need to persuade Congress that the mighty dollar was in fact overvalued would have been a political embarrassment; throwing the odd billion dollars into the defence of sterling was much simpler. The net result was that a policy which in the longer run did Britain nothing but harm was encouraged and financed by the Americans, to the accompaniment of self-congratulation on the part of British Ministers on their success at getting American support.

ALTERNATIVE COURSES OF ACTION

If the balance of payments was to be put right, and if devaluation was ruled out as a method of doing it, there were only two possible courses of action. One was the time-dishonoured remedy of deflation. As this would produce rising unemployment, and be inconsistent with Labour's central theme of raising the growth rate, not to mention its fragile majority, it was ruled out. This left import controls. But there were grave difficulties about this final option. Since the late 1940s, trade barriers – in the form of tariffs as well as of quantitative restrictions – had been progressively dismantled, particularly on trade between developed countries, and any unilateral move on Britain's part to re-introduce them would certainly annoy foreign governments and might lead to retaliation. As a country which needs to export a great deal simply in order to pay for the food and raw materials which cannot be produced at home, Britain has always been chary of any policy that might lead to foreign restrictions on its exports. A more practical difficulty was that controls over imports require an elaborate administrative structure of a kind that had existed in the war and early post-war years, but existed no longer. Moreover such controls are the more difficult to administer, the greater the differentiation of the product controlled; and the variety of manufactured and semi-manufactured goods that Britain was importing in the mid-1960s was much greater than in the late 1940s. Some people in the Labour Party may have wanted to move towards a siege economy; but the means to do so were missing, and would take time to construct.

All effective courses of action for curing the balance of payments deficit thus being ruled out, Labour settled for some ineffective ones. The least ineffective was the imposition of a 15 per cent tariff surcharge on all imports of manufactured and semi-manufactured goods. This was equivalent to a devaluation confined in its effects to imported manufactures, and as such was rational and useful – or would have been had it lasted for any length of time. But, being in breach of both GATT and EFTA treaties, it provoked a storm of protest, and within a month the Government had given private assurances that it would be reduced.[1] The knowledge that the surcharge was to be temporary reduced its effectiveness: some foreign suppliers absorbed the charge themselves rather than lose their grip on the British market, and some of the fall in imports that did take place reflected a running down of stocks, which were later built up again when the charge was removed. The Chancellor's estimate that the surcharge would cut the import bill by about £300 million a year looked optimistic.[2] On the export side, the Government announced that arrangements would be made to rebate to exporters various indirect taxes (such as purchase tax on stationery) which increased their costs. It was reckoned that the effect might, on favourable assumptions, be to reduce export prices by about 1½ per cent. There was a general feeling – not only about the export rebate, but about the package as a whole – of the mountain having laboured, and brought forth a mouse. The need for drastic action to get the balance of payments right might have been postponed; it had not been avoided.

LABOUR AND THE CITY'S HANGUPS

It was not only Labour that suffered from hangups: the City of London had some too. The City had been forced to take a back seat during the war and early post-war years; but with the election of the Conservative Government in 1951, it had once again come into its own. A political philosophy which assumed that the man in Whitehall knew best was replaced by a political philosophy which assumed that the market knew best. Exchange controls were relaxed, government intervention reduced, cheap money abandoned. The City loved it. Share prices surged ahead, invisible earnings boomed, fortunes were made (and occasionally lost), huge sums of capital flowed in and out of the country. Before long, London was well on the way to resuming its role as the world's greatest financial centre. And now all this was being put at risk – as the City saw it – by the election of a doctrinaire socialist government bent on reintroducing all sorts of

[1] Wilson, 1971, p. 63. It was cut to 10 per cent in April 1965, and ended in November 1966.
[2] For two subsequent verdicts, see footnote 1 on p. 80.

controls and restrictions, and on raising income tax and profits tax to pay for a higher level of public expenditure. Far more than industry – which had welcomed the emphasis Wilson had been putting on the need for an end to stop-go and the importance of harnessing technology and increasing investment – the City viewed the prospect of a Labour government with a jaundiced eye. *Don't Let Labour Ruin It,* Conservative posters had proclaimed during the 1959 election campaign. That was exactly how the City felt about it in 1964.

The City had, in a superficial sense, some grounds for its complaint that Labour's behaviour was making the economic situation even more difficult. Wilson's attacks on the weakness of the balance of payments during the later stages of the election campaign undoubtedly affected confidence in sterling, and may have aggravated the subsequent run on the pound. Similarly, the failure to consult other countries about the proposed import surcharge, and the clumsy handling of the Concorde issue,[1] unnecessarily hardened foreign opinion against the measures the Government took to improve the balance of payments. Nevertheless, the myth that soon developed in the City, that the Labour Government had inherited a perfectly manageable economic situation and rendered it unmanageable by its own incompetence, was entirely unjustified. Had the Conservatives been re-elected, they would have been faced by the same problems and the same need for emergency action, as Maudling himself had the grace to admit;[2] indeed the temporary import surcharge which Labour imposed had been worked out by the Treasury during the summer at Maudling's request.

It seems fair to say that in the autumn of 1964 many people in the City allowed their dislike of the Labour Government to distort the judgment they pronounced on the measures the Government was taking; and that these adverse judgments – about which foreign holders of sterling, as well as domestic opinion, were left in no doubt – made Labour's task more difficult. It is true that Wilson himself over-reacted to the City's hostility by attacking 'speculators' in the City as largely responsible for the successive sterling crises of the

[1] In the White Paper on the economic situation it issued ten days after taking office (HMG 1964 (ii)), the Government talked of 'cutting out expenditure on items of low economic priority, such as "prestige projects" ', and went on to say that it had already communicated to the French Government its wish to re-examine urgently the joint Anglo-French project to build the Concorde supersonic airliner. But when it read the small print of the agreement, it decided – quite wrongly, in the light of the subsequent escalation of costs – that it would be more expensive to cancel than to continue, and the project proceeded.

[2] Brittan, 1971, p. 296.

next three years. These attacks infuriated the City, to whom the activities described by Wilson as speculative and unpatriotic were simply sensible precautions on the part of those charged with managing their clients' money. If a business thinks that sterling may soon be devalued, it is not only legitimate but in accordance with common business prudence for it to accelerate payments abroad denominated in sterling, and delay receipts from abroad denominated in foreign currencies. These 'leads' and 'lags', together with the underlying balance of payments deficit which prompted them, were far more important in accounting for the sterling crises of the mid-1960s than the activities of international speculators with which Wilson became obsessed, and the City's knowledge that this was so intensified its dislike of the Government. Nevertheless, there was more than a grain of justification in Wilson's attitude towards the City. In the early 1970s the Conservatives were sometimes to complain that they were being denied the degree of co-operation from the trade union movement which, as the duly elected Government of the day, they had the right to expect. Labour could make the same complaint of the City in the mid-1960s.

The City's attitude was well illustrated by the hostility with which it received the autumn Budget introduced by Mr Callaghan on 11 November 1964. A prime feature of this was the announcement that old-age pensions and other social security benefits would be increased by approximately 20 per cent the following March, and that prescription charges for National Health Service medicines would be abolished. To the Government, these steps were an earnest to its supporters of its determination to press ahead with its programme despite its small majority and despite the difficult economic situation. To many in the City, the measures appeared irresponsible and inflationary. What such critics did not understand – or did not wish to understand – was that most of the increase in pensions was to be financed by an increase in National Insurance contributions, and that the residual cost of the package to the Exchequer – some £130 million in a full year – was more than covered by Mr Callaghan's simultaneous announcement of an increase of 6d. in the standard rate of income tax, and 6d. a gallon in the duty on petrol. The net result of the changes was to increase revenue in a full year by £100 million more than expenditure, so that the measures, taken as a whole, were mildly deflationary. This was not something which casual opinion would have grasped from the tone of City comment. In the same way, there was much criticism of the Chancellor's announcement that he intended in his next April budget to replace the existing system of company taxation by a Corporation Tax, a change which would have the effect of encouraging profits to be retained in the business rather than distributed to shareholders; and greatly to strengthen the recently-introduced tax on capital gains. Lay opinion at home and abroad, observing the state of agitation into which the City worked itself over these two proposals, would never have guessed that Callaghan was merely introducing in Britain taxes that had operated for many years in that great exemplar for much City opinion, the United States.

The efforts of the City and other parts of what was sometimes called 'the Establishment' to prevent the Labour Government from doing what it had been elected to do had their comic side: in November, for example, the *Daily Mail* suggested that what was needed was a National Government, in which men of good will from all parties would join forces to conquer the economic crisis. Calls for a national government always cause some amusement in the Labour Party, partly because they are based on such ignorance of the Party's temperament and history, and partly because they are so predictable: whenever a new Labour government really seems to mean business, the cry goes out that what is needed is a National Government. But the situation had its serious side too. In a speech at the annual Mansion House dinner on 3 November, Lord Cromer, Governor of the Bank of England, made a thinly-veiled attack on government expenditure, both domestic and overseas, called for a reduction in the pressure of demand in the economy, and criticized the steps the Government was taking to cut down the outflow of private capital. On this and other less public occasions Cromer was in effect telling the Government that unless it cut its expenditure, dropped its proposed curbs on overseas investment, and perhaps introduced a wage freeze, he would not be able to organize enough support from other Central Banks to defend the pound at its existing exchange rate.

The crunch was not long in coming. In a speech at the annual Lord Mayor's Banquet on Monday 16 November, the Prime Minister talked of his Government's determination 'to keep sterling strong and see it riding high'. This was widely interpreted to mean that Bank Rate would be raised the following Thursday, the normal day for such changes. When this did not happen, the exchange rate dropped rapidly to \$2-78¼ – the level below which, under the IMF rules, the Bank of England could not permit it to fall. From now on

any sales of sterling in excess of purchases would have to be absorbed by the Bank of England, which would have to draw on the nation's dwindling reserves of foreign exchange to pay for it. At a meeting at Chequers over the weekend senior Cabinet ministers decided that Bank Rate must be raised from 5 to 7 per cent on Monday morning. But this unusual – some said panic – action was counterproductive: the run on the pound accelerated. Cromer came to see the Prime Minister and told him that there must be immediate and sweeping cuts in public expenditure, and a reversal of various other aspects of Labour's policies, if confidence in sterling was to be restored. Given Wilson's apparently obsessive determination to preserve the existing exchange rate, Cromer must have felt that he was batting on an easy wicket.

Not so; the wily Yorkshireman spreadeagled his stumps with a googly. In what was obviously a moment of intense drama – although much underplayed in Wilson's own deadpan account of the confrontation[1] – Wilson replied that unless the necessary international support for the pound was rapidly forthcoming – and there would be no deviation from Labour's programme as the price of securing it – he would float the pound, dissolve Parliament and go to the country on the issue of a bankers' ramp. The British people would be told that international bankers were trying to dictate to a democratically-elected British government. He would win by a landslide. The new government would have little patience with City obstructionism.

If Wilson was bluffing, then it was a bluff backed up in depth. Detailed plans were worked out, at feverish speed, for the floating of the pound and the announcement of the Dissolution of Parliament. Cromer decided not to call the bluff. Within twenty-four hours he had organized $3 billion support for Britain's reserves from the Central Banks of the U.S. and the EEC. For a while at any rate, the exchange rate was safe.

Wilson had routed the enemy in battle. But in a way he had lost the war. He had spiked the City's guns. But the City's guns – perhaps unknowingly – had been bombarding an indefensible position. If they had been allowed to do their work properly, sterling's defences would have been breached. For a few weeks things would have been very messy; but then order would have been re-established, under a

[1] Wilson, 1971, pp. 64–6. The inside story of what actually happened was not known by – or not revealed by – Brandon, 1966, or Crossman, 1975. There is no reason to doubt Wilson's own account.

regime with a viable exchange rate. As it was, immediate surrender had been staved off, but only at the expense of three exhausting years of siege, which would bring capitulation in the end.

THE DEPARTMENT OF ECONOMIC AFFAIRS

While the Treasury and the Bank of England were coping with the short-term problem of financing the balance of payments deficit and maintaining confidence in sterling, the Department of Economic Affairs was beginning to grapple with the long-term problem of Britain's laggard growth rate. At least that was the idea; it all turned out rather differently.

The DEA had both an intellectual and a practical origin. The intellectual origin lay in the conviction that had been growing on Labour leaders and advisers for some years that Britain's growth rate would never improve as long as the Treasury remained the unchallenged centre of economic decision-making. By temperament and by experience the Treasury's main interest lay in short-term demand management, in the manipulation of fiscal and monetary instruments, in worrying about the outlook for the balance of payments and the position of sterling. It could not, Labour felt, be given the job of raising the growth rate. However tough and committed to faster growth any incoming Labour Chancellor, he would soon become the prisoner of his awe-inspiring officials, and the spokesman for the Treasury's traditional views. Therefore another central economic department should be set up, with power and prestige equal to that of the Treasury, charged with the job of getting the economy on to a sustained path of faster growth. Out of what Wilson described as the 'creative tension' that would exist between the two departments would emerge a coherent policy which emphasized growth without neglecting the day-to-day needs of stabilization policy and the balance of payments.

The intellectual origin of the DEA stemmed from a view of the Treasury that was, perhaps, a little unfair: certainly some Treasury officials and economists had always deplored the chopping and changing of the stop-go cycle. But the practical origin was decisive: a job had to be found for George Brown. In the leadership struggle in 1963 Brown had run Wilson a fairly close second; and he had subsequently become Deputy Leader of the Parliamentary Party. If Labour came to power, he must clearly be given a top job. But the Treasury had already been bagged by Callaghan, who had come third in the ballot for the leadership, who had already been acting as Shadow Chancellor under Gaitskell, and who had shown the seriousness with which he took his prospective duties by frequently travelling down to Nuffield College, Oxford to be instructed in the mysteries of economics. And many felt Brown's temperament to be unsuited to the delicate job of Foreign Secretary.[1] Hence the neat solution of setting up a Department of Economic Affairs and putting George Brown at the head of it.

INCOMES POLICY

Although Brown's main task was to get the growth rate up, his first priority was to construct a workable incomes policy. The need for an incomes policy had been foreshadowed as early as the 1944 White Paper on *Employment Policy*. Full employment, free collective bargaining, and stable prices are unlikely for long to be compatible with each other. Once the government has guaranteed that it will maintain full employment – as the war-time coalition government had done in the 1944 White Paper – there is nothing to stop trade unions demanding, and employers conceding, wage increases far in excess of the average rise in productivity in the economy. Unions need not fear that by insisting on higher wages they are pricing themselves out of their jobs – because full employment is guaranteed. Employers have more to lose by resisting wage demands and suffering the loss of output and profits occasioned by a strike than they have by paying higher wages and passing the higher costs on in higher prices. They will not price themselves out of the market because other firms are doing the same – and because full employment is guaranteed. And so the merry-go-round goes on: higher wages are passed on in higher prices; higher prices become the justification for further wage increases. Although the strong may benefit from this process for a while, the weak will suffer; and in the long run everyone is likely to be worse off. For what determines the rise in a nation's living standards is the rise in output, not the rise in money incomes; and the periodic need to deflate in an attempt to slow down inflation slows down the long-term growth of output. Hence – so the argument went – the need for a policy which kept the growth in money

[1] In April 1956, during the visit to Britain of Bulganin and Khrushchev, Brown had indulged in a widely-publicized slanging match with Khrushchev over the imprisonment of social democrats in Eastern Europe. Brown did in fact become Foreign Secretary in July 1966, but resigned in March 1968; he was not generally rated a success in the job.

incomes in line with the growth of productivity. This meant that wages, instead of rising by 7 or 8 per cent a year, as had been usual in the 1950s and early 1960s, should rise by no more than 2½ or 3 per cent a year. And this could be achieved – if it could be achieved at all – only with the active co-operation of the trade unions.

The unions, although they had acquiesced for a while in Stafford Cripps' policy of voluntary wage restraint in the late 1940s, had never liked the idea of a policy which called for moderation in wage demands. One reason for this lay in the conviction of most trade unionists that higher wages meant lower profits. This is a perfectly plausible idea; indeed if the national income is divided up between wages and profits – as it is in some simple economic models – the point is self-evident. Profits are regarded by many people as a bad thing. In the economic theories of Karl Marx, for example – which have been immensely influential in conditioning the way in which twentieth-century socialists perceive the world – profit is called 'surplus value', and represents that part of the value of the workers' output which is appropriated by the capitalists. Any wage increase restores some of the surplus value to the workers and reduces the degree of capitalist exploitation. Non-Marxists, too, can perfectly reasonably welcome an increase in wages (or salaries) at the expense of profits. Whatever form they take – rent, interest or dividends – profits represent in the main a return to capital, and the distribution of capital in most Western countries is highly unequal – more unequal than most people would care to justify. To many trade unionists, therefore, wage increases mean a rise in the living standards of the workers at the expense of the idle rich, and any restraint on wage increases, enabling the rich to hold on to their privileges, is unacceptable.

More sophisticated trade unionists might agree that it is not really like that: that big wage increases are often fully passed on in big price increases; and that even if rising wages do succeed in squeezing the share of profits in the national income, the eventual result, in a mixed economy, can be lower investment and a slower rise in workers' living standards. But awareness of these facts does not necessarily make such union officials willing to engage in a policy of wage restraint. Wage restraint is a fundamental contradiction of the original function of trade unions, which is to fight for better pay and conditions for their members. How can a union, whose main activity for over half a century has been to use its bargaining skills and strength to secure from employers higher wages, shorter hours and better conditions of work, suddenly accept that in a fully democratic society in which the government is pledged to maintain full employment such an activity can do little to promote a rise in living standards and can very easily hold them back? How can union officials be persuaded that their chief skill, on which they pride themselves and on which their standing in the eyes of their fellows depends, has been rendered obsolete and even anti-social by a fundamental change in the role of the government in the economy? Yet until trade unions are willing to accept the need for a drastic alteration in their traditional role an incomes policy will not work.

Difficult though the task of persuading trade unions of this might be, it had to be tackled by the new Labour Government if inflation was to be brought under control without sacrificing full employment. Indeed the decision not to devalue had made the need to secure agreement on an incomes policy particularly urgent: for if sterling was overvalued and the Government refused to correct this by changing the exchange rate, competitiveness in world markets could be restored only if for some years prices rose more slowly in Britain than in other countries. Without a successful incomes policy, past experience suggested that there was little likelihood of that.

If anybody could pull it off, it was felt, it was George Brown; and so the job was included among his functions. Into it he threw all his formidable energy and all his vigorous powers of persuasion. He had something to build on: at the Labour Party's annual conference at Scarborough the previous year, Frank Cousins, the most influential of all the trade union leaders, while repudiating wage restraint, had talked approvingly of 'a planned growth of wages' (Labour Party, 1963, p. 197). What he appeared to mean was that if a Labour government went both for a policy of economic growth – implying more planning of the economy – and a policy of fair shares – implying controls over the growth of profits and dividends, reforms to make the taxation system more equitable, and measures to raise the relative incomes of the poorest sections of the community – then the unions would co-operate in an incomes policy. It was a reasonable and responsible pledge – provided it was interpreted realistically, in the light of Britain's short-term economic difficulties; and provided it could be made to stick at the shop-floor level, and not remain simply an honourable intention on the part of the TUC.

Brown's first task was to persuade the unions that the Labour Government was determined to keep its part of the bargain: hence the importance attached by him and many other Ministers to the various measures taken or announced during the Government's first few weeks in office: the increase in old-age pensions, the abolition of prescription charges, the rise in income tax, the proposals to introduce a Corporation Tax and an effective Capital Gains Tax, and so on. These measures may have upset the City, but they reassured the unions, and on 16 December 1964 the TUC, together with the Government and the employers' associations, signed a *Joint Statement of Intent on Productivity, Prices and Incomes.* In this document the unions accepted that it must be a major objective of national policy to keep increases in wages, salaries and other forms of income in line with the increase in real national output. In the absence of any marked change in the terms of trade – and they changed very little during the 1960s – such a policy, were it to be adhered to, would mean that the general level of prices would be stable.

But how to translate intent into reality? No one believed that wages would rise in line with productivity just because the TUC said it would be a good idea. The ultimate problem lay in getting people to behave in a way consistent with the policy. But this came later; the immediate problem lay in determining just what consistency with the policy meant for individual unions or groups of workers. Any fool could work out what the *average* increase in pay should be – the 2½–3 per cent or so by which national productivity had grown on average each year during the past decade. But it was unrealistic to imagine that all groups of workers would, or should, get the *same* percentage increase, regardless of whether they were high-paid or low-paid, in industries or occupations which were expanding or contracting, or where productivity was rising or stagnating. Britain is still an economy in which changes in relative wages and salaries are an important device for encouraging labour to leave occupations or industries where demand is falling, and to enter occupations or industries where demand is rising. At the same time, it is an economy in which the existing structure of wages and salaries bears no very close or consistent relationship with either the pattern of productivity and efficiency, or the needs of equity and social justice: some people are paid far more than can be justified by the value of what they produce, others far less; some people receive far more income than is required to satisfy reasonable human needs, others far less.

If, therefore, the normal process of economic development and growth is to continue, and resources are to move from one industry to another in response to changes in tastes or technology, an incomes policy must permit the pay of some groups to rise faster than the pay of others. Similarly, if groups which are relatively underpaid in relation to their needs or qualifications, either because they have always been underpaid or because they have recently fallen behind, are to be treated in a way that most people would regard as fair, their incomes must be permitted to rise faster than the average.

As with pay, so with prices. Overall price stability cannot mean that all prices remain stable. In those sectors of the economy – such as fruit and vegetable markets – where something akin to perfect competition obtains, prices will be determined by the interplay of supply and demand: severe drought will put up the price of potatoes, and a feeling of national penury may bring a fall in the price of strawberries. But in a modern industrial economy the majority of prices are 'administered' – determined at relatively infrequent intervals by large corporations. In some industries, where for technical reasons productivity cannot rise fast enough to absorb even moderate increases in wages, prices must rise over time if profits are not to fall to zero. Correspondingly – if the overall price level is to remain stable – other prices must fall; this will apply particularly in sectors where the rise in productivity is relatively fast and price reductions are needed to prevent a disproportionate increase in profits.

With both pay and prices, however, the general principles to be observed if overall price stability is to be achieved are easier to enunciate than to put into practice. Some wages and salaries will have to rise by more than 3 per cent, others by less. But which groups of workers will fall into which category? While some prices will rise, others will have to fall. But which? And since the whole idea of an incomes policy is to have these decisions made *not* by the market-cum-collective bargaining mechanism, because experience demonstrates that with full employment that leads to inflation, but by some other mechanism, the question arises: what is this other mechanism going to be?

George Brown's answer was that it was going to be the Prices and Incomes Board.[1] This body, composed mainly of independent members under an independent chairman, Aubrey Jones, a former Conservative Minister of moderate views, and backed by a fairly large expert staff, would consider particular pay claims or settlements referred to it by the Government, and form a view on whether they were consistent with the 'norm' for increases in money incomes,

[1] As it was usually called. Its actual title was the National Board for Prices and Incomes.

which the Government set at 3–3½ per cent. A White Paper[1] laid down four sets of circumstances in which pay increases above the norm might be permitted: where this would be associated with a big increase in productivity; where it was needed to help with a change in the distribution of manpower; where a group was particularly low paid; and where a group's pay had fallen seriously behind the pay of other groups doing similar work. If the Board reported that a wage claim above the norm could not be justified under one of these criteria, the union in question was expected to lower its sights and settle in accordance with the norm. The same principles would apply to prices. Businesses, including nationalized industries, were to keep their prices stable unless increases would be justified under certain criteria; but this was balanced by the requirement that where certain other criteria applied, a firm should cut its prices. In cases where the Government was not satisfied that these rules were being observed it could refer the matter to the PIB; and firms were expected to comply voluntarily with the Board's findings.

In short, an expert body was going to pronounce on whether the behaviour of particular unions and particular businesses was consistent with the prices and incomes policy which both the TUC and the employers' organizations had set their names to. But where such behaviour was not so consistent, the matter would be left to the conscience of the union or the firm: no sanctions would be applied to get them to confirm. At a time when the pressure of demand in the economy was very high, and shortages of many kinds of labour acute, it needed a real optimist to suppose that a voluntary policy of this kind was going to work for very long. But optimists were, perhaps, more numerous in the mid-1960s than they were ten years later.

THE GROWTH PROBLEM

Before long, Gargantua-like, the prices and incomes policy was swallowing up increasing amounts of the time of George Brown and his officials. This was not intended; it just happened: a centralized incomes policy of the kind the Government had devised takes a lot of administering. The fact remained, though, that the DEA's main job was to secure a faster rate of growth. This was the key to all Labour's plans: the 1964 Manifesto made no sense without it. Towards the end of the decade, doubts would increasingly be ex-

[1] HMG, 1965 (April).

pressed about the desirability of faster growth; at best, it was to be claimed, economic growth had all sorts of adverse consequences that were insufficiently recognized, and at worst it would lead to an ecological catastrophe and a dead or dying planet. But there were few such doubts in 1964. In relation to comparable countries, Britain had experienced a deplorably low rate of growth, and something must be done to speed it up if living standards were not to fall further and further behind those in the rest of Western Europe.

But if a remedy was to be found, the nature of the disease must first be understood: prescription must be based on diagnosis. Why was Britain's growth rate comparatively low? By 1964 the question had been exercising economists for the best part of a decade, and a wide spectrum of answers had been canvassed. Although there are various overlaps and linkages between them, it is possible to distinguish five essentially separate explanations.

One explanation attributed Britain's slow growth to the fact that it had not been 'export-led'. The exports of Germany and Japan, to cite the obvious examples, had grown rapidly, perhaps because of the happy accident of currencies that were initially undervalued, perhaps because these nations were determined to regain by economic success the place in the world they had lost by military defeat. Rapidly rising exports, mainly of manufactured goods, led to rapidly rising output and investment in manufacturing industry; this led to rapidly rising productivity, and rapid growth of the economy as a whole. British exports, by contrast, rose too sluggishly to pull up the output of manufacturing industry very much or to induce any very substantial new investment: output and productivity rose only slowly, both in manufacturing and in the rest of the economy.[1]

The second explanation had something in common with the first, in that the absence of a strong and sustained rise in the demand for exports was an important ingredient. But blame was attached not so much to the fact that Britain's growth had been led by consumers' expenditure rather than by exports, as to the fact that this domestic consumer demand fluctuated so much from one year to another. Continuous government intervention, it was argued, expanding consumer demand when unemployment rose too high, and cutting it back when the balance of payments swung into deficit, made it impossible for businessmen to plan their future investment in any rational way. The sudden stops administered to the economy from

[1] For different versions of the export-led growth argument see Lamfalussy, 1961, Beckerman, 1962 and Kaldor, 1971.

time to time not only had the short-run effect of making businessmen postpone or abandon plans for new investment; over the years there was a cumulative effect, with Britain's capital stock becoming older and more obsolescent than that of competitor countries. And just as the suddenness of the stop phases had bad effects, so did the sharpness of the go phases: whenever the government expanded the economy it did so much too fast, with the result that British industry could not cope, and much of the rise in consumer and investment demand was satisfied by a surge in imports. This weakened the balance of payments further, while doing little to encourage a sustained rise in British investment.[1]

The third explanation laid the responsibility for Britain's slow growth rate fairly and squarely on its relatively low rate of investment – though this low rate of investment was not necessarily blamed on sluggish exports or 'stop-go', but on other mistaken policies leading to a misallocation of resources at home and excessive government spending and private investment overseas (PEP, 1960). One study (Hill, 1964) showed that among advanced industrial countries there was a very strong relationship between a country's growth rate and the share of national income it devoted to investment, particularly investment in machinery and equipment. The obvious explanation of this relationship was that technical progress, one of the main engines of economic growth, can become operative only if it is embodied in new machinery and equipment. A subsequent study (OECD, 1970 (ii)) came up with similar findings, concluding that 85 per cent of the variation in growth rates among the main industrial countries was explained by variations in the proportion of national income invested. But although the sheer simplicity of this explanation of Britain's slow growth rate made it persuasive (why look for a complicated explanation when a simple one will do?), it had certain drawbacks. One was the awkward fact that such investment in machinery and equipment as was undertaken in Britain seemed to be less productive than in other countries (Sargent, 1963). Another was the suspicion, always lurking around the social sciences, that the direction of causality may be the opposite of what appears, and that a high share of investment in the national income may be at least as much a consequence as a cause of a high rate of growth (Denison, 1967).

The fourth explanation was not fully formulated until a couple of

[1] Among those who subscribed to this kind of explanation were Dow, 1964 and Brechling and Wolfe, 1965.

years later (Kaldor, 1966), but its origins derived from a much earlier piece of research (Verdoorn, 1949), and it formed part of the climate of economic opinion in 1964. The basic hypothesis was that the growth of productivity, particularly in manufacturing industry, was positively correlated with the growth of production. This meant, in effect, that one would get a rapid rise in productivity in manufacturing only if one got a rapid rise in production – the reason being that the dynamic economies of scale required if output per man is to rise rapidly can be reaped only if output itself is rising fast. But manufacturing output cannot rise fast unless manufacturing employment is rising fast as well. In other industrial countries – Kaldor argued – this was happening: labour had been flowing into the manufacturing sector from the agricultural sector (and, in the case of West Germany, from East Germany). Not only did this result in rising productivity in the manufacturing sector as a result of the operation of Verdoorn's Law; it contributed in a second and quite separate way to increasing the growth rate, because output per man in manufacturing was higher than in agriculture, and moving men out of low productivity jobs into high productivity jobs automatically increases the national income. In Britain, however, neither factor could operate. Britain had reached a stage of development in which output per man was as high in agriculture as in manufacturing, and in which the proportion of the population still working in agriculture had fallen so low that no flow of labour out of agriculture and into manufacturing was any longer feasible. In short, Britain was suffering from 'premature maturity': it had exhausted its potential for rapid growth before achieving very high levels of productivity or real income.

This rather chilling explanation of Britain's slow growth rate has not been without its critics. One problem has been the usual one of the direction of causality: maybe a rapid rise in productivity, leading to very competitive prices and hence a rapid increase in sales, *causes* the rapid rise in production. If it is this way round, then a strong rise in the manufacturing labour force would not be a necessary condition of a rapid rate of growth of manufacturing productivity, and hence of the national income as a whole. Another criticism has queried the statistical validity of the close relationship between production and productivity on which the theory rests (Rowthorn, 1975). Nevertheless, the theory was to have a considerable impact on British economic policy in the second half of the 1960s.

The fifth and final explanation of Britain's slow growth rate was not so much a single explanation as a set of arguments which stressed the importance of a number of social and structural factors. Less fundamental perhaps than the apparently ineluctable laws of economic development which Kaldor was to invoke, these factors were nevertheless too fundamental to be swept aside simply by altering the exchange rate or lurching less violently from stop to go. They included ignorant, untrained and unadventurous management – a legacy of the long-standing distaste of the English upper classes for 'trade', and the traditional reluctance of the best minds to go into industry, rather than the Civil Service or the professions; a trade union movement resistant to change, and particularly hostile to innovations that would mean redeployment out of some jobs into others; the wrong sort of educational tradition, with an over-emphasis on non-vocational courses and inadequate provision for the training of scientists and engineers; above all, perhaps, an inheritance of class antipathies which at best meant that bosses and workers were inhabiting different worlds, speaking different languages, and at worst meant reckless confrontation: antagonists locked in deadly combat, oblivious of the chasm opening beneath their feet.

Sooner or later, in economics, it all comes back to supply and demand. Of these five explanations of Britain's slow rate of economic growth, the first two – sluggish exports and stop-go – stressed factors on the demand side, the last three – too little investment, labour shortages and out-of-date attitudes – stressed factors on the supply side. Its interventionist, anti-laissez-faire philosophy made Labour suspicious of demand-side factors; it was more inclined to believe that the fault lay on the supply side. The moral of accepting one of the first two explanations was that one should simply alter the exchange rate and leave the rest to the market; or cease to intervene continuously in the economy in order to maintain full employment, and leave the economy much more to itself. Neither moral commended itself to the Labour Party. Much more consonant with its instincts was the message that followed acceptance of one of the three supply-side explanations of slow growth: that investment must be increased, labour trained and re-trained and assisted to move from low-productivity sectors to high-productivity sectors, the quality of management improved, the educational system broadened and democratized, and social and economic inequalities reduced. In short, faster growth could not be achieved simply by manipulating demand; it could be achieved only as a result of widespread and continuous government intervention. And it is a short step from believing that what is needed is widespread and continuous government intervention to believing that what is needed is a National Plan.

NEDDY AND THE NATIONAL PLAN

Underlying the revived interest in economic planning at the beginning of the 1960s was a growing disillusionment with the results of the kind of *ad hoc* economic policies pursued throughout the 1950s. With the economy being alternately expanded and deflated like an accordion, business found it difficult to formulate or carry out sensible long-term investment plans – as indeed did the government itself. What was needed, it was increasingly felt in both industry and government, was some kind of economic strategy that would look four or five years ahead, and constitute a framework within which tactical day-to-day decisions could be made.

They seemed able to do it on the other side of the Channel. Since the 1940s France had had a series of national economic plans, and a very impressive growth rate. *Post hoc,* many people felt, *ergo propter hoc.* French planning was not 'imperative' planning, of the kind that takes place in what is sometimes called a 'command' economy, where the government specifies a large number of targets for output, investment, prices and so on in different sectors of the economy, and operates a system of punishments and rewards to ensure that the targets are met. French planning was 'indicative' – a much more flexible type of planning, appropriate to mixed economies like France and Britain where a large part of the national income is allocated by market forces, where producers and consumers are free to decide what to produce and what to spend their money on, and where economic growth, though an important objective of policy, is not given absolute priority over other objectives.

An indicative plan is neither a statement of what the government intends to happen (because its power to make things happen is limited) nor simply a forecast of what it expects to happen (for that would hardly be a plan) but something between the two. It is an ambitious but realistic indication of what might be achieved – in terms of the overall growth rate, the level of employment, the balance of payments, increases in private and public consumption and so on – provided that appropriate courses of action are followed both by the government itself and by private firms and individuals. The overall and sectoral growth rates in the plan, chosen after consultation with all the interests involved, enable different industries to determine their investment plans on the basis of common assumptions about the development of the economy; with luck this will avoid a situation in which too much capacity is installed in some industries and too little in others. An even more important feature of an indicative plan – according to some enthusiasts – is the way in which it can 'talk up' the growth rate. If the main constraint on growth is the belief that demand will not grow very fast – as perhaps it was in the early days of French planning – firms will be slow to expand their capacity, and the prophecy will be self-fulfilling. But if the government sets an ambitious growth target, and this makes firms believe that they will be able to sell more if they expand their capacity, they *will* expand their capacity; and this process, writ large, will itself bring about a faster rate of growth.

And so economic planning became all the rage – the panacea for Britain's lagging growth rate. By the time that Harold Wilson called for a four-to-five year plan in August 1961, the idea was quite well established. In 1959 Mr Heathcoat Amory had set up a committee under Sir Edwin Plowden to consider the longer-term planning of government expenditure, and in 1961 the committee recommended that both in total and in some detail government expenditure should be planned five years ahead; and since the government could not be indifferent about the proportion of the national income it spent, this implied a five-year view about the growth of the economy as a whole (HMG, 1961). In 1960 the Federation of British Industries urged the establishment of machinery that would enable the government to consult employers and unions about the longer-term needs of the economy. In January 1961 Selwyn Lloyd talked about the advantages of economic planning;[1] in September he proposed the setting up of a National Economic Development Council; and by the end of the year – although the Council did not itself meet until March 1962 – recruitment of staff for the NEDC Office was in full swing.

The basic task of NEDC (or 'Neddy') was to identify obstacles to faster growth, and to get the co-operation of both sides of industry, as well as of government, in efforts to remove them. As Selwyn Lloyd said in his Budget speech in April 1962,

> What the Council must do is to set an ambitious but realistic target figure. Both sides of industry, the Government and indeed all sections of the

[1] He may have had his elbow jogged by Macmillan, who had always been more of an interventionist than the typical Conservative. As Macmillan observed in a debate later in the year, 'I have nothing against planning; I once wrote a book about it' (Hughes, 1962, p. 231).

community must be prepared to face up to the practical consequences involved in its achievement.

The 'ambitious but realistic' target figure chosen by Neddy was 4 per cent; in a report published in 1963 (NEDC, 1963 (i)) it examined the implications of a 4 per cent growth in GDP over the five-year period 1961–66, compared with the 2.7 per cent growth rate over the previous five years. It concluded that such a growth rate was feasible provided that output per man rose by 3.2 per cent a year (the working population was expected to rise by 0.8 per cent a year) and provided that the volume of exports rose by 5 per cent a year, compared with the past trend rate of 3 per cent. Various requirements were identified: there would have to be a rise in the proportion of the national income invested, and therefore saved; there would have to be more of the right kind of education and training; and so on.

This was all quite enlightening stuff; Neddy (or rather the Neddy Office) met the first half of Selwyn Lloyd's requirements, and set an ambitious but realistic target. The trouble was that the other parties – notably the government – did not live up to the second half. Nothing much was done to *ensure* that productivity would rise by 3.2 per cent, or the volume of exports by 5 per cent. Although Maudling's 1963 Budget was based on the assumption of a 4 per cent growth rate, this was really an exercise in wishful thinking; the Conservative Government never undertook to do the things that would be needed to speed up the growth rate to 4 per cent. Perhaps this was because of Macmillan's failing grip during 1963, ending with his retirement in October; perhaps it was because the Conservatives were not at bottom very interested in faster economic growth; perhaps it was because, as political realists, they recognized the formidable difficulties of laying down plans for faster growth in a mixed economy, and getting these plans implemented. Whatever the reason, it was clear by 1964 that Neddy pronouncements had become, as one observer put it, 'merely useful propaganda support when they were in accordance with departmental policy; and words which could be safely ignored when they were not' (Mitchell, 1966, p. 144). In many ways Neddy has proved extremely useful – not least the work of its twenty or so industrial sub-committees (or 'little Neddies') where government experts, employers and unions thrash out issues pertaining to their particular industry. But in no sense was Neddy in 1964 doing the kind of planning job that was done by the *Commissariat du Plan* in France.

Hence, in Labour eyes, the need for a National Plan, which would be prepared not by some outside body but – in consultation with both sides of industry – by the government itself, and to which the government would be committed. The task of drawing up the Plan, and getting it implemented, was seen as the central function of the DEA. Work on preparing the Plan started immediately after the 1964 election, and, despite incomes policy distractions, was completed within a year: the Plan itself was published in September 1965. And an impressive-looking document it was, too. The basic projection was of a 25 per cent increase in national output over the six-year period 1964–70 – a compound rate of 3.8 per cent a year. (Although this might seem less ambitious than the 4 per cent growth rate sanctified by Neddy and the Conservatives, it was in fact slightly more ambitious, because a slower expected growth in the labour force required productivity to rise by 3.4 per cent a year, compared with 3.2 per cent under the Neddy projection.) The possible implications of the 25 per cent increase in GDP were worked out in great detail for different components of the national income, such as private consumption and private investment, and for different industries; and a checklist was drawn up of the action required by government, management and unions if the overall and sectoral targets were to be attained. To anyone who thought that something like French planning was required if Britain's growth rate was to be speeded up, it all looked like an encouraging start.

Alas, it was all a dream. Exactly the same thing was wrong with the National Plan as had been wrong with the Neddy projections: no action was taken to get exports rising fast enough to pay for the rise in imports that a 3.8 per cent growth rate would require. Under the Plan, the volume of exports would have to rise by 5¼ per cent a year. It is true that an Industrial Inquiry conducted by the DEA, in which industries were asked what a 25 per cent rise in the GDP between 1964 and 1970 would mean for them, suggested that the volume of exports would rise slightly faster than required – by 5½ per cent a year. But this was nearly double the rate achieved in the past, and at a time when Britain had lost competitiveness in world markets, and ruled out devaluation as a way of restoring it, to build the whole Plan on the assumption that an export growth rate of 5¼ per cent would be achieved with existing policies required an act of faith big enough to move mountains. The Industrial Inquiry also suggested that productivity would rise by only 3.2 per cent instead of the 3.4 per cent assumed in the Plan; if this were true, the 3.8 per cent growth rate could only be achieved if the labour force rose by 0.2 per cent a year faster than seemed likely. The manpower gap, like the credibility gap in the balance of payments, was swept discreetly under the carpet.

The National Plan was not formally interred until 20 July 1966 (see pages 72–3 below); but to close observers it had been stillborn, denied lifeblood by the decision not to devalue, and fatally damaged before birth by the measures of July 1965 (see page 53 below). To Harold Wilson, it was overwhelmed by 'short-term speculative factors' (Wilson, 1971, p. 186). George Brown was probably nearer the truth when he said that the Plan would have worked if growth had been given the priority Labour had promised it. Certainly the failure to accord growth priority over the preservation of the exchange rate doomed the Plan from the start. An indicative plan can only work if decision-makers at key points throughout the economy believe in it and act accordingly, utilizing the information in the plan to undertake an adequate amount of investment, avoiding too much capacity in some sectors and too little in others. In the face of the deflationary measures taken by the Government in 1965 and again in 1966, the National Plan was simply not credible, and decision-makers did not act as though it was. At the same time, it may have been a little naive to imagine that a 3.8 per cent rate of growth would have been achieved if only the Government had devalued, and if only everyone had believed that it would happen, and therefore acted in a way that made it happen. The forces of inertia and resistance to change are strong in the British economy, and the ability to talk up the growth rate may be limited. Evidence was to accumulate in the late 1960s and early 1970s that Britain's problem was not so much one of over-timid expectations depressing the growth rate, as of over-confident expectations about the growth rate being used to justify a faster rise in private and public consumption than the economy could afford.

ON THE TIGHTROPE

The negotiation of the $3 billion credit in November 1964 was followed by a $1 billion IMF drawing, and sterling steadied; for a few months there were no real crises. All the same, Wilson was walking a tightrope. Having pinned his colours firmly to the existing exchange rate, he was at the mercy of foreign creditors if he was to obtain the funds required to maintain it: nothing must be done to diminish foreign confidence in Britain's ability to get its inflation under control and its balance of payments back into the black. As against this, the Left of the Labour Party was impatient with the need to appease foreign bankers and international speculators, and determined that, after thirteen years in the wilderness, Labour should push firmly ahead on the road to socialism. Even Labour moderates felt that the critical economic situation should not be allowed to prevent the Government from putting some of its distinctive policies into operation. Hence a series of measures whose economic justification may not – to put it mildly – have been very strong, but whose political pay-off within the Labour movement was high: an embargo on arms sales to South Africa; a ban on office-building in central London (which, ironically, made millionaires out of those who had got permission to build just before the ban); and the announcement in February 1965 that public expenditure over the period 1964–65 to 1969–70 would rise by 4¼ per cent a year in real terms. Although the form of the last announcement stressed that public expenditure would rise by *no more than* 4¼ per cent a year, the intention that it should rise by as much as 4¼ per cent a year – i.e. considerably faster than total output, according to the National Plan – indicated the emphasis that Labour was putting on its social and egalitarian objectives.

On the balance of payments front, meanwhile, stringent action was taken to curb the outflow of long-term capital. Labour has always been hostile to overseas investment by British firms, taking the view that the money should be invested in Britain, thus raising productivity and providing employment at home instead of abroad. This is a rather over-simplified view, since if investment is prevented from taking place abroad it does not necessarily take place in Britain; and in any case much of the investment carried out abroad by British firms is designed to provide British industry with essential materials and components, or assist in the assembling, selling or servicing of British exports. Moreover such investment increases Britain's invisible income in the form of profits and dividends from abroad. Nevertheless the Labour Government, mindful of the fact that nearly half the £800 million deficit in 1964 had been accounted for by the net outflow of long-term capital, took the view that the nation could no longer afford a large outflow now for the sake of a relatively small inflow in the future.[1] Accordingly, various steps were taken, both in

[1] It was subsequently estimated that for each £100 cut in overseas direct investment, the subsequent annual loss to the balance of payments in terms of lower exports and lower invisible income would only be about £9 (Reddaway, 1968).

April 1965 and at various times thereafter, to discourage overseas investment, both direct and portfolio.[1]

There can be little doubt that these measures had a considerable effect: over the next four years the net outflow on long-term capital account fell away almost to zero. Nevertheless, they did nothing to help with the immediate problems of the deficit on the current account of the balance of payments, and the rate of inflation. By early May, in spite of the slightly deflationary Budget and a number of other steps to restrict credit, sterling was in trouble again, under the influence of bad trade figures in March and April and accumulating evidence that the incomes policy was not working, with wage settlements running at twice the 3–3½ per cent norm. The $3 billion credit, renewed for another three months in February, was soon due to expire, and it was clear that if the sterling exchange rate was to be maintained a great deal more foreign support would be needed.

Although the Americans continued to be willing to support sterling, President Johnson was far too shrewd not to see the corner into which Harold Wilson had painted himself: Wilson needed him a lot more than he needed Wilson. If Britain was to get support from the U.S. she would have to agree not to cut her defence commitments in Western Germany; she would have to reduce the high level of demand in the economy; and she would have to take some more effective steps to slow down the rise in wages. These last two conditions were also stressed by the main European countries whose participation would be needed in any further rescue operation for sterling.

The immediate upshot – the price that had to be paid for getting a further $1.4 billion from the IMF in May 1965 – was the set of 'July measures' – the first of many July measures to be taken by Labour governments over the next ten years. This particular package included the postponement of various public sector investment projects, action to delay certain kinds of private sector investment projects, and a tightening of hire purchase controls. But foreign

[1] Portfolio investment overseas (i.e. investment in securities) was discouraged by a new requirement that 25 per cent of the proceeds of the sale of overseas securities should be surrendered to the Bank of England at the official rate of exchange, instead of being sold at a premium in the 'investment dollar' market where all currency for purchases of overseas securities had to be obtained. Thus at a stroke the price of investing in overseas securities was raised and the ultimate return on such investment was lowered. Direct investment overseas, which in any case would be less profitable under the new Corporation Tax, had to be financed – after July 1965 – either out of profits or by overseas borrowing, unless it was in the sterling area; and even the latter concession was modified in April 1966.

opinion was not particularly impressed, and foreign exchange markets remained in a highly jittery condition. With great reluctance the Government came to accept that if the necessary foreign credits were to be obtained, the prices and incomes policy could no longer remain a voluntary operation: it must be given some teeth. The Americans – already puzzled by the absence in Britain of an equivalent of the Taft-Hartley Act, which enables an American Administration to order the postponement of a strike to allow tempers to cool and further negotiations to take place – wanted lion-size teeth: a wage freeze. The Labour Government resisted this, but agreed to introduce legislation which would require unions and employers to give early warning of wage claims and price increases. These proposed wage or price increases could then be referred by the government to the Prices and Incomes Board; and the parties involved would be required to defer increasing wages or prices until the Board had reported on the implications.

Selling this idea to the CBI took some doing;[1] selling it to the unions called for a miracle. George Brown duly obliged. For twelve hours on 2 September 1965 he battled with the General Council of the TUC. In the end, exhausted, it agreed to accept the proposed legislation. A week later the Chancellor announced that substantial new funds had been made available by the United States and the main European countries to support the pound. Once again, for a while, the exchange rate was safe. But at what cost? What did the willingness to tailor both domestic and overseas policies to the requirements of foreign creditors really mean? It meant that the decision to give the preservation of the existing exchange rate priority over other objectives, particularly growth, had been reaffirmed. It is small wonder that when the National Plan was published a few days later, close observers gave vent to a cynical laugh.

UNHAPPINESS IN THE UNIONS AND ON THE LEFT

The extreme reluctance of the TUC, in September 1965, to agree to George Brown's very modest proposals for inserting a statutory element into the prices and incomes policy contrasted with the hopefulness with which it had signed the Declaration of Intent nine months earlier, and was one indication of the growing unhappiness of many Labour activists during this period. Another indication was the

[1] The various employers' organizations merged in 1965 into the Confederation of British Industry.

increasingly critical tone of the articles in the left-wing weekly *Tribune*. In October and November 1964 the emphasis was on the desperate economic situation the Government had inherited and the very limited room for manoeuvre which it enjoyed. A year later the Government's policies on the economic front – and on other fronts – were under severe attack.

These criticisms of the Government's economic policies sprang from differing degrees of contact with reality. To some extent they represented no more than the hammering which any incoming government, which has to cope with the complexities of the real world, always receives at the hands of its more simple-minded supporters. Those Labour enthusiasts, for example, for whom the extension of public ownership was the touchstone of a socialist economic policy, were incensed that the Government did not proceed forthwith with the renationalization of steel, which had been promised in the manifesto. But not only would the speedy renationalization of steel have done little to help the nation's immediate economic problems (indeed it would probably have aggravated them, by convincing foreign opinion that Labour was fiddling while Rome burnt); it was also impossible in parliamentary terms. Two right-wing Labour MPs made it clear that they would vote against the proposal, and this would have denied the government a majority.[1] Similarly, there were many in the Labour Party who had – and still have – a highly exaggerated idea of the amount of resources which went into defence, and believed that the padlock on the gates of the socialist paradise was the Government's refusal to slash defence expenditure. The Labour Government's fairly bold decision in 1965 to hold defence spending at the same absolute level (in real terms) for the next five years – so that it would pre-empt a steadily diminishing proportion of the national income – was regarded by these people as quite inadequate.

More fundamental, more widely-based and, in the long run, more serious in its effects, was the increasing criticism of the Government's prices and incomes policy. The critics were of two kinds, who might be described as the toughies and the utopians. The toughies – mainly trade union leaders – were those who refused to accept that rising

[1] The careers of these two MPs never recovered from what was widely regarded in the Labour movement as an act of betrayal. Neither ever achieved office; Woodrow Wyatt lost his seat in 1970 and never found another one; Desmond Donnelly was eventually ousted by his local Labour Party, and subsequently lost his seat when he fought as an Independent in 1970.

wages were a prime cause of inflation, and who were hostile to any kind of incomes policy on the kind of grounds discussed earlier – that it would mean a rise in profits, or deprive trade union officials of their main function. By an unfortunate coincidence in the timing of the business cycle, events played into the hands of these critics. During the downswing of the cycle, profits usually fall as a proportion of the national income, as overheads and other fixed costs are spread over a lower volume of output; correspondingly, during the upswing of the cycle, they rise. The cyclical upswing set off by the Conservative measures of 1963 had been accompanied, in the usual way, by a big rise in profits; and it was these profits which were being reported by companies during late 1964 and early 1965. It was money for jam, as far as the critics were concerned, to point out that in the first quarter of 1965 profits were 40 per cent higher than in the first quarter of 1963, and to contrast that with the 3–3½ per cent a year wage increase for which workers were expected to settle under the incomes policy. The same critics would turn a blind eye to the fact that in the first quarter of 1963 profits had been 15 per cent lower than in the first quarter of 1960, whereas average earnings were 10 per cent higher. Those who had been afraid that wage restraint would mean higher profits seemed to be having their fears confirmed.

The utopians – usually left-wingers in the constituency parties – were more positive. They had a vision of the ideal society – which was understandable enough; and they thought that this society could soon be brought into existence if only the Government would do the right things – which was less understandable. The prices and incomes policy, as it developed during 1965, seemed to them to be unfair, because prices continued to rise, because the rich stayed rich, and because (though this objection was not unanimous) the lower-paid did not become significantly better off in relation to the higher-paid. Similarly, the rest of the Government's economic policies, and in particular the National Plan, seemed to them to be a betrayal of socialism. The increases in interest rates, the cuts in public expenditure, the efforts to jolly along private industry, all represented not a move towards socialism, but a willingness to co-exist with capitalism. What was needed were socialist measures: somehow (never mind exactly how) speculators must be clobbered, luxury consumption cut, unnecessary imports eliminated, wealth redistributed, the outflow of capital stopped, public ownership extended, investment increased, exports increased, wages increased and expenditure on the social services increased.

Nevertheless, for all the vulnerable woolliness of its idealism, in some ways the utopian Left had a firmer grasp of reality than the Government had. At least it understood that the era when Britain could police the world had gone for ever, and that even the maintenance of a significant military presence 'East of Suez' was now beyond the nation's means. In the same spirit, it had little interest in prolonging Britain's role as world banker and centre of the sterling area; and if its desire to appropriate private holdings of overseas securities in order to sell them and add their proceeds to the reserves struck many in the City as akin to peasant revolutionaries chopping up the Chippendale for firewood, it must have struck some more objective observers as an overdue attempt to subordinate private to social interests. The Left had, above all, got the basic point, which was that the Government's economic strategy was unviable. The Government was relying mainly on market forces to secure the faster rate of growth on which all its policies depended; yet it was refusing to let market forces determine one of the key variables in the system – the exchange rate. The Left's strategy was equally unviable, for it ignored the complexity of the mixed economy and of its relations with the rest of the world; but at least it refused to accept that growth should be sacrificed to the preservation of the existing exchange rate. Throughout 1965 devaluation, together with tougher exchange and import controls, was one of the remedies advocated by contributors to *Tribune*.

HEATH REPLACES HOME

The Labour Party was not alone at this time in suffering from internal dissension: so did the Conservatives. But whereas what divides the Labour Party is usually ideology and policy, what divides the Conservative Party is generally the question of how to win power or, having won it, to retain it. So it was on this occasion. Although Sir Alec Douglas-Home had only narrowly lost the 1964 election, the fact remained that he had lost it; and few Conservatives believed that he would do any better in any future election – an impression reinforced by the fact that as Leader of the Opposition Sir Alec cut an even poorer figure on the floor of the House of Commons than he had as Prime Minister. What was needed, many Conservatives felt, was somebody more able to cope with Harold Wilson – perhaps somebody more like Harold Wilson himself. And buried within this general determination to seek a new leader was a particular desire to oust Sir Alec on the part of those more modern-minded Tories who had been outraged by the way in which what Iain Macleod had called the 'magic circle' had conspired to foist Sir Alec on the party as successor to Harold Macmillan. To avoid another case of a highly stage-managed 'emergence' of the new leader, these Tories insisted that the choice be made – as in the Labour Party – by secret ballot of Conservative MPs, and of them alone. Sir Alec himself being quite prepared to give up the job, Butler having retired from the scene, Maudling – though a strong contender – being under a cloud as the main culprit in bringing the economy to the brink of disaster, and Enoch Powell already looking too weird and maverick a figure to entrust with the leadership of the party, the choice fell upon Edward Heath.

Heath was to a minor extent the inheritor, and to a major extent the creator, of a sharp change of trend in the conduct of politics in general and economic policy in particular. The consensus approach to the economy of the early 1950s had continued throughout the rest of the decade and into the early 1960s, reflecting the leading role played in the Labour Party throughout this period by Hugh Gaitskell, and – even after Macmillan had become Prime Minister – the pervasive influence in the Conservative Party of Mr Butler. But just as the consensus or Butskellite approach to politics had come under fire in the Labour Party after the 1959 election – notably over nationalization and nuclear disarmament – so it had been rejected by many Conservatives; the foundation in 1961 of the right-wing Monday Club signalled the belief that the Conservatives must demonstrate that their values and policies were quite distinct from those of the Labour Party. Although Heath was not regarded as being on the right wing of the party, he seemed much more likely to fill the required role than Maudling – in terms of personality as well as outlook. Maudling was ruminative and easy-going; Heath was full of drive and aggression. Maudling was firmly in the Buskellite tradition; Heath believed in efficiency, and in vigorous competition as the way to secure it. To this end, as President of the Board of Trade in 1963–64, he had forced through the abolition of resale price maintenance in the teeth of opposition from more traditional Conservatives who were reluctant to see the corner shop put out of business by the supermarket. To this end, too, he had from the beginning been a fervent supporter of British membership of the EEC, and had been put in charge of negotiating Britain's entry after Macmillan's application in 1961. His belief in competition went hand-in-hand with his belief in incentives and self-help: taxes must be lowered in order to ensure a proper reward for those whose ingenuity and energy were the mainsprings of economic growth, and welfare benefits should not be spread around indiscriminately, but concentrated on those in genuine need.

Sentiments of this kind are, of course, the small change of Tory rhetoric. But Heath, a man of stubborn integrity, really subscribed to them. Any doubts about his determination to break with the consensus politics of the last decade and a half should have been allayed by the publication in September 1965 of *Putting Britain Right Ahead* – a Conservative policy statement with Heath's hallmark firmly stamped on it. This pamphlet clearly dropped two commitments which had been in the 1964 manifesto, and which had underlain Conservative policy for several years before that – the commitment to national planning and the commitment to an incomes policy. So the publication of the much-heralded National Plan, already greeted by Labour critics as a futile exercise because the Government was not following the policies needed to make the Plan work, was greeted by the official Opposition with the much more fundamental criticism that planning was the wrong way to go about getting faster growth. Similarly, George Brown's achievement in persuading both employers and unions to agree that the prices and incomes policy must be given certain statutory teeth was dismissed as irrelevant: an incomes policy would have no place in the armoury of a future Conservative government.

It was a real change. The experiences of the late 1950s and early 1960s had brought the Conservatives, painfully and reluctantly, to the conclusion that there must be more economic planning and some kind of incomes policy. The Labour Government agreed, and had embarked on the most ambitious economic plan and the most comprehensive incomes policy so far attempted. And now the Conservatives had repudiated both exercises. It was very confusing for the unbiased observer. And it was very ominous for the rational future conduct of economic policy.

MANOEUVRING TOWARDS THE NEXT ELECTION

As 1965 wore on, the political aspects of what the Government did – and failed to do – loomed increasingly large. Life with an overall majority of five (down to three after the Leyton by-election) was not, as many had predicted, impossible; but it was very difficult.

Plainly Wilson must go to the country before long to secure a larger majority. At first, the auguries were not good. The shock of the Leyton result in January 1965 was followed by disastrous results in the local council elections in May, which showed a swing against Labour of some 10 per cent compared with the year before. Any possibility of a June election was ruled out. From May until September, the Conservative lead in the opinion polls increased, perhaps because of the rows going on in the Labour Party not only over economic policy and steel nationalization, but also over the Government's immigration policy and its support for the American position in Vietnam; and perhaps because of the replacement of Home by Heath. In September, however, the tide began to turn. One factor here may have been the Labour Party conference's massive endorsement of the statutory strengthening of the prices and incomes policy. Probably more important was the highly-publicized way in which George Brown succeeded in persuading the bakers not to increase the price of bread, and the building societies not to increase the mortgage rate: at last the Government was seen to be doing something about inflation. Labour's confidence that it might win the next election began to return. When Harold Wilson flew to Balmoral on 13 October it was widely assumed that he was going to ask the Queen for a dissolution. In fact he appears to have made the trip solely to knock Heath's keynote speech to the Conservative Party conference off the front pages of the following day's newspapers.[1] Politically, the moment had not yet come. Yet the underlying economic problem remained unresolved, and could erupt again at any time.

In November came a new problem of major dimensions – the Unilateral Declaration of Independence announced by the white Government in Southern Rhodesia. Because he had foreseen the acute difficulties this would create for the British Government, Wilson had gone to great lengths to prevent UDI, and seems to have convinced himself that in the last resort it would not happen. When it did, the Government had made no preparations to cope with it. Although bold military action might have shocked the whites into submission, this course of action was rejected: to send in British troops to fight 'our kith and kin' on behalf of the Rhodesian blacks could have cost Labour many votes. Moreover, such military action might have been halted by a torrential outflow of foreign exchange of the kind that had stopped the Suez operation ten years earlier. If UDI were not simply to be accepted as an unfortunate *fait accompli*

[1] Crossman, 13 October 1965.

– a course which would probably have split both the Labour Party and the Commonwealth – the only remaining option was economic sanctions. These did not have much of a track record – many still remembered the fiasco when the League of Nations tried to organize economic sanctions against Mussolini – but Wilson put a brave face on the matter and talked of sanctions bringing Rhodesia to its knees 'in weeks rather than months'; not one of his more successful predictions.

The main effect of the Rhodesia crisis on the British economy lay in the enormous amount of Ministerial and official time it took up. In December 1965, according to one estimate,[1] the Chancellor was spending more than a third of his time on Rhodesia, and the Prime Minister more than a half. For a nation whose house needed to be put in order as badly as Britain's, this was far too much. The economic outlook remained unpromising. There seemed little likelihood of any significant improvement in the balance of payments: in November 1965 the NIESR predicted that the current account would still be in substantial deficit in 1966. Prices continued to rise at an annual rate of about 4 per cent, but wages and salaries were rising at a rate of 8–10 per cent. This was doubly ominous: it meant – despite some increase in the savings ratio – that extra resources were going into private consumption rather than into investment or exports; and it meant that before long these higher wages would feed through into a further rise in prices. But in spite of the rise in real incomes, the incomes policy became increasingly unpopular as particular groups felt that they had been discriminated against. In February 1966 it took the eleventh-hour intervention of the Prime Minister to avert a national rail strike which the National Union of Railwaymen had called in protest against a PIB report on rail pay. Another significant point was reached in March when Britain's largest union, the Transport and General Workers' Union, whose former General Secretary, Frank Cousins, was a member of the Cabinet, announced that it would boycott PIB enquiries which were purely concerned with wage questions. The incomes policy was tottering. The idea that Britain could regain her international competitiveness by holding down the rise in her costs more effectively than other countries began to look madder than ever.

On 27 January Labour won a decisive victory in a by-election at Hull, the result showing a 4½ per cent swing to Labour since 1964. By his own account, Harold Wilson had firmly decided on a March

[1] Crossman, 9 December 1965.

election before Hull had polled (Wilson, 1971, p. 259). If so, the result can have done nothing to change his mind. An advantage of a March election for Labour was that it would be fought on a new electoral register.[1] A disadvantage, perhaps, was that it would come before the Budget, and lay the Government open to the charge that it was trying to get re-elected before taking the harsh and unpopular measures that the failure of its policies had made inevitable. To forestall this charge, Callaghan made a pre-Budget statement on 1 March, the day after Wilson had announced that the election would be held on 31 March. In this, in addition to proposing a betting tax and promising 4½ per cent mortgages for those not already benefiting from tax relief, he said that the balance of payments was rapidly improving, short-term overseas debt was being repaid, and that he did 'not foresee the need for severe increases in taxation'. The judgment was in line with what Wilson claims was the Treasury's advice: that the situation required 'a neutral Budget, with little, if any, net increase in taxation' (Wilson, 1971, p. 262). The NIESR, too, saw no need at this time for further deflation, even though it expected the improvement in the balance of payments to be very slow, with the current account no better than in balance in the first half of 1967 (NIER, February 1966).

A much more sombre view of the situation was taken at this time by Richard Crossman. Ruminating into his tape recorder on 17 February, he said:

> The main trouble is that we haven't delivered the goods; the builders are not building the houses; the cost of living is still rising; the incomes policy isn't working; we haven't held back inflation; we haven't got production moving. We are going to the country now because we anticipate that things are bound to get worse and we shall need a bigger majority with which to handle them.

This prediction proved much more accurate than the Treasury's or the National Institute's.

'YOU *KNOW* LABOUR GOVERNMENT WORKS'

Although the problem of Rhodesia hovered uneasily overhead, and although the question of whether or not Britain should again apply

[1] New electoral registers are issued each February. It is generally acknowledged that the older the register the greater the disadvantage to the Labour Party, which is much less efficient than the Conservatives at organizing a postal vote for those of its supporters who have moved away.

to join the Common Market was heard faintly in the background, and although people's concern about the cost of living featured prominently in the opinion polls, the election was not really about any of these things. It was about whether Harold Wilson should be given a clear mandate to get on with the job. Projecting something of the image of the trusted family doctor,[1] Harold's friendly but resolute visage looked out at the nation from a thousand hoardings. 'A vote for me is a vote for Harold Wilson', proclaimed hundreds of Labour candidates through their loudspeakers. 'You *know* Labour government works', insisted the campaign literature, and whatever the inner qualms felt by the more fastidious at such a claim, the nation seemed to agree, laying the blame for the current economic difficulties on the previous Conservative Government rather than the present Labour one. This was especially noticeable among the younger and more middle-class elements in the electorate, which swung quite markedly towards Labour (Butler and King, 1966). To them particularly the Labour Government seemed responsible without being stuffy, progressive without being wild, and Wilson himself appeared a reassuring figure.[2] The election result, declared on April Fools' Day, gave Labour an overall majority of ninety-seven. Provided the Party did not split, this would give Labour an unassailable parliamentary majority for four or five years – long enough to make some big and lasting changes in British society. The Left of the party looked forward to some full-blooded socialism. The social democrats wanted some radical changes too – starting with a solution of the balance of payments problem and going on to the achievement of a rapid rate of growth. The nation as a whole, numb from electioneering, and probably more interested in the World Cup than the balance of payments, kept its fingers crossed.

[1] Theodore White had apparently told Wilson that he was not a father figure but a doctor figure (Crossman, 1 February 1966).

[2] 'They think they've got a Prime Minister like them', Wilson told Crossman (Crossman, 1 April 1966).

Chapter 4
THE LIGHT THAT FAILED
April 1966-June 1970

Returning to their desks at the beginning of April 1966, exhilarated by the size of the Labour majority, Ministers found that there had been no improvement in the economic outlook while they had been away; indeed it had grown worse. New figures indicated that incomes, consumption and imports had all been higher in the early months of the year than had been anticipated; one consequence of this was that the balance of payments deficit seemed likely to be bigger in 1966 than in 1965, and to continue into 1967.

From an economic point of view, this was not a good time to devalue: there was no slack in the economy out of which could be created the extra exports and import-substitutes which it is the object of devaluation to encourage. But from a political point of view the time was ideal. This was an issue on which Labour's huge majority was unlikely to be split: for some time influential voices on the Left had been quietly demanding devaluation (while calling for a number of other, less realistic, measures); and it was an issue on which the Centre and Right, broadly speaking, would do what they were told. The City and the Conservatives might not like it, but they would have to lump it. Nevertheless, the Government did not devalue. This was not, it seems safe to say, because Harold Wilson's decisions were typically influenced more by economic considerations than political ones. It seems more probable that Yorkshire obstinacy, admirable in a good cause, was being deployed in a bad one.

The Government was now in a slightly embarrassing situation. If the existing exchange rate were to be held, it looked as though fairly drastic deflationary measures were going to be needed; yet only a month before, at the start of the election campaign, Callaghan had denied the need for severe increases in taxation. What was to be done? To turn round and increase taxes would look incredibly cynical. Monetary policy was too uncertain, cuts in public expenditure too slow-acting.

To the Chancellor's rescue – as it must have seemed to him – came Nicholas Kaldor, a Cambridge economist of high distinction who was an expert on taxation policy, and one of the large number of sympathetic economists brought into Whitehall as advisers when Labour took office in 1964.[1] Within a remarkably short space of time, Kaldor succeeded in selling Callaghan something which came to be known as the Selective Employment Tax (SET) – a device which would seemingly take money out of the economy without making the Chancellor break his word.

SELECTIVE EMPLOYMENT TAX

SET was a very interesting tax. While bringing in more revenue for the Government, it also represented an attempt to harness market forces to a socially useful end. Basically, it was a *per capita* tax on employment in the service industries, equivalent to a payroll tax of 6–7 per cent.[2]

The tax was advocated at three different levels of sophistication – not all consistent with each other. The first argument derived from the fact that consumers' expenditure on *goods* was quite heavily taxed by purchase tax and excise duties, whereas expenditure on *services* bore no tax at all. SET – assuming it was passed on in higher prices in the service industries – would thus have the effect of reducing distortions in the tax structure. This argument was widely accepted as plausible, though in fact its plausibility was somewhat suspect.[3] The second argument was that SET, provided that some of the revenue was used – as it was – to subsidize employment in manufacturing industry, would help the balance of payments. About 25 per cent of manufacturing output was exported, compared with only about 5 per cent in the service industries; it was reckoned that the adverse effect on exports of higher labour costs in the service sector would be more than offset by the favourable effect of lower labour costs in manufacturing.

The third argument was the most persuasive of all, though unlike the first two it depended on the tax *not* being passed on in higher

[1] The other most notable recruit was Thomas Balogh, for long a close friend and adviser of Harold Wilson, who became Economic Adviser to the Cabinet.

[2] It was accompanied by a small subsidy to employment in manufacturing industry.

[3] The argument assumes that the degree of monopoly is the same in both service and manufacturing sectors. If this is not the case, it follows from the theory of the second best (Lipsey and Lancaster, 1956) that it may *not* be optimal policy to align tax rates in the two sectors more closely.

prices of services. According to this third argument, the price of the output of a large part of the service sector – particularly in distribution – is determined by a traditional gross mark-up on the price of the inputs which it receives from the manufacturing sector. A tax levied on employment in the distributive sector will therefore not lead to higher prices, but will result either in a squeeze on profit margins, eliminating the least efficient firms, or in economies in the use of labour. Either way, labour productivity in the service sector will rise, and labour will, in the slightly longer run, be released for employment in the manufacturing sector. This extra inflow of labour into manufacturing will, in line with Verdoorn's law (see p. 45) increase output and productivity in that sector, and thus lead to higher exports and faster growth.

On this third interpretation, then, SET was rather a magical tax. Without all the apparatus of detailed government intervention – simply by raising the price which employers in the service sector had to pay for their labour – it would increase productivity in both the service sector and the manufacturing sector. By the same token, the Government's tax revenue would increase without the real disposable incomes of the rest of the community being reduced.[1]

Whether SET really did have these magical properties remains a matter of considerable controversy. There is no doubt that in both wholesale and retail distribution productivity did show an abnormally big rise in the years immediately after the introduction of SET. But the most exhaustive investigation which has been conducted on the effects of SET (Reddaway, 1970) found it very difficult to say how far this rise in productivity was the result of SET and how far it stemmed from other factors, such as the progressive elimination of resale price maintenance (following Edward Heath's Act of 1964), which might have been expected to have the same effect. Another study (Whitley and Worswick, 1971) found evidence that the abnormal increase in productivity in retailing in the years immediately after the introduction of SET had been accompanied by an abnormal increase in productivity in manufacturing. Since this latter increase in productivity happened too soon to be the consequence of the Verdoorn-type mechanism propounded by the advocates of SET, the hypothesis suggested itself that there was some common cause behind the abnormal increase in productivity in both sectors, and that SET had little to do with it. It was subsequently

[1] There would thus be what economists call a 'Pareto improvement': some people would be better off without anyone else being worse off.

argued, however (Reddaway, 1971), that the Whitley and Worswick study rested on inappropriate figures of manufacturing employment, and that the abnormal increase in manufacturing productivity had been very small. Other studies were critical of SET from other points of view, arguing that though it might have had the effect of increasing productivity in the service sector, the labour thus released was often geographically and occupationally immobile, and instead of moving into the manufacturing sector either became unemployed or left the labour force altogether (Hutton and Hartley, 1966).

Despite the advantages claimed for it – some at least of which were probably true – SET came under heavy fire, particularly from the business community. This was partly because it was introduced in such a hurry that it created many anomalies on which it was easy for the Conservatives to capitalize. It was partly because the very act of striking at the soft under-belly of the British economy was regarded in many quarters as hitting below the belt: perhaps, deep down, Britain is still a nation of shopkeepers. And it was by no means universally popular within the Labour Party itself. Although the Left welcomed it at first, partly on the puritanical grounds that it was penalizing the service sector, which was candyfloss and bad, and favouring the manufacturing sector, which was real and good, a certain amount of disillusionment soon set in. Even in the Cabinet it seems to have had some enemies: Richard Crossman recorded the sense of outrage he felt not only at the 'disastrous' measure, but also at the way it had been sprung on the Cabinet at the last moment, when it was too late to stop it (Crossman, 2 May 1966).

However the immediate disaster about SET was not the philosophy behind it or the rather arbitrary way in which it might work, but the fact that any deflationary effect it would have would not even begin to operate until September. For a Budget introduced on 3 May, consisting of little but the announcement of SET, in a situation which called for swift-acting deflationary measures if the exchange rate was to be preserved, this was too long a time-lag. The statement that SET would increase government revenue by £315 million in 1966–67 cut little ice with those whose horizon was limited to the likely performance of sterling during the next few weeks. The Chancellor may have welcomed SET as a way of reducing the pressure of demand without reneging on his pre-election pledges, but he was actually making the same mistake that Labour made more than once during 1964–70: using a weapon that was designed to bring about long-term structural changes in the economy as if it was a weapon suitable for coping with a short-term crisis. There was much in Crossman's subsequent verdict that the SET Budget had been an 'absolutely fatal mistake' (Crossman, 24 July 1966).

THE SEAMEN'S STRIKE

Mr Callaghan's SET Budget was only the beginning of the summer's troubles. A fortnight later, for the first time in more than fifty years, Britain's seamen went on strike. A week after that, for the first time since 1955 (and only the fourth time since the General Strike in 1926) the Government proclaimed a State of Emergency. Another crisis had arrived.

Although the seamen had various long-standing grievances, the immediate background to the strike lay in the prices and incomes policy. For some time Callaghan and Brown had been worried about the way this was being flouted, not only by settlements above the 3½ per cent norm, but by reductions in the length of the standard working week which had the same effect in raising labour costs as a straight wage increase. They believed that if foreign confidence in the pound was not to be rapidly eroded again, the Government would have to pick a particular wage claim on which to stand and fight. And the claim on which they chose to fight was that of the seamen. In the middle of April the National Union of Seamen had rejected the employers' final pay-and-hours offer, and had announced its intention to strike on 16 May. The Government decided to exert no pressure on the employers to improve their offer, and to throw its weight behind an effort to defeat the strike, starting with a broadcast by the Prime Minister on the day the strike started.

Even at the time, the decision to take on the seamen seemed unwise. It is true that their claim, for an immediate reduction in the working week from fifty-six to forty hours, represented a substantial breach in the incomes policy: conceding the claim would make little difference to the number of hours actually worked – ships at sea cannot be left to their own devices between Friday evening and Monday morning – but would mean that the last sixteen hours work each week would be paid at overtime rates. It was calculated that this would mean an increase in average weekly earnings of about 17 per cent. As against this, the seamen had quite a strong case, being relatively overworked and underpaid. They also packed a powerful punch: they could – and very soon did – bring a large part of Britain's export trade to a standstill. (Naturally enough, ships on the high seas were not affected by the strike immediately, but only as they arrived back in Britain. The effect was that imports continued to arrive for many weeks, whereas exports stopped immediately.) On the other hand, it can be argued that in a complex and sophisticated economy like Britain many unions have the power to inflict severe damage, and that there are several groups of workers – miners, railwaymen, dockers, power station workers – whose thumbs are as close to the nation's windpipe as the seamen's. On this reading, the seamen were not necessarily the worst group for the Government to take on.

As the strike dragged on from one week to another and the damage it was doing became more and more apparent, increasing pressure was brought on the seamen by both the Government and the TUC – but to no avail. A hastily-convened Court of Inquiry recommended that the reduction in the working week should be introduced over one year, compared with the employers' final offer of two years. This the union instantly and flatly rejected. Wilson became convinced that the strike – stemming initially from legitimate grievances – was now being orchestrated by 'a tightly knit group of politically motivated men' – by which he meant the Communist Party; and he named eight Communists or near-Communists who, although not themselves members of the forty-eight-man NUS executive, were exercising ruthless pressure on the executive in order to secure 'what is at present the main political and industrial objective of the Communist Party – the destruction of the Government's prices and incomes policy'.[1] Charges of this kind are always regarded with grave distaste within the Labour Party and trade union movement, being reminiscent of right-wing smear campaigns aimed at discrediting perfectly legitimate industrial action. They are also viewed with suspicion by liberal intellectuals, who recall the accusations the late Senator Joe McCarthy used to make about Communists in the American State Department. Thus, at a time when the Government's handling of the strike was already being bitterly criticized by the Left, it took considerable courage for Wilson to take the stand he did – a stand which seems to have been largely justified by the facts. Happily, it paid off. Almost immediately, the moderates on the NUS executive reasserted themselves, and the union settled on terms very close to those it had rejected three weeks earlier. George Woodcock, the General Secretary of the

[1] The quotations are from Wilson's statements in the House of Commons on 20 and 28 June respectively.

TUC, played a valuable role in settling the dispute; but the outcome was generally regarded at the time as a personal triumph for the Prime Minister.

But courage and an isolated personal triumph were not enough. It was the wider picture that Britain's creditors were looking at, and this was still bleak. The Government's willingness to fight the seamen to the death was supposed to demonstrate its determination to make the incomes policy stick. What the seven-week strike actually demonstrated was the alarming vulnerability of the British economy and of the Government's strategy for putting it to rights. The cost of the strike to the shipping industry alone was estimated at tens of millions of pounds; and export markets had been lost, some probably irretrievably. And at the end of the day, although the hard-line extremists had been visibly defeated, the settlement – involving the equivalent of a 17 per cent increase after a year instead of immediately – was still very inflationary. Foreign opinion was not impressed.

THE JULY MEASURES

Large amounts of money left the country in May and June, and it cost the Bank of England many hundreds of millions of pounds to support the exchange rate. Increasing pressure was put on the Government by the IMF, OECD and the Bank for International Settlements (BIS) to cut back expenditure and tighten the incomes policy. By the beginning of July it was obvious to all but the most feckless optimists that some kind of crunch was coming. As Crossman put it on 3 July: 'Very soon we shall be faced with a choice between devaluation or intensive deflation.' Wilson was later to talk of the economy being 'blown off course' by the seamen's strike, but this was mere self-deception.[1] Nothing had really changed since the Budget two months before. The economic situation was unviable now because it had been unviable then.

Which of the two options – devaluation or deflation – would be chosen was not entirely a foregone conclusion. Although Wilson himself was still adamantly, even pathologically, opposed to devaluation, there was less disposition than there had been in the heady days of October 1964 to accept his *diktat* without question. In some ways his position had been weakened by the Government's much increased

[1] Statement to House of Commons, 20 July 1966.

majority; he could no longer be regarded as utterly indispensable in the way he was between October 1964 and March 1966. Moreover the consequences of refusing to devalue were now more apparent than they had been: for two years now the economy had been living from crisis to crisis, and things were in as much of a mess as ever. As the signs began to accumulate that the Treasury was preparing yet another deflationary package, a small but influential group of Cabinet Ministers, including Crossman, Roy Jenkins and Anthony Crosland, started to argue the case for devaluation.[1] On their side they not only had economic common sense but also – not necessarily the same thing – the virtually unanimous view of the Government's economic advisers, and the regular support of some of the left-wingers who wrote for *Tribune.* And George Brown, though he fatally failed to give a firm and consistent lead, had become pretty well convinced that devaluation was necessary. At one point Callaghan himself seems to have wavered, agreeing with Brown to present a common front to Wilson in demanding devaluation – a demand which the Prime Minister might have found it difficult to resist. But Wilson got wind of this plot and managed to bring Callaghan round, promising in the process that he, and not the Chancellor, would announce the unpopular deflationary measures which would be needed if devaluation was to be staved off.

In the end, Wilson's view prevailed. In the immediate sense this was because, with the Chancellor and a number of other ministers on his side, he was able to convince a majority of his Cabinet colleagues that it could be disastrous to float the pound from a position of weakness, and promised that once the immediate crisis was over a top-level Cabinet committee would be set up to examine the whole question of the Government's economic strategy and the floating of the pound.[2] But there were two other reasons for Wilson's victory. One lay in his control, through Sir Burke Trend, the Secretary of the Cabinet, of the Whitehall machine. As comes out vividly from Crossman's account of this period, Whitehall was already far ad-

[1] In fact they wanted to float the pound for a while rather than devalue immediately to a new fixed exchange rate. Floating would have resulted in a substantial devaluation, but would have had the advantage of allowing market forces, rather than government guesswork, to determine the new rate. (It would also have had the advantage, one cannot help feeling, of permitting Wilson to exercise his unique skill of rationalizing defeat in the language of victory: 'as an ultimate sign of our determination not to devalue the pound', one can almost hear him saying 'we have decided to float it'.)

[2] Crossman, 19 July. When the committee was eventually set up its composition caused Crossman, who strongly supported the idea, to describe it with disgust as a 'panjandrum committee' unlikely to achieve anything – which indeed proved to be the case.

vanced in planning the cuts finally announced on 20 July at a time when Ministers were still arguing whether such cuts were needed.[1] In the end, the Prime Minister and the Chancellor effectively presented their colleagues with a *fait accompli.* The second, and ultimately decisive reason why devaluation was rejected lay in the internal politics of the Labour Party. By and large the pro-devaluers in the Cabinet and among other Ministers were in the centre or on the right of the party, and were also in favour of Britain joining the EEC. Early in July, President Pompidou had dropped a broad hint to the effect that Britain would have to devalue if it joined the EEC, and members of the Cabinet who were neutral or opposed to EEC membership were suspicious that the pressure for devaluation was a first step in the direction of British entry. Even more important was the fact that Harold Wilson, despite the increasing body of evidence to suggest that he was a centrist pragmatist, was still regarded by the Left as one of themselves. Although left-wing members of the Cabinet such as Richard Crossman and Barbara Castle wanted devaluation, they were not willing to press the issue to the point at which Wilson might resign and be replaced by Brown or Callaghan. So Wilson got his way.

On 14 July Bank Rate was raised by 1 per cent, a call was made on the clearing banks for special deposits,[2] and Wilson announced in the House of Commons that the Government was reviewing the economic situation and that 'in the near future' he would be announcing some deflationary measures. This announcement about an announcement had the same perverse effect as it was to have exactly nine years later (see p. 211): everybody became more jittery than ever, the outflow of capital became a torrent, and the timetable had to be drastically telescoped. On 20 July Wilson unveiled the deflationary package the Government had decided on, which aimed at reducing demand by £500 million. All indirect taxes were increased, by use of the 'regulator', by 10 per cent. Hire purchase restrictions were further tightened, as were building controls in the private sector. Public investment was to be cut by £150 million, though houses, schools and hospitals were to be exempted. Government overseas

[1] Wilson himself initiated the whole exercise by drafting a remarkable memorandum in which he listed no fewer than twenty-eight steps which he thought should be taken. To those who remembered the famous Fourteen Points of an earlier Wilson this document immediately became known as 'the double Woodrow'.

[2] Special deposits are cash deposits which the clearing banks are required to make with the Bank of England. By reducing the banks' liquidity, a call for special deposits leads to a tightening of credit.

expenditure, both civil and military, was to be reduced by at least £100 million. The personal travel allowance was to be reduced to £50 from the autumn. A 10 per cent surcharge was to be imposed on 1965–66 surtax liabilities. And – most dramatic of all – there was to be a six-month standstill on wages, salaries and dividends, to be followed by a further six-month period of 'severe restraint'. With certain exceptions, arising mainly from any increased price of imports, prices, too, were to be frozen.

REACTIONS TO THE JULY MEASURES

It is hard to imagine a more complete *volte-face* in policy than that represented by the July measures. The Labour Party, when in opposition, had spent the early 1960s vigorously denouncing the deflationary package of July 1961, the Selwyn Lloyd pay pause of 1961–62, and the heavy unemployment of 1962–63. In the election campaigns of 1964 and 1966 it had promised full employment and faster growth, and in September 1965 had published the National Plan, showing how the GDP might grow by 25 per cent between 1964 and 1970. Now it had introduced the biggest deflationary package ever, and had imposed a compulsory freeze on all wages and prices. The consequence was bound to be rising unemployment, stagnant output, and the complete abandonment of the National Plan.[1]

What was particularly infuriating about the July measures was that they led up a blind alley. Had they been accompanied by devaluation, or even a firm decision to devalue a few months later when slack had started to appear in the economy, they would have made some sense. As it was, they presaged only a short-term improvement in the balance of payments, via a fall in imports as domestic activity levelled out, which would soon be reversed – as it had been in 1959–60 and 1963–64 – when heavy unemployment forced the Government to reflate the economy again. Similarly, the freeze on wages and prices made little sense in the absence of devaluation: it could not possibly last long enough to restore Britain's competitiveness, yet used up a large amount of Labour's invaluable political credit balance with the trade unions, which would have been better stored up against the day – after devaluation – when it was really

[1] The NIESR predicted in August 1966 that the rise in GDP between 1964 and 1970 might be 'perhaps 15 per cent', compared with the target of 25 per cent; in the event the figure was 14 per cent.

needed. Yet, despite the fact that the July measures made nonsense of everything Labour had been saying for the past few years, and despite the fact that by themselves these measures offered no solution to Britain's problems, not a single member of the Government resigned – except for George Brown, who resigned and then, after a few hours, de-resigned. Only some of those Labour supporters who had entered Whitehall after the victory of 1964 as advisers, and a few civil servants who had hoped that under Labour things would be different, regarded the July measures as the last straw, and started looking for other jobs.

The TUC reluctantly acquiesced in the measures: despite George Woodcock's warning that the freeze could not work, the General Council voted twenty to twelve in the Government's favour on 27 July, and this decision was subsequently endorsed, though only by a very small majority, at the TUC Annual Congress in September. The CBI, too, agreed to co-operate in implementing the wage and price freeze. In a technical sense this co-operation on the part of the TUC and the CBI was essential, because the standstill did not become law until 12 August, when the Prices and Incomes Bill received the Royal Assent.[1] But in a deeper sense the co-operation, or at any rate the acquiescence, of the TUC and the CBI was a necessary – though not a sufficient – condition of the success of the standstill. Despite their own misgivings, and the outright hostility of many of those they represented, both bodies rallied round in what they were persuaded was Britain's hour of need.

The Left was less obliging. On 13 July fifty Labour MPs, led by Frank Cousins, had called for the rejection of the original, rather modest, Prices and Incomes Bill. The extended Bill, including the new Part IV, which contained the implicit threat that workers could be fined, perhaps even imprisoned, for bringing pressure to bear on employers to make them grant a wage increase, raised their hackles even more. They objected violently, too, to the cuts in public expenditure and the other deflationary measures making up the

[1] The original Prices and Incomes Bill (see p. 54) which had lapsed with the dissolution of the previous Parliament in March, which required employers and unions to notify wage claims and proposed price increases to the Prices and Incomes Board, and empowered the PIB to defer the implementation of such wage and price increases for up to three months, had been published again on 4 July (occasioning the resignation from the Government of Frank Cousins, who rejected the idea of having a statutory element in the incomes policy). After the 20 July announcement, the Government tacked a new Part IV on to the Bill at Committee stage, giving effect to the standstill. It was this extended Bill which became law on 12 August.

package, and advocated the familiar triad of import quotas, tougher controls over the outflow of long-term capital, and cuts in defence expenditure overseas. These criticisms were subsequently set out, in September, in a pamphlet (Kerr *et al.*, 1966) in which it was argued that if import and exchange controls, accompanied by action to appropriate and liquidate privately-owned holdings of foreign shares and securities, did not work, then the pound should be devalued.

The Left was perhaps a trifle muddled: import quotas and devaluation are essentially alternative ways of curing a balance of payments deficit – if one needs both of them then neither is being used properly. It was also somewhat naive: the introduction of legislation to tighten exchange controls or take over privately-owned foreign securities would have been much more likely to weaken the pound than strengthen it. Nevertheless, the Left was at least plugged in to the point that much of the Right was not: that if the balance of payments was the constraint on growth then the answer was to take direct action to get the balance of payments right, not to deflate the economy. But the Left was largely impotent. Left-wing MPs could – and several did – abstain when the Government's legislation came before the House; but the Government still had a comfortable majority. They could, perhaps, have brought the Government down by voting against it; but that was something neither their consciences nor their constituency parties would have stood for.

Conservative criticism of the July measures was rather more muted, as was only decent; Labour had inherited an adverse balance of payments from them, and was now taking much the same steps to cope with it as they themselves had taken in 1961. Mr Maudling agreed that the Government had been right not to devalue or introduce import quotas. The best that he and Heath could do was to argue that Labour's inept handling of the economy, and in particular its tax reforms, had caused foreigners to lose confidence in Britain, and that the loss of confidence was the main cause of the trouble.

Each criticism – that from the Left and that from the Right – contained a grain of truth. There were two coherent strategies open to the Government when it was returned with a large majority at the beginning of April 1966. One was to take a giant stride down the road towards completely centralized control of the economy. This could have meant, among other things, the state acquiring all overseas assets owned by British citizens, and allocating all foreign exchange only in accordance with centrally-determined priorities. The sterling balances held in London by foreign governments and businesses could have been blocked. In this way, a process of explicit choice, rather than general deflation, would have kept imports down to the level that could be paid for by exports; and the danger of a loss of reserves caused by a run on the pound would have been averted by simply refusing to convert sterling holdings into foreign exchange. Thus, at any rate in theory, deflation, stagnation and heavy unemployment could have been avoided.

Although this was a coherent strategy, and was very much what the Left was calling for, there never seemed much likelihood of the Government adopting it. It would have meant an abrupt reversal of the policy of progressively reducing restrictions on international trade and payments which Britain and other Western countries had been pursuing for the previous twenty years. It would also have meant an outright repudiation of Britain's role as an international banker. Moreover, so complex are Britain's trading and financial links with the rest of the world that the transition to such a siege economy would probably have been much slower and more painful than its proponents imagined: in the short run at least, scarcities of key items as a result of cuts in imports, and loss of foreign markets as a result of retaliation, could have led to just as much unemployment as deflation did.

The other coherent strategy was to roll with the punch: to accept that for the time being at any rate Britain was not only a mixed economy but an open economy, and that trade and capital flows in to and out of the country are determined very largely by market forces. But if market forces are to work, supply and demand must be brought into balance by the price mechanism. Refusing to devalue was to refuse to allow the price mechanism to equate the supply and demand for sterling.

So the Government fell between two stools. It neither went boldly for a socialist or collectivist solution, nor did it play the mixed economy game properly. The result, as exemplified by the 20 July measures, was effectively an abdication of its responsibility to maintain full employment and a satisfactory rate of growth.

EEC: SECOND SHOT

The period from the autumn of 1966 to the autumn of 1967 witnessed not only the terminal phase of Labour's attempt to stave off devaluation, but also a further instalment in the lengthy epic of its love-hate relationship with the EEC. Harold Macmillan's original application to join the Common Market in 1961 had been greeted with cautious approval by Gaitskell, then Leader of the Labour Party, who took the view that although the economic arguments were probably evenly balanced, there were important political considerations which favoured entry. But a year later, partly perhaps as a way of uniting the Labour Party, but mainly as a result of personal reflection, he swung the Party against entry in a famous speech at the annual conference at Brighton, proclaiming that British membership of the EEC would mean 'the end of a thousand years of history'. Although there was from the start a sizeable element within the Labour Party, particularly on the centre-right of the Parliamentary Party, strongly in favour of entry, hostility tinged with indifference remained broadly the party's official line for the next three or four years, and the Common Market was barely mentioned in the 1964 manifesto.

However, high office brings new perspectives. Wilson had for long believed that there was great scope for an expansion of trade and economic co-operation between Britain and the Commonwealth – a belief which found enthusiastic expression in Labour's 1964 manifesto. But nothing much came of this. Commonwealth countries were unwilling to extend new preferences to British exports – or even maintain existing ones: they might feel some sentimental attachment towards the old mother country, but they also wanted value for money. Britain, for her part, had little to offer: she could no longer afford to give the Commonwealth unrestricted access to the London capital market, and she could play no more than a subsidiary role in creating and financing something Wilson himself was keen on, international commodity agreements to stabilize the price of Commonwealth primary products.

If closer links with the Commonwealth were a pipe dream, what were the alternatives? Could Britain continue to stand alone? She could, but the on-going 'Kennedy round' of negotiations on tariff cuts, which were dominated by the two huge blocs of the United States and the EEC, underlined the increasing dangers of economic isolation. One way of avoiding this would have been for Britain to attach itself in some way to the U.S., and at one point Whitehall, on Wilson's initiative, and for the most part with undisguised scepticism, conducted a brief investigation of the possibilities of launching a North Atlantic Free Trade Area (NAFTA). But even Wilson himself does not seem to have taken this option very seriously. The only real alternative to going it alone seemed to be entry into the EEC. No doubt other, less elevated, considerations than those concerned with

Britain's economic future were also at work. Wilson may have looked forward to a leading role on the larger European stage; he may, like Macmillan before him, have welcomed the opportunity to divert attention away from current economic problems; he may have found irresistible the temptation to pinch Mr Heath's clothes – for Heath, now the vociferously pro-EEC Leader of the Opposition, had been the chief negotiator of Britain's previous attempt to join the Common Market, which had been stopped dead by de Gaulle's sudden veto in January 1963.

Whatever the cause, Wilson announced during the 1966 election campaign that 'given a fair wind, we will negotiate our way into the Common Market, head held high, not crawl in. And we shall go in if the conditions are right' (quoted in Wilson, 1971, p. 283). After the election, apparently undeterred by the fact that de Gaulle was still President of France and that there was no reason to suppose that his love for the British had grown during the previous three years, he put George Thomson in charge of the delicate task of opening up the subject of a new membership application by Britain with both the Six and with Britain's partners in EFTA. Gradually, the pace began to accelerate. Whitehall was again put to work on the detailed implications of EEC membership for the U.K.; in July, tentative discussions were held with Pompidou; in October the Cabinet agreed that early in the new year Wilson and Brown should tour the capitals of the Six, testing the water; in December the EFTA heads of government gave their provisional blessing; in March and April 1967 the Cabinet had endless discussions of the pros and cons of membership; in May Wilson announced the decision to apply for membership, and the House of Commons endorsed this decision by a massive majority of 488 to 62 (only thirty-five Labour MPs voting against); and in October the Labour Party conference backed Wilson's initiative by a majority of two to one.

The only thing missing in this triumphal progress, cynics must have felt, was the proverbial banana skin. They need not have worried: it soon made an appearance. On 27 October 1967 de Gaulle made it clear that he was totally opposed to British membership, and on 19 December he formally imposed the veto. If applying to join the Common Market was a game of snakes and ladders, Britain was once again back at square one.

THE BUMPY ROAD TO DEVALUATION

Meanwhile, the nation was learning to live with its first full-blown prices and incomes freeze – and doing so with remarkably good grace. At first, at any rate, the freeze was distinctly popular (Behrend, 1972), people's dislike of having their own wages frozen apparently being outweighed by their relief that other people's were frozen as well. The policy was also notably successful. During the year from July 1966, wages rose by only 2 per cent. Prices, too, rose by 2 per cent, but this largely reflected the increase in indirect taxes which formed part of the July measures: there was little substance in the criticisms from the Left that the policy was being applied more stringently to wages than prices.

However a complete freeze cannot last for long if the working of a mixed economy is not to become seriously distorted, and in March 1967 the Government published a White Paper on the arrangements to succeed the period of severe restraint from July 1967. Essentially, it proposed that there should be a year of 'moderation', meaning that no one could expect as of right to receive a wage or salary increase during the coming year, and that increases should be confined to worthy cases – the low-paid, those who co-operated in raising productivity, and so on. The powers to prevent increases in wages and prices under Part IV of the 1966 Prices and Incomes Act would be allowed to lapse; henceforth reliance would be placed on an amended Part II, which would do no more than defer proposed wage or price increases for a maximum period of seven months. These arrangements were accepted with resignation by the TUC and CBI, though the Conservative Opposition voted against the proposals in the House of Commons, and thirty Left-wing Labour MPs abstained.

This abstention by Labour MPs reflected not only their dislike of government interference with collective bargaining but also their continued disenchantment with the Government's economic policy as a whole. The deflationary package of July 1966 had had its anticipated effects. Output had stagnated and unemployment had risen: by mid-1967 it was 2.2 per cent, compared with 1.2 per cent a year earlier. The trade figures showed some improvement, but this reflected the fall in imports always associated with the stop part of the stop-go cycle rather than any marked surge in exports; and some boost was given to imports of manufactured goods by the final removal in November 1966 of Labour's much-criticized temporary import surcharge.[1] Although Callaghan, introducing his neutral Budget of April 1967, had talked confidently of combining 3 per cent growth with a satisfactory balance of payments surplus, this was all pie in the sky as long as the Government neither moved to a more realistic exchange rate nor introduced a real siege economy. There was no prospect, as the Government seemed to imagine, of the incomes policy and the additional restraining effect on wages of running the economy at a higher rate of unemployment improving Britain's competitiveness either far enough or fast enough to permit both growth and a balance of payments surplus. The fatal contradiction at the heart of the Government's economic policy remained. Stagnating output could keep the balance of payments problem at bay, but only at the expense of unemployment rising to a level that would soon become politically impossible to sustain; and any attempt to reverse the rise in unemployment would lead to renewed trouble with the balance of payments.

To its credit the Government, in late 1966 and early 1967, did announce two measures which had the effect of mitigating this central contradiction in its economic policy. One was the Regional Employment Premium (REP), an employment subsidy of £1.50 a week (about 6 per cent) for adult men, and correspondingly smaller amounts for other workers, paid to manufacturing industry in the development areas. It was hoped that this labour subsidy would lead to a fall in the price of goods manufactured in the North and West, diverting demand away from factories in the Midlands and South East. There would be an easing in the pressure of demand in the low-unemployment areas, thus weakening the forces making for demand-pull inflation, and an increase in the pressure of demand in the development areas, thus reducing their politically embarrassing rate of unemployment. There might even be a bit of a balance of payments bonus, as cheaper output from manufacturing industry in the North and West found its way into export markets.[2] The other measure was the announcement in December 1966 of a temporary increase in the

[1] Estimates of the effect of the surcharge vary considerably. The Chancellor's forecast in November 1964 was that the saving on the import bill would be 'approaching £300 million a year'. One *ex post facto* analysis (Johnston and Henderson, 1967) put the saving on imports over the whole two-year period of the surcharge at no more than £100–150 million; another (NIER, Nov. 1967) put the effect over the two years at about £350 million. Even by this latter tally, the saving achieved seems to have been significantly smaller than the Government had expected.

[2] REP and regional policy generally are discussed further on pp. 100–2.

rate of investment grants paid to manufacturing and certain other industries: investment undertaken before the end of December 1968 would attract an extra Government grant. The idea here was to encourage manufacturing industry to re-equip itself at a time when there would otherwise be spare capacity in the capital goods industries.[1]

Like SET – though less controversially – both measures represented an intelligent attempt to identify some of the things wrong with the British economy and to put them right, not by detailed intervention in industrial decision-making, but by effecting a simple change in the parameters within which industry worked. Both deserved to be – and within limits were – successful in securing their main objectives. But like so much else that Labour did at this time, neither measure had much direct bearing on the nation's fundamental economic problem.

During the later part of 1966 and the early part of 1967, as it became apparent to foreign opinion that the freeze was holding and that deflation was beginning to bite, there was a considerable reflux of the funds that had left Britain during 1966; there was some strengthening of sterling and most of the short-term assistance which had been received from other Central Banks was repaid. But despite the usual month-to-month fluctuations, no evidence appeared of any sustained improvement in the trade figures. There seemed little prospect of even a modest current account surplus in the foreseeable future, let alone a surplus big enough both to repay the $2.4 billion that Britain owed the IMF, and at the same time to strengthen the reserves. The pound remained in the same condition as it had been for more than three years: vulnerable.

The extent of this vulnerability was demonstrated in May, when the combination of Britain's application for membership of the EEC, which it was variously estimated would increase the nation's balance of payments deficit by anything between £450 million and £900 million (Brittan, 1971, p. 349), and the announcement of bad trade figures for April, signalled the beginning of yet another massive run on the pound. Matters were not improved by the Six Day War which broke out in the Middle East on 5 June. Egyptian accusations – later agreed to have been wholly unfounded – that Israel's devastating initial attack had been made under cover of British and American air support led the Arab oil producing nations to impose an embargo on

[1] Sweden had for some time been using taxes and subsidies to influence the timing of investment expenditure (Lindbeck, 1975, pp. 97–102).

shipments of oil to the U.S. and U.K. The embargo actually lasted less than a month, being called off as a result of pressure from Saudi Arabia and Kuwait, who were afraid – ironically, in the light of what happened after the next Middle East war six years later – that if it were continued any longer it might lead to the collapse of their *own* economies. But the temporary embargo further weakened confidence in the pound. Much longer-term in its effects was the closure of the Suez Canal, an action bound to increase the cost of some of Britain's essential imports and damage her export trade with the Far East. It was hardly surprising that an outspoken OECD report published on 24 July underlined the weakness of the British balance of payments and her relatively low ratio of reserves to liabilities. Unfortunate, too, were dock strikes in London and Liverpool which broke out in September and continued for some two months; these had much the same effect as the 1966 seamen's strike in hitting exports immediately, but imports only after a time-lag.

During late October and early November the crisis built up. The trade figures for September (published on 12 October) were bad; the EEC countries made it increasingly clear that there was no prospect of British membership at the present exchange rate; the pound was on the floor, and only prevented from falling through it by large and increasing intervention by the Bank of England in both spot and forward markets, at the cost of many hundreds of millions of pounds to the nation's gold and foreign exchange reserves. The Treasury's autumn economic forecasts, which became available to Ministers in late October or early November, apparently showed an overall balance of payments deficit of £500 million in 1967 and not much less in 1968 (Brittan, 1971, pp. 356–7). The writing was now on the wall in such large letters that not even Harold Wilson could fail to see it. The only conceivable way to avert devaluation would have been a savage further deflation. Quite apart from the sheer senselessness of this, it would not have been politically possible. Labour MPs were already up in arms about the high and rising level of unemployment, which in October had reached a rate of 2.4 per cent – the highest October figure for twenty-five years; and early in November seventy Labour MPs, by no means all on the Left of the party, signed a motion deploring Callaghan's apparent willingness to countenance a permanently higher level of unemployment than had become customary during the previous couple of decades.

The question now was not whether, but when and by how much. The answer came at 9.30 p.m. on Saturday 18 November, when

James Callaghan announced a change in the pound's dollar parity from \$2.80 to \$2.40, a devaluation of 14.3 per cent.

REACTIONS TO DEVALUATION

The Government had talked and acted for so long as if devaluation was a fate worse than death that it is hardly surprising that when it came many people should have regarded it as a major national defeat and humiliation. A second setback to the nation's morale came ten days later when President de Gaulle made it clear at a press conference that great changes would be needed in Britain's economy and attitude of mind before she could be regarded as fit for membership of the EEC. Wilson himself contributed to the general unease and demoralization by a television broadcast in which he assumed something of the air of a Sir Galahad who had battled gallantly in a noble cause, and finally been overwhelmed by tremendous odds. 'We were right to fight', he said, attributing defeat to 'successive waves of speculation'. In fact, he had been quite wrong to fight, and what had defeated him were the realities of the situation.[1]

Predictably, it was the City of London which reacted worst of all. Obsessed with its traditional role as a world financial centre, and with the traditional role of sterling as a world reserve and trading currency, it had failed to notice that Britain had become a second rank industrial power with a sluggish growth rate and an uncompetitive exchange rate. Devaluation was seen not as a belated and essentially technical adjustment to changed economic conditions, but as a crushing blow to the City's self-esteem. There was much talk of dishonourable betrayal of overseas holders of sterling, as if these were ignorant natives, keeping their money in London out of sentimental gratitude to the mother country, rather than hard-headed central bankers keeping their money in London because interest rates there were much higher than anywhere else. Particularly absurd was

[1] It was typical of the general bewilderment that criticism of Wilson's broadcast should have fastened not on his Walter Mitty fantasies but on his statement that 'the pound in your pocket' had not been devalued. While clumsily phrased, this was a perfectly legitimate attempt to explain to people who did not understand what devaluation meant that it was in terms of foreign currency that a pound note had lost 14.3 per cent of its value, not in terms of what it would buy in the shops the following morning. (In practice the actual extent of the devaluation was closer to 11.5 per cent than 14.3 per cent, because it was accompanied by the abolition of the export rebate (see p. 31) and of the SET subsidy to manufacturing industry outside development areas (see p. 65).) It was estimated that devaluation would eventually add about 3 per cent to the retail price index.

the reaction of Lord Cromer, who had ceased to be Governor of the Bank of England in June 1966, and now retaliated for his defeat by Wilson in November 1964 by talking of the tragic consequences of 'the promotion of party political dogma' (a description of the Government's activities which must have caused some surprise to the Labour Left); asserting – as if the huge balance of payments deficit inherited by Labour in 1964 had never existed – that devaluation was 'the outcome solely of the Government's policies'; and asking 'how can those responsible for the default, and those who condone the default, command respect as worthy leaders of this nation?'[1]

Predictable, too, was the reaction of the Conservative Party. If the Government itself admitted that devaluation was a defeat for its policies, it was hardly for the Conservatives to disagree. Yet there was a certain hollowness to their attack. Not only had they handed Labour a large balance of payments deficit in October 1964; they had failed ever since to offer any coherent strategy for dealing with it. Maudling had specifically rejected both devaluation and import controls,[2] and such action as the Labour Government had taken to restrict overseas investment and cut back overseas defence expenditure had been greeted with a chorus of horror from the Opposition front bench. Conservative spokesmen had largely fallen back on ritual incantations about the need to cut public expenditure and reduce direct taxes, though just how this would have restored the balance of payments to surplus was not entirely clear – a lack of clarity which the enactment of the doctrine by the next Conservative Government (see Chapter 5) did nothing to dissipate. They were now reduced to arguing that devaluation was the consequence of a loss of confidence in the Labour Government, and in particular of such iniquitous socialist innovations as its capital gains tax and corporation tax.

More surprising was the reaction of the CBI. One consequence of devaluation that most economists are agreed about is that it increases profits as a proportion of the national income[3] – indeed this was the reason for the announcement, at the time of devaluation, of an

[1] House of Lords debate, 21 November 1967.

[2] Letter to *The Observer*, August 1967.

[3] In the present case, if the dollar price of British exports was left unchanged, the sterling price would rise by 16.7 per cent – far more than any rise in a firm's costs as a result of higher sterling import prices. Alternatively, if a British firm kept its sterling price unchanged and thus reduced its dollar price by 14.3 per cent, the consequent increase in the volume of its sales would reduce overhead costs per unit of output and thus raise profits per unit of output.

increase in corporation tax from 40 to 42½ per cent. Initially, at any rate, the CBI seems to have failed to understand this, and put out a statement that industry would be 'out of pocket' as a result of devaluation (Brittan, 1971, p. 377).

One quarter from which the Government might have expected an enthusiastic welcome for devaluation was the Labour Left; contributors to *Tribune* had, after all, been calling for it long enough. Indeed Norman Atkinson, long-standing Tribunite and several times left-wing challenger for the party Treasurership, said that he backed the move '100 per cent', and Eric Heffer, who was to emerge in the 1970s as one of the leading figures on the Left, welcomed the fact that at last 'the interests of our people are being placed before the sacred cow of maintaining the pound'. But, alas, not everyone who had called for devaluation seems to have appreciated what it meant. This became clear from the reactions of the Left when James Callaghan's Letter of Intent to the Managing Director of the IMF, which had been sent on 23 November, was published on 30 November.[1]

Underlying the Letter of Intent was the brute fact that if Britain was to make the new rate of $2.40 to the pound stick, it needed the help of the international financial community. In a rational world speculation against a currency might be expected to cease once the worst has happened and the currency has been devalued, but the world of exchange rate changes and short-term capital flows is far from rational, and it was to be nearly two years before sterling's new parity could be regarded as really firmly established. In the meantime Britain needed to be able to draw on large amounts of foreign currencies if it was to be able to fight off speculative attacks which might have forced another – and in terms of international competitiveness quite unjustified – devaluation which might have caused the Government to lose control of the situation altogether. And if the international financial community – meaning the IMF and particularly those members of it known as the Group of Ten[2] – was to provide the necessary help, it wanted an assurance that Britain was going to stop messing about and really put its house in order.

The Letter of Intent provided this assurance. The Government was

[1] On 29 November Roy Jenkins became Chancellor of the Exchequer, James Callaghan – to emphasize that his inevitable resignation was an honourable one – replacing Jenkins as Home Secretary.

[2] The Group of Ten comprised the main countries in what is loosely termed 'the West': the United States, Canada, Britain, France, West Germany, Sweden, Italy, Belgium, the Netherlands and Japan.

aiming – said Callaghan – to improve the balance of payments by 'at least £500 million a year', and it recognized that this meant freeing resources from domestic use to the extent of perhaps £800 million – the extra £300 million being required to make good the worsening in the terms of trade involved in devaluation. It was thought that the deflationary measures announced at the time of devaluation (see p. 88 below), together with the contractionary effect that devaluation itself would have on real incomes, by increasing the sterling price of imports, would achieve this; but if not, further steps would be taken – steps which would be discussed in advance with the IMF. Pledges were also given to keep the money supply and the public sector borrowing requirement (PSBR) under strict control, and to continue to operate a firm prices and incomes policy.

The Letter of Intent thus recognized one of the key consequences of devaluation: a worsening in the terms of trade. To a double extent, after devaluation, must exports be increased, or imports reduced, or both; for one not only has to eliminate the balance of payments deficit which has made the devaluation necessary; one also has to make up for the fact that each object exported is now earning less foreign currency, and so more of them must be sold. Until the balance of payments was put right – and at long last devaluation had, it was to be hoped, provided the necessary price incentives for this – the increase in resources available at home for raising consumption or public expenditure was going to be very limited. It was the Left's somewhat belated recognition of this fact which made it so unhappy about the Letter of Intent, speakers such as Michael Foot and John Mendelson bitterly criticizing the Government's pledge to cut borrowing, and claiming that although the Conservatives had been defeated at the polls, Conservative policies were now being imposed on the nation by outside bodies.

For all the objections and the rhetoric, the fact remained that at last the Government had embarked on a course which promised, for the first time in fifteen years, to rid the nation of the incubus of a chronic balance of payments deficit. The question was, could the Government hold down domestic demand sufficiently firmly, and for a sufficient time, to shift the necessary resources into extra exports?

TWO YEARS' HARD SLOG

In the event, the Government pulled it off. In 1970 there was a current account surplus on the balance of payments of £735 million, and in 1971 of £1,058 million.[1] In real terms, these were the largest surpluses since at least 1950; in money terms, the largest ever. Because of a return of confidence in sterling and the consequent unwinding of leads and lags, the improvement in the external debt position was even more dramatic. As late as the end of 1968, when the success of devaluation was still very much in the balance, short- and medium-term external debt was £3,363 million and reserves only £1,009 million – a net adverse position of £2,354 million. By April 1970, when Roy Jenkins introduced what was to be his last Budget, the external debt had been more than halved, and there had been a substantial rise in the reserves; at £525 million the net adverse position had been reduced by nearly four-fifths, and was soon to be eliminated altogether.

But if the destination had eventually been reached, the road had been long and arduous. Defeat had often seemed to lie around the next corner, and a number of scars were collected on the way which were to last long after the journey had ended. The outcome of two years' hard slog was a triumph; but those two years had exacted a heavy toll.

The real difficulty lay in depressing domestic demand enough to make available sufficient resources for the extra exports – and import-substitutes – which devaluation had now made profitable. In order to do this on the scale required the Government had to take no fewer than five bites at the cherry. This was partly because, probably for political reasons, the initial action taken at the time of devaluation was simply not tough enough – it was absurd, for example, that not until the Budget of March 1968 should any really effective steps have been taken to restrain consumer demand. But it was partly because of the sheer uncertainty of the forecasting process: nobody really knew how long it would take for the demand for exports and imports to be affected by devaluation, or what would be the reaction of business and consumers to the new situation.[2] Some impression of the determination of the Government to get the balance of payments

[1] The 'basic' or 'overall' balance was in even bigger surplus, and it was on this that the Government had promised the IMF an improvement of at least £500 million (the actual improvement between 1967 and 1970 was about £2,000 million). But this indicator of the balance of payments situation went rather out of favour during the late 1960s, because of the somewhat arbitrary distinction between long-term capital flows, which were included, and short-term capital flows, which were not. The balance on current account, which indicates the difference between income and expenditure, is a more useful indicator of the state of a country's balance of payments.

[2] Forecasting problems are discussed more fully on pp. 143–50.

right – and, perhaps, of the influence of the ever-open eye of Big Brother, in the form of the IMF – can be gauged by briefly listing these five bites at the cherry.

First was the package of measures announced at the same time as devaluation: Bank Rate was raised by 1½ per cent to 8 per cent; severe restrictions were imposed on bank lending to the private sector (other than priority customers such as exporters); hire purchase terms on cars were tightened; and, for 1968–69, defence expenditure was to be cut by over £100 million, other government expenditure was to be cut by £100 million, and corporation tax was to be raised to 42½ per cent.

The second bite at the cherry came two months later, with Harold Wilson's announcement on 16 January 1968 of drastic cuts in public expenditure in 1968–69 and 1969–70. As well as substantial further cuts in defence, including an acceleration of the withdrawal from East of Suez, these incorporated such politically sensitive items as the reintroduction of prescription charges, the postponement of the long-planned raising to sixteen of the school-leaving age, and the ending of free milk in secondary schools. The total effect of these cuts (designed to save £700 million in 1968–69) was to reduce the growth of public expenditure to below 3 per cent a year, in real terms, between 1967–68 and 1969–70, compared with a rise of about 4½ per cent a year during the Government's first three years of office.

The next blow to domestic spending was the Budget introduced by Roy Jenkins on 19 March 1968, which aimed to convert what was expected to be a 2 per cent rise in private consumption during the next year and a half into a 1 per cent fall. Purchase tax and excise duties on drink, tobacco and petrol were increased; SET was raised by 50 per cent and, with some exceptions, a 3½ per cent ceiling on pay increases was announced (see p. 105).

The fourth bite at the cherry came in November 1968, when it became clear that consumption and imports were running at a considerably higher level than expected, against a background of severe international currency fluctuations, and a good deal of anxiety about the apparent failure of exports to start moving up the longer arm of the predicted 'J-curve'.[1] The regulator was used to increase indirect taxes by 10 per cent; hire purchase controls were tightened

[1] The immediate effect of devaluation is a reduction in the value of exports, in terms of foreign exchange, as the same volume is sold at lower prices in terms of foreign currency. It is only when this effect has been outweighed by a significant increase in the volume of exports that the value of exports rises beyond its former level.

even further; banks were instructed to cut the level of their advances to 2 per cent below the level of November 1967; and importers of most manufactured and semi-manufactured goods were required to deposit 50 per cent of the value of imports before customs would release them, these deposits being repayable after six months. This latter was an ingenious new method, subsequently tolerated if not positively welcomed by the IMF, both of restraining imports and of further tightening credit in the domestic market.

Finally came the Budget of April 1969. This was relatively mild compared with some of the earlier steps; even so, it reduced demand by a further £200–250 million, mainly by raising SET and corporation tax, and extending purchase tax to a wide range of domestic articles.

The net effect of this marathon of taxing and squeezing was pretty much what had been intended: a substantial shift of resources into the balance of payments at the expense of private consumption and government expenditure. Between 1967 and 1970 the GDP rose by 7.7 per cent, but private consumption rose by only 5.4 per cent and public consumption by less than 1 per cent. The volume of exports, by contrast, grew by 27 per cent, compared with a 17 per cent rise in the volume of imports.

If the results of the policies of 1967–70 were satisfactory in terms of the Keynesian constant price calculations which had been used to forecast and regulate the economy since the war, they were no less so in terms of the monetary aggregates which were becoming increasingly fashionable in the late 1960s, and in terms of the public sector borrowing requirement which was to become such a focus of attention in the mid-1970s. The money supply[1] grew by 7 per cent during 1968, and although this was a slower rate of expansion than in 1967, it was still faster than intended. During 1969, however, it was held down to a growth of less than 3 per cent. More dramatic still was what happened to Domestic Credit Expansion (DCE), a new-fangled concept invented in 1968 by the IMF, which had the advantage of taking account of the automatic effect on the money supply of a surplus or deficit on the balance of payments, but the disadvantage that no one could ever quite remember exactly what it meant; not entirely surprisingly, it fell out of fashion after a few years.[2] DCE had been £1,225 million during the financial year

[1] On the broader (M_3) definition. See p. 138.

[2] Essentially, Domestic Credit Expansion is the increase in the money supply *plus* the deficit (or *minus* the surplus) on the balance of payments current account. In other words, if the balance of payments is in deficit the increase in the money supply must be smaller than DCE.

1968–69; in a second Letter of Intent sent to the IMF in May 1969, Jenkins had promised that it would be no more than £400 million in 1969–70; in the event the figure was negative to the extent of over £500 million. This represented a very tough monetary policy.

Similarly, marked progress was made in reducing the borrowing requirement of the central government, and of the public sector as a whole – both of which are related to changes in the money supply, though in a highly complex and variable way. The November 1967 Letter of Intent promised to bring down the central government borrowing requirement, which turned out to be £1.4 billion in 1967–68, to no more than £1 billion in 1968–69; in the event the figure was only £280 million. More significantly, the borrowing requirement of the public sector as a whole (PSBR) was brought down from almost £2 billion in 1967–68 to £450 million in 1968–69, and was actually negative in 1969–70, when the public sector ran a surplus of over £500 million. This £2½ billion turnround in two years mainly reflected the combination of tax increases and rigid restraint on the growth of public expenditure which characterized the Government's policy between late 1967 and early 1970. Although this change was not quite the mirror image of the change in the balance of payments current account later claimed by the New Cambridge School,[1] the relationship between the two was more than a coincidence.

In recent years, something of a myth has grown up to the effect that the big balance of payments surpluses of 1970 and 1971 owed less to devaluation than deflation. It is true that the very large surplus of some £1,060 million in 1971 would have been smaller had the economy not been moving into a recession that year, though it would still have been very respectable. But there is little truth in the charge as far as the 1970 surplus of £735 million is concerned. The pressure of demand in that year was not enormously lower than it had been in 1967, unemployment in Great Britain averaging 2.5 per cent compared with 2.2 per cent. Between 1967 and 1970 total demand increased very much in line with the growth of productive potential, at a rate of 2½–3 per cent a year, but with exports increasing much faster than demand as a whole, and consumption and public expenditure more slowly.

The rapid growth in the volume of British exports at the end of the 1960s certainly owed something to the rapid growth of world

[1] See pp. 194–8.

trade in manufactures at that time, but it was notable that during this period Britain's share of world exports of manufactures declined significantly more slowly than usual. It is very difficult to attribute this to anything except devaluation. Just how much the balance of payments surplus in 1970 owed to devaluation, compared with other factors, is impossible to say; but there is nothing in the evidence inconsistent with the commonsense answer: a great deal.[1]

And so, after many trials and tribulations, the Labour Government finally got the balance of payments to come good. Not that everything in the garden was lovely by the spring of 1970: there were some pretty murky thickets here and there, and some of these are investigated later in this chapter. Nevertheless, for the first time for many years there was a healthy balance of payments surplus, against the background of a pressure of demand that was neither particularly high nor particularly low. Now, if ever, the nation was poised to embark on a process of sustained, export-led, reasonably rapid growth.

IN PLACE OF *IN PLACE OF STRIFE*

It had been apparent for many years when the Labour Government took office in 1964 that one of Britain's biggest problems was industrial relations, and particularly industrial stoppages. The problem lay not so much in official strikes – though these could be very damaging, as the 1966 seamen's strike was to demonstrate – as in unofficial or unconstitutional strikes. In many industries – of which the motor industry is an obvious example – the dependence of the final product on a large number of different components and

[1] One well-known study (NIESR, 1972) concluded that devaluation had improved the balance of payments current account by something between £200 million and £650 million in 1970, two-thirds of the improvement coming, surprisingly, on invisible account. But one feature of this study was the perverse result that devaluation had led to an *increase* in the volume of imports. This finding probably resulted from a substantial underestimate of the trend rate of growth of imports of manufactured goods, in which case the favourable effect of devaluation on the balance of payments was also underestimated.

Another study (Hague *et al.*, 1974) found that eighteen out of nineteen firms surveyed had been able to increase both the value and the volume of their exports after devaluation, though they were in general reluctant to ascribe these increases to devaluation. However none of the nineteen firms had switched to British substitutes for imports on any substantial scale, claiming that home market conditions were sufficiently buoyant to enable them to pass on higher import costs in higher prices. These findings suggest that most of the benefit of devaluation came from higher exports rather than lower imports, a result consistent with the overall figures.

processes means that the whole operation can be halted if a handful of men down tools over some real or imagined grievance. It was difficult to deny, in the 1950s and early 1960s, that the frequency with which this happened had something to do with the long and often unhonoured delivery dates of which Britain's foreign customers complained. The obvious answer might seem to be to deprive unconstitutional strikes of the protection the law had long afforded to official ones. But this was a nettle that even the Conservative governments of 1951–64 had been reluctant to grasp. The new Labour Government, with its close ties to the unions, was even more reluctant, and accordingly fell back on an age-old device: in April 1965 it appointed a Royal Commission on Trade Unions and Employers' Associations under the chairmanship of Lord Donovan. At best, it was hoped, the Royal Commission would be an instrument for prodding the unions into putting their own house in order; at worst it would gain time.

Gain time it certainly did: it did not report until June 1968, and in the atmosphere of statutory prices and incomes policies and harsh economic measures to which people had in the intervening three years become accustomed, its recommendations seemed to be very tame. Although there was plenty of admirable analysis and sensible suggestions for long-term reform, there was not much help on what seemed the key issues. Two frequently canvassed panaceas, strike ballots and cooling-off periods, were rejected on the grounds that they had not made much difference in America. Lord Donovan himself, in an Addendum to the Report, discussed the importance of finding a solution to the problem of unofficial strikes – but admitted that he had not himself found such a solution. To the Government, the advantage of the Donovan Report was that it called for little that might upset the Labour Party's delicate equilibrium between trade unionists and middle-class intellectuals. The disadvantage was that it offered no clear way forward in an area where public opinion was increasingly demanding action, and increasingly hearkening to the Conservative cry that the Labour Government was the creature of the unions, and unwilling or unable to restrain their power. Compared with *Fair Deal At Work*, a policy statement published by the Conservatives earlier in the year, Donovan seemed feeble indeed; and unless Macleod's jibe that the Report was 'a blueprint for inaction'[1] could be refuted, Wilson for one was con-

[1] *Sunday Telegraph*, 16 June 1968.

vinced that Labour would lose the next election: the unions were distinctly unpopular at this time, and Labour's appalling performance in by-elections and opinion polls during 1968 and 1969 owed much to its close association with the unions in the public mind.

Meanwhile, in a Cabinet reshuffle in April 1968, Wilson had sent the redoubtable Barbara Castle to a newly-created Department of Employment and Productivity,[1] where she rapidly came to the conclusion that something really had to be done. The result was *In Place of Strife*.

Shown, rather tactlessly, to the TUC before the Cabinet, this was a White Paper published in January 1969, proposing legislation for the reform of industrial relations. Although containing a number of proposals that were welcome to the unions, in other respects it went well beyond Donovan. In particular, it proposed that in certain cases the Minister could require a union to hold a ballot of its members before going on official strike;[2] that in the case of unofficial strikes which threatened to be especially damaging, the Minister could, if the normal conciliation procedures had failed, order a twenty-eight-day Conciliation Pause before strike action could take place; that in the last resort the Minister could impose a settlement in cases where unofficial strikes were the result of inter-union disputes; and that where unions failed to respect these provisions, an Industrial Board should have the power to impose fines, recoverable if necessary by attachment of earnings (care was taken to ensure that in no way could failure to pay a fine result in a trade unionist being sent to prison).

Although to much middle-of-the-road opinion these proposals appeared reasonable, even modest, that was not how they looked to the unions or to a large number of Labour MPs. Although successive versions of a statutory incomes policy had been swallowed by the unions and the Left, at least these could be regarded as a temporary expedient in a critical economic situation. This new and permanent threat to the freedom of working men to band together and fight for their own interests was regarded as intolerable; coming as it did from a Labour Government, it was regarded as a betrayal. Although the

[1] This was basically the old Ministry of Labour, but took over from the DEA the responsibility for incomes policy, and was therefore supposed to see the problem of industrial relations not simply as one of securing agreement between employers and employees at any cost, but in the wider context of the effect on prices and the economy generally.

[2] During the Budget debate, on 16 April 1969, Mrs Castle announced that this provision would be dropped from the legislation the Government intended to introduce.

TUC was initially acquiescent,[1] this first reaction was evidently ill-considered. Before long, most of the trade union movement was up in arms. Not a single prominent trade unionist could be found to defend the proposals of *In Place of Strife*. Early in March fifty-three Labour MPs went to the length of voting against it in the House of Commons, and later in the month it was rejected by the Party's National Executive Committee. The incipient revolt within both the Parliamentary Party and the Party in the country was much more serious than anything which had so far happened since October 1964, because it was not a simple Left-Right split, but one in which virtually all trade unionists – a great many of them traditionally in the centre or on the right of the party – were ranged against the leadership. The leadership, too, was badly divided, with Callaghan, who since his resignation as Chancellor had been steadily moving in an increasingly pro-union and anti-incomes policy direction, apparently assessing his chances of ousting Wilson on the industrial relations issue. In the event Callaghan, though willing to wound, was afraid to strike; but the threat he represented, together with the virtually unanimous opposition of the unions and the increasing pressure exerted by centre opinion within the Parliamentary Party which believed that the proposed legislation would split the party irrevocably, proved too strong. Although at one point Wilson had described the proposals as 'essential to our economic recovery; essential to the balance of payments; essential to full employment',[2] he found himself, together with Barbara Castle, virtually isolated at the crucial Cabinet meeting in June, and had to climb down. To save face, a 'solemn and binding' undertaking was given by the TUC to exert its influence to prevent damaging unofficial strikes,[3] and this was somehow represented by the Prime Minister, with typical Wilsonian panache, as what he had really been after all the time.[4] But few people were deceived. The Prime Minister had been defeated on an issue which he had classified as of major importance: and as far as the Labour Party was concerned, any attempt to legislate against trade union actions, unofficial or otherwise, was off the agenda for a long time to come.

[1] See Jenkins, 1970, for a well-informed and entertaining account of this whole episode. An account rather more sympathetic to the union point of view is to be found in Robinson, 1972.

[2] Speech to Parliamentary Labour Party, 17 April 1969 (quoted in Wilson, 1971, p. 808).

[3] 'Mr Solomon Binding', a character invented for the occasion by Peter Jenkins (op. cit.) was to make several appearances in subsequent years.

[4] To be fair, Wilson argues this case with great skill in his account of the period (pp. 806–35).

What is one to make of this strange episode? Although staunch trade unionists on the one hand, and committed union-bashers on the other, knew where they stood on the issue from the start, it was possible for moderate men of goodwill to take two different views. One view was that trade unions had indeed become too powerful, and that it was high time some sort of curb was applied, particularly to unofficial strikes. It was not lost on those who took this view that such unofficial action was very much less common in other countries where industrial relations were more closely governed by legislation, and where indeed Britain's record of unofficial strikes was viewed with amazement tinged with hilarity.

The other view – which on the whole had been taken in the Donovan Report – was that reforming trade unions, like reforming so much else in Britain, was a long-term task that had to be done by agreement (perhaps even a little by stealth) and not by rushing through legislation in the face of widespread and bitter opposition. It was particularly suicidal for the Labour Party, most of whose funds come from the unions and a third of whose MPs are sponsored by trade unions, to propose legislation to which the unions themselves – shortsightedly or otherwise – were so adamantly opposed. And from a purely party political point of view, while failure to grasp the nettle of industrial relations reform might, as Wilson feared, lose votes in the centre, an attempt to push through legislation might alienate far larger numbers of Labour's traditional supporters, already disillusioned by the Government's incomes policy, and demonstrating this disillusionment by massive abstentions in by-elections.[1]

In the light of hindsight, it is this second view which seems the more persuasive. The legislation proposed by Wilson and Barbara Castle never seemed likely to get through Parliament except on the basis of Conservative support – and this would surely have split the Labour Party more damagingly than anything since 1931. Moreover, even if the legislation had been enacted, it seems highly doubtful whether it would really have had much effect – at any rate if the Industrial Relations Act passed by the Conservatives in 1971 is anything to go by.

In retrospect, the whole episode seems a strange and uncharacteristic aberration on the part of a Prime Minister whose main genius always lay in his ability to avoid damaging confrontations, to keep a miraculous balance between the multitude of different interests and

[1] In three by-elections held on 27 March 1969 the average swing from Labour to Conservative was 16 per cent, and the average fall in the number of Labour votes was 60 per cent.

values represented in the Labour Party, and to be all things to all men. His conduct on this occasion was reminiscent less of anything in his own earlier record than of Gaitskell's conduct over Clause Four and nuclear disarmament. Perhaps for once he wanted to show that he, too, could slug it out when he had to; that the disparaging opinions held of him by the ex-Gaitskellites in the party were wrong and unfair. Whatever the reasons, Wilson learnt his lesson from the experiences of the spring and summer of 1969. Never again was he to take action which would bring him into serious conflict with the unions. And in the mid-1970s this hard-learnt caution was, arguably, to bring the nation to the verge of disaster.

INDUSTRIAL POLICY

If the main objectives of economic policy discussed in Chapter 2 – full employment, growth, price stability and a satisfactory balance of payments – are to be achieved, then a government has to get its macroeconomic policies right. But although such policies, involving particularly the use of fiscal and monetary instruments, and of the exchange rate, may be a necessary condition of achieving success, they may not be a sufficient condition. Some, particularly Conservatives, argue that a government's task should be confined to creating a satisfactory macro framework within which market forces can operate. This framework would involve the government more or less balancing its own budget – at least in normal circumstances – and taking action to prevent the emergence of monopolies and restrictive practices; but not intervening in any more detailed way. The traditional Labour view is that the role of the state must be much more positive. At one end of the Labour spectrum are those who advance the attractive slogan 'production for use and not for profit', and who believe, in the phrase of the famous Clause Four of the party's constitution, in 'the common ownership of the means of production, distribution and exchange' – in other words in nationalizing everything. At the other end are those who believe little more than that in a modern economy there will be cases where social and private costs, and benefits, diverge – where behaviour that maximizes the profits or the welfare of the firm or the individual may have adverse effects on others, and in some cases reduce the welfare of society as a whole. In cases of this kind, they argue, steps must be taken, by imposing taxes or granting subsidies, to bring social and private costs – and benefits – into line with each other, so that those who make decisions purely on the basis of the private costs and benefits to themselves are also, willy-nilly, making decisions in the interests of society as a whole. Somewhere between this position and the position of the out-and-out nationalizers lies the main area of debate. How much direct intervention should there be? What form should it take? Given Britain's slow rate of growth and low rate of investment, it was particularly in the industrial field that answers to these questions were needed in the 1960s.

With the single exception of steel, where a political commitment stretched back to the 1940s, and where there was a strong economic case for bringing the whole industry under unified control, nationalization was not an instrument used by the 1964–70 Labour Government. (Steps were taken, however, to improve the framework within which pricing and investment decisions were taken in the existing nationalized industries, notably by encouraging greater use of marginal cost pricing and more sophisticated techniques of investment appraisal.)[1] Thus the main problem lay in the field of private industry. What steps should be taken to get private industry to invest more, to expand faster, to raise productivity and generally to operate more efficiently?

To some extent Labour's answers to these questions took the orthodox form of changing taxes and subsidies. The main argument advanced for the new system of Corporation Tax was that it would encourage firms to retain and plough back a larger proportion of their profits. Similarly, the system of investment allowances which the Government had inherited from the Conservatives was replaced by a system of investment grants, on the grounds that this was a more direct and effective way of encouraging investment in manufacturing industry.[2] And SET and REP were, respectively, examples of a tax and a subsidy designed to affect business behaviour. But these blanket measures were not thought sufficient on their own. To some extent, of course, the energizing of industry was supposed to be the job of the National Plan, and the effective abandonment of the Plan inevitably knocked a large hole in Labour's industrial policies, even though useful work continued to be done by the little Neddies, which under Labour grew in number.

[1] HMG, 1967 (ii).

[2] Evidence submitted to an official enquiry in 1963 suggested that most British businesses paid little attention to the level of taxes on profits when making pricing and investment decisions (HMG, 1964 (i), paragraphs 261–6). This being so, their incentive to invest could not be much affected by investment allowances – which had the effect of reducing the proportion of profits paid in tax. It was hoped that such businesses would, however, be able to see that they would benefit from an investment grant.

Labour's main innovation was the establishment in January 1966 of the Industrial Reorganization Corporation. Underlying the formation of this body – which had been strongly pressed for by Wilson's own economic adviser, Thomas Balogh – was the idea that in many of Britain's industries there were too many firms of sub-optimal size. The IRC's job was to take the initiative in getting some of these firms to merge into larger and, it was hoped, more efficient units – and it was primed with funds of £150 million in order to sweeten the pill. And so GEC took over AEI, English Electric merged with Elliott Automation, and this new entity subsequently merged with GEC. In another part of the field British Motor Holdings merged with Leyland Motors to become British Leyland; and – though not without a good deal of dust being raised in the process – a similar rationalization was achieved in the ball-bearing industry. Whether these big new units were any more efficient – or less inefficient – than the small old ones has been hotly debated.[1] But at least the IRC represented a coherent point of view: that state intervention in the market system *was* needed, but only in order to make private firms bigger than they otherwise would be. While this is not a wholly unreasonable line to take, people on the left of the Labour Party felt that it had very little to do with socialism.

However, while the IRC was busy encouraging some mergers, the Monopolies Commission was busy discouraging others. So far from this apparent contradiction causing the Government concern, steps were actually taken to strengthen the Monopolies Commission; and many of the activities of the PIB took the form of searching enquiries into the profit margins of firms in a monopolistic or oligopolistic position. The contradiction was, in fact, more apparent than real: there is no basic inconsistency between wishing to create larger and more efficient units, particularly in industries subject to fierce foreign competition, and wishing to ensure that in industries where one or two firms have a very large share of the market, this market power is not being abused. Nevertheless, the situation provided ammunition for the Government's critics.

The main reason why the IRC represented a rather timid departure from orthodoxy was that it was expected to 'earn a commercial return *overall* on its operations'[2] – in other words to have no truck with activities which, however beneficial on wider economic or social

[1] For some of the difficulties in making an assessment, see Young, 1974.

[2] Quoted in Graham, 1972, p. 211. Graham gives a very comprehensive account of the Labour Government's industrial policies, and of the difficulties in evaluating their effectiveness.

grounds, seemed unlikely to make a profit. This omission was made good in 1968 by the Industrial Expansion Act, which gave the Minister of Technology power to make grants or loans available to particular firms where he was satisfied that this would 'improve the efficiency or profitability of an industry' or 'create, expand, or sustain productive capacity'. This represented a big departure from orthodoxy – bigger, perhaps, than many people realized at the time – and raised two very acute problems, neither of which has as yet been satisfactorily resolved.

One problem is that if a privately-owned firm is to be given or lent public funds (or 'taxpayers' money', as opponents of the idea, not always correctly, describe it) in order to improve the efficiency or expand the capacity of the firm, the shareholders of the firm stand to benefit. How can this quite uncovenanted benefit be offset, or at any rate minimized? There are various possibilities, such as the government, or a state holding company, taking a stake in the firm's equity; but this can lead to further difficulties over what part, if any, the state should play in the management of the firm. And this still does not necessarily resolve what many people would regard as a basic difficulty about such *ad hoc* state intervention. This is that in a country in which equality of all before the law is a cherished tradition, it is one thing for the state to favour particular *categories* of people or institutions – old-age pensioners, or workers in areas of high unemployment, or manufacturing firms, or dog-lovers; it is quite another thing for it to favour *this* firm rather than *that* firm, simply because the Minister says so.

This links up with the second problem. If a firm cannot survive except on the basis of a government grant or loan, how does one decide whether or not it should be allowed to survive? The orthodox commercial – and, particularly when in opposition, Conservative – answer is that it should be allowed to go under in the interests of the general efficiency of the system. But this answer assumes that the test of the market is always the correct one, and thus begs the entire question. If, however, one goes to the opposite extreme and lends a perennially sympathetic ear to requests for government assistance on the grounds that if it is not forthcoming men will lose their jobs without any immediate prospect of re-employment, or exports will fall and imports rise, one may indeed slow down economic progress, propping up inefficient and dying industries and preventing resources flowing into efficient and expanding ones. It can be argued that there is no general solution to this problem: that each case must be dealt with in an *ad hoc* way, by the exercise of informed judgment. But a judgment which may involve large amounts of public expenditure can only, in the last resort, be exercised by a Minister. If the judgment to be exercised is a discretionary one, and not bound by clearly-defined criteria, there will always be the suspicion that short-term political considerations (the need to avoid redundancies in a marginal constituency, or at a time when delicate negotiations are in progress with the unions) may be given more weight than an objective assessment of the prospects and social usefulness of the firm or industry involved. An attempt to grapple with these problems was made by the next Labour Government, in 1975 (see pp. 214–20). But at the time the 1966–70 Labour Government left office, they were still very much unresolved.

REGIONAL POLICY

Another respect in which market forces manifestly fail to solve a pressing problem is attested by the persistence of above-average rates of unemployment, and below-average levels of income, in Scotland, Wales and the North of England. The need for some kind of regional policy to deal with this situation has been accepted by both main political parties since the Special Areas Act was passed in 1934. Unfortunately regional policy has been operated with different degrees of enthusiasm at different times – not only in terms of the inducements offered to firms to locate or expand in the North and West but also in terms of the firmness with which they have been prevented from locating or expanding in the Midlands and South. Moreover, the exact areas to be assisted, and the type and rates of assistance available, have been changed with bewildering rapidity, not only each new government, but each new Minister being apparently unable to resist tinkering with the existing arrangements. Although it is impossible to quantify, this constant chopping and changing must have had an adverse effect on the willingness of firms to set up or expand in the assisted areas.[1]

The Conservatives had largely neglected regional problems during the 1950s, and although they started to step up assistance to the depressed areas in the early 1960s, this had borne little fruit by

[1] As one observer (Hardie, 1972, p. 245) has said, 'This uncertainty makes a company very unwilling to relocate. If it invests now in a Development Area it will get free depreciation, or investment grants, or whatever the current incentive is: but there is no way of telling whether this differential will exist in ten years' time when plant has to be replaced or expanded.'

1964: unemployment in the development areas in June of that year was 2.21 times as high as in Britain as a whole – the highest multiple for a decade (Hardie, op. cit., p. 241). Labour had a double incentive to bring down regional unemployment: the extra labour resources that had to be mobilized if the National Plan was to succeed mainly had to come from the areas where unemployment was high; and the majority of Labour's parliamentary seats were in the development areas of Scotland, Wales and the North of England.

The new government's regional policy took various forms: the size of the areas which qualified for assistance was increased, the form of assistance to investment projects was changed, and Industrial Development Certificates were granted less readily for new investment in the Midlands and South-East. But Labour's main innovation was the introduction in 1967 of the Regional Employment Premium (see p. 80). Unlike most existing regional incentives which subsidized capital – with the incongruous result that some of the most capital-intensive industries had been located in the areas of highest unemployment – REP subsidized labour. This was rational. By reducing labour costs in manufacturing industry, it was hoped to make the development areas more attractive to labour-intensive projects. It was also hoped that existing firms would be enabled to reduce their prices and increase their profits, and that this would lead to a rise in output and employment. The effect would be not unlike that of a devaluation of the development areas in relation to the rest of the country.

Labour's regional policies certainly seemed to meet with some success: by June 1970 the relationship between unemployment in the development areas and the nation as a whole was as good as it had ever been (the multiple had fallen to 1.67). The contribution to this of REP is very difficult to quantify. An early prediction (Brown, 1967) was that after three to five years REP might result in an increase in employment in development areas of 60–80,000. A later study (Moore and Rhodes, 1973) came up with a rather uncertain and qualified estimate of 40–50,000 extra jobs in 1970. On this latter reading, unemployment in the development areas might have been reduced by something up to a fifth as a result of REP. The effect would probably have been greater but for two factors. One was that the value of REP, being fixed in money terms, depreciated over time: by 1974, when the incoming Labour Government doubled it, its value had fallen by a half. The other was that although the Conservative Opposition tacitly agreed in 1967 that the scheme should run for seven years, since an ongoing subsidy to labour which could be abolished overnight would be a useless incentive, it soon made clear that a Conservative government was unlikely to renew it when it expired in September 1974. Although, in response to criticism from the CBI, the Conservatives later showed signs of repenting this hasty and doctrinaire decision, the apparent impending end of REP must have reduced its effectiveness.

THE DISTRIBUTION OF INCOME AND WEALTH

One of the economic aims of a Labour government is an improvement – i.e. a reduction in inequality – in the distribution of income and wealth. Although the available data are less comprehensive than might be wished, and are by no means easy to interpret, it does seem that under the 1964–70 Labour Government there was some improvement in the distribution of *income,*[1] if this is defined – as seems reasonable – as income after taking account of all taxes paid and all benefits received.[2]

To only a slight extent, if at all, was this the result of an improvement in the distribution of original, or pre-tax, income, despite the fact that in the Government's successive incomes policies low pay was always a criterion for obtaining increases in wages above the norm. There does appear to have been a slight improvement in the relative earnings of low-paid workers during the first four or five years of Labour's term of office, but this was lost in the wage explosion of 1969–70,[3] when differentials that had been compressed were opened up again. To a large extent the improvement is attributable to changes in taxes, on the one hand, and benefits, on the other.

Between 1964 and 1970, the share of the national income collected by the Government in taxation rose substantially – from 32

[1] *Income* is a flow over time (a week or a year), whereas *wealth* is a stock at a particular moment.

[2] I have argued this at length elsewhere (Stewart, 1972), on the basis of data for 1964 and 1969 (Labour's last full year in office). This slight improvement in income distribution was subsequently confirmed by the First Report of the Royal Commission on the Distribution of Income and Wealth (Diamond, 1975, table G. 15). The extent of the improvement is *reduced* if relative price changes for goods and services consumed by different income groups are taken into account (Muellbauer, 1974, pp. 44–5), but *increased* if changes in household composition over the period are taken into account (Semple, 1975, table 2).

[3] See pp. 107–9 below.

per cent to 43 per cent.[1] Much of this rise reflected the Labour Party's philosophy, which emphasises the importance of goods and services which can only be provided communally, and of redressing the balance between – in Galbraith's celebrated phrase – 'private affluence and public squalor'; though some of it reflected the need to remove purchasing power from domestic consumers as a counterpart to shifting resources into the balance of payments. One of Labour's achievements – at least from an egalitarian point of view – was to ensure that more of this extra tax revenue came from direct taxes, which are progressive, than from indirect taxes, which are regressive. Between 1964 and 1970 the yield of taxes on income rose by 104 per cent, whereas the yield of taxes on expenditure rose by 90 per cent. Within the latter category, attempts were made to load tax increases on to goods consumed to a large extent by the higher income groups. Thus the extra taxes imposed on beer and tobacco – which form a much higher proportion of the expenditure of low than of high income groups – were relatively modest; the extra taxes imposed on such commodities as wine, furs and jewellery, on the other hand, were fierce. In addition to the shift from indirect to direct taxation, Labour put through a number of lesser tax changes, which may not have helped the poor very much but – wisely or unwisely – did a good deal to discomfit the rich. Chief among these was the capital gains tax; but there were also various measures which had the effect of increasing the amount of taxation borne by unearned incomes.

Benefits, too, increased under Labour in a way which had a favourable effect on the distribution of income. The real disposable incomes[2] of those relying wholly or mainly on national insurance benefits (mainly retirement pensioners) rose somewhat faster than the real disposable income of the average wage or salary earner; and family allowances, which when Labour took office in October 1964 had been at a lower level, in real terms, than when first introduced in 1946, were doubled, more than restoring their original real value. Overall, cash benefits as a percentage of original income rose for virtually all households between 1964 and 1970, and to a much more significant extent for poorer than for richer households. Benefits in kind, too, increased in a way that probably had a favourable effect on income distribution, though there are many conceptual and

[1] Taxes on income and expenditure, including national insurance contributions, as a percentage of GDP.

[2] i.e. incomes after allowing for taxes and price increases.

statistical problems in allocating these benefits – mainly health and educational services – to different income groups. Between 1964 and 1970 the proportion of the GNP spent on health rose from 3.9 per cent to 4.9 per cent and on education from 4.8 per cent to 6.1 per cent. Although there is a lot of evidence that the middle class is better at using the social services than the working class (in terms of getting satisfaction out of the Health Service or getting their children into the best local schools and later into universities), it seems unlikely that this can outweigh the fact that the value of the health and educational services received represents a much higher proportion of low than of high incomes, and consequently that an overall increase in the proportion of the national income devoted to health and education has a favourable effect on income distribution.

The distribution of *wealth* became distinctly less unequal while the Labour Government was in office, though the Government could take very little credit for the fact: its only action to reduce the very unequal distribution of wealth in Britain was in 1968, when Roy Jenkins increased from five years to seven years the length of time a man had to survive, after giving all his money to his children, before totally escaping estate duty on it. The main factors behind the improvement were a marked increase in house values (the value of owner-occupiers' houses accounting for a very big proportion of the wealth of the bottom 80 per cent or so of wealth-owners) and a rather static trend in the price of equity shares – which account for a large proportion of the wealth of the richest 10 per cent of the population. If wealth is measured as including pension rights,[1] the improvement in the distribution of wealth over the period may have been slightly greater.

Surprisingly, it was on this issue of the distribution of income and wealth, where its record was relatively good, that Labour came under the fiercest fire from some of its own supporters during its last few months in office. In an attempt to persuade the Chancellor to increase family allowances again in the 1970 Budget, a campaign was started to convince people that 'under Labour, the poor had got poorer'. On closer inspection, it turned out that all that was meant by this highly inflammatory phrase was that the incomes of certain disadvantaged groups had, or perhaps had, risen less than the average since 1964. Although this was certainly regrettable, there are so many different disadvantaged groups in the community that it is

[1] For a discussion of the pros and cons of counting pension rights as part of wealth (which significantly reduces wealth inequality) see Atkinson, 1972 and Diamond, 1975.

almost inevitable that some of them will do less well than the average over any given period of time; that is, after all, the nature of an average. This is not to say that the Labour Government could not have done more to help the poor: no doubt it could – though the very slow growth of real incomes consequent on the need to restore the balance of payments, and the political unpopularity of such measures as family allowances, were dismissed far too readily by the critics. But the charge that under Labour the distribution of income worsened simply cannot be sustained. There was some improvement, albeit less than both socialists and social democrats had hoped for.

THE INCOMES POLICY AND THE WAGE EXPLOSION

Meanwhile, come rain come shine, the prices and incomes policy continued on its weary way. The Government was fully aware that, with devaluation, the policy had become more vital than ever. Any rapid rise in money incomes would both have eroded the competitive edge gained by devaluation and fuelled a rise in consumption which could have pre-empted the resources needed for extra exports. Accordingly, early 1968 saw the introduction of a tough new stage in the incomes policy. In the Budget on 19 March – the same in which he sharply increased indirect taxes – Jenkins announced that from the following day there would be a 3½ per cent a year ceiling on increases in wages, salaries and dividends. The only exception to this ceiling would be 'productivity agreements', where workers co-operated in promoting a marked and genuine increase in productivity. In all other cases, wage increases would have to be justified under one of the four criteria of the original 1965 White Paper (see p. 42), and the same went for price increases. In addition, the Government would take powers to require firms to reduce prices when the PIB judged it appropriate. In order to make this policy effective, the Government would need to introduce new legislation giving it the power to defer wage and price increases for twelve months (compared with seven under its existing powers); and Jenkins announced that this legislation would need to cover 'at least eighteen months, with freedom to renew it'.

Although the Government managed to get this legislation passed, it came under very heavy fire in the process. For the Opposition, Mr Robert Carr denounced the Bill during the second reading debate in the House of Commons on 21 May, saying that his party rejected the whole economic and political philosophy on which the Bill was based, including the use of statutory and legal compulsion. Only within a 'radically different economic context', in which government expenditure had been cut back, direct taxation reduced, industrial relations reformed, and competition sharpened by every available means, would an incomes policy – *without* statutory powers – have a minor, but nevertheless significant role to play. The Government got even less aid and comfort from the unofficial opposition on its own left wing. At various stages thirty or more Labour MPs abstained, and at one point twenty-three of them voted with the Conservatives, reducing the Government's majority to eighteen. The Left's basic objection to the legislation was voiced in a speech in the House of Commons by Ian Mikardo, who remarked on 'the grossly mistaken theory that wage levels are the cause of the nation's economic difficulties', and rejected the idea of penal sanctions on trade union officials 'for doing the job they were elected or appointed to do'. Although the new Prices and Incomes Act finally reached the statute book in July, the Government had been served notice of its unpopularity with its own supporters; and this point was heavily underlined in September, when motions calling for the repeal of the new Act were carried by overwhelming majorities at both the Trades Union Congress and the Labour Party Conference.

In 1969 the Labour Government in effect abandoned its statutory incomes policy. In his April Budget Roy Jenkins announced that when the Government's powers under the 1968 legislation expired at the end of 1969, they would not be renewed. In December fairly modest proposals were put forward: a 2½–4½ per cent norm for wage and salary increases, backed by nothing stronger than the three months delaying powers under Part II of the 1966 Act. Despite the modesty of these proposals, the Conservatives were again up in arms, Edward Heath asserting in the Commons on 17 December that the Conservatives had been proved 'absolutely right' in their opposition to the system of compulsion from its first introduction in 1966, and even claiming that the policy had resulted in wages being pushed up further than they otherwise would have been. For the Labour Left, Norman Atkinson called for free wage bargaining coupled with price restraint controlled by the Government: certainly a trade unionist's idea of paradise. Atkinson seemed to imagine that this would lead to an orderly transfer of wealth from those who had it to those who did not; a more realistic prediction might have been wholesale bankruptcies and massive unemployment. But whatever one thought of the quality of the arguments deployed, there can be no doubt that by this time the anti-incomes policy forces were very strong.

The jettisoning of the incomes policy in 1969 was followed by a wage explosion: between the fourth quarter of 1969 and the fourth quarter of 1970 weekly wage rates and average earnings both rose by about 13 per cent, a significantly bigger increase than had ever occurred before. This wage explosion, together with the great commodity price boom of 1972–73, sowed the seeds of the 25 per cent rate of inflation from which Britain was suffering in the mid-1970s. It is therefore pertinent to ask whether this wage explosion was inevitable, or whether it could have been prevented if Labour had, despite the heavy bombardment it was receiving, stuck to its guns on incomes policy.

There is much to be said for the view that the wage explosion was inevitable. The big wage increases conceded in France and a number of other countries after the student and worker unrest of 1968, and the acute inflationary pressures which had developed in the United States as a result of its ever-deepening involvement in the war in Vietnam, had between them set in motion a process of world cost and demand inflation from which Britain could not hope to be immune. In Britain itself, the absence of any increase in living standards over the past two years, as resources were fed into the balance of payments, had caused growing discontent, and put growing pressure on the incomes policy.[1] People were by now much more conscious of the restraints the policy imposed on themselves than of the benefits they received from the restraints it imposed on others. Moreover by this time quite a respectable intellectual case was being developed against continuing the incomes policy. A number of commentators had argued that the effects of the various incomes policies which had been in force since 1965 were very modest – certainly by comparison with the vast amount of ministerial and official time and energy which had been deployed in operating them. The PIB itself had concluded in mid-1968 that so far the policy had probably done

[1] It was suggested by some observers (e.g. Jackson and others, 1972) that a kind of 'tax-push' inflation had begun to come into play, with increases in the effective rates of direct taxation (through failure to offset fiscal drag) causing unions to demand even bigger gross wage increases in order to secure a modest improvement in their real net-of-tax incomes.

no more than reduce the rise in earnings by about 1 per cent a year;[1] and Hugh Clegg, for two years a member of the PIB, considered that the productivity agreement loophole had much reduced the effectiveness of the policy (Clegg, 1971, ch. V).

According to this interpretation, then, the incomes policy had been pretty ineffective anyway, the wage explosion was bound to happen, and any attempt by the Labour Government to contain it by continuing a tough incomes policy would have led to the same kind of ignominious defeat that it suffered over *In Place of Strife*. Discretion, on this reading, was the better part of valour.

This argument, though plausible, does not carry complete conviction: it is too fatalistic, and too impressed by what did happen, compared with what might have happened. If two factors had been different, so might have been the wage explosion and much of subsequent history. First, the Labour Government took its eye off the ball in 1969, by concentrating on *In Place of Strife*, and tacitly (and in the event unsuccessfully) agreeing to trade in its incomes policy in return for legislation on industrial relations. If the unions and the Left had not been alienated by the *In Place of Strife* episode, and if the Government had stuck to its incomes policy instead, the policy – albeit in more flexible form – might have been successfully

[1] Prices and Incomes Board, 1968, p. 67. In spite of this interim view – which the PIB report added was 'probably an underestimate of the true effect' – the actual figures were not unimpressive. During the freeze and period of severe restraint (July 1966–July 1967) average earnings rose by less than 2 per cent, compared with an annual rate of 7½ per cent between April 1965 and July 1966. There was a rebound to an annual rate of 9 per cent from July 1967 to March 1968, but this was brought down to 8 per cent during the rest of 1968 and 6½ per cent during the first nine months of 1969 (the figures, which are seasonally adjusted, are taken from the December 1969 White Paper (HMG, 1969 (ii)).

Many subsequent attempts were made by econometric methods to test the effect of incomes policy. One of the best-known of these (Lipsey and Parkin, 1970) in effect agreed with Mr Heath's view, suggesting that when unemployment was above 1.8 per cent, incomes policies actually made inflation worse – presumably because weaker unions tended to secure at least the minimum increase permitted by the policy. However, various technical weaknesses in this analysis (see Wallis, 1971), and the crucial reliance on the distinction between 'policy on' and 'policy off', when in some sense the Government always has some policy for incomes, whether statutory or not, reduced its plausibility. A later and particularly exhaustive study (Dept. of Employment, 1971) concluded that over the three years 1965–67 the earnings of manual workers rose by about 4 per cent less than expected, but during the two years 1968–69 rose by about 4 per cent more than expected, so that the policy was effective only in the short run. But this study, like all such econometric studies, depended in the last resort on the extrapolation of relationships which had existed in the past, and did not necessarily give a more correct answer than impressionistic evidence or 'hunch'.

continued.[1] However, for this to happen, a second factor would have had to be different too: the Conservatives would have had to refrain from making all-out attacks on the policy. The hostility to the incomes policy that had developed among the Conservatives by 1968 was a typical instance of the Jekyll and Hyde syndrome. The Conservative Governments of 1951–64 had been brought by the intractability of events to accept the need for an incomes policy, and although the first example of this – Selwyn Lloyd's 1961 pay pause – was unfair and unfortunate, the lesson had been learnt, and much of Mr Maudling's efforts as Chancellor had been directed towards getting the unions to co-operate in a fair and workable incomes policy. But by 1968 all this had been forgotten: the Tory party was deep into the Hyde phase of the cycle, wild, irresponsible and baying for blood. And so the Labour Government was on a hiding to nothing. At least, with *In Place of Strife,* there was some prospect of winning ground in the centre to compensate for losses on the left; but the continuous criticism of the incomes policy by the Conservatives – and the Liberals – reduced the chances of the policy gaining votes for Labour anywhere. And so, as election year approached, it was dropped.

THE EMERGENCE OF SELSDON MAN

As the date of the next election grew nearer, attention began to focus on the Conservatives, and the kind of alternative government they offered. By the end of the 1960s, the Conservative Party was a somewhat different animal from the one it had been at the beginning. The change was most visibly manifested in the aggressive and edgy personality of Heath himself – 'abrasive' was the adjective often used about him at this time – which contrasted sharply with the languid insouciance of Macmillan and the aristocratic informality of Sir Alec Douglas-Home.[2] This change in style was itself a reflec-

[1] This seems to have been the view taken in 1970 by Aubrey Jones, for five years chairman of the PIB (Jones, 1970). He also criticized the weakening effect on the incomes policy of transferring responsibility for it in 1968 from the DEA to the DEP. A related view (Brittan, 1971, p. 406) was that the announcement in the 1969 Budget that at the end of the year the 1968 powers would be allowed to lapse 'acted as an advertisement for wage claims'.

[2] Heath suffered the disadvantage of having been elected leader of his party while it was in Opposition; he was thus the first Conservative Leader of the Opposition since Bonar Law (though not the last, since his successor, Margaret Thatcher, was in the same case) who lacked the standing of being a former Prime Minister.

tion of an underlying shift in the balance of power within the party, away from the great old Tory families and towards a new breed of men who had made their own way in the world; away from the rural areas and towards the suburbs; and even, to some extent, away from the City of London and towards industry. With this shift in the balance of power went a shift in the emphasis of policy, away from the easy-going consensus approach of a Maudling and towards the tough-minded competitive attitudes of a Sir Keith Joseph.

The main factor behind this change in the emphasis of policy lay in the personal philosophy of Heath, and his belief in the virtues of competition, of incentives, of reducing state intervention in industry and of abolishing state grants or subsidies for those who did not really need them. But although this new thrust of policy did not escape all criticism from the Maudling faction, it was in no sense imposed on an unwilling party: on the whole, Heath had a receptive audience. The interventionist policies of the early 1960s, with their emphasis on incomes policy and planning, had become increasingly unpopular with many Conservatives, and Heath's victory over Maudling in the 1965 election for the leadership was a demonstration of this.

There seem, however, to have been two other factors behind the Tory change of direction during the second half of the 1960s. One – impossible to quantify, but widely remarked upon at the time – was the personal antipathy that developed between Heath and Wilson. Heath intensely disliked the gimmicky and flashiness which seemed to him to characterize Wilson's performance as Prime Minister; and his temper cannot have been improved by the frequent humiliation to which he was subjected on the floor of the House, at any rate in his early days as Leader of the Opposition, by Wilson's unparalleled dialectical skills. As time wore on, and Heath's contempt for Wilson deepened, he moved towards a posture of almost automatic opposition to anything Wilson said or did.

The second factor was Enoch Powell. Ever since his resignation from Macmillan's government in 1958, Powell had been proclaiming the importance of reducing the role of the state in the economy. He had also – and eventually with far more spectacular results – started to denounce Commonwealth immigration, playing on the fears aroused, particularly in working-class areas and in the Midlands, by an influx of coloured people from India, Pakistan and the West Indies. In April 1968, he made a particularly outrageous speech in which he said he was 'filled with foreboding' and, like the Roman, seemed 'to see "the River Tiber flowing much with blood" '.[1] This speech earned him – to Heath's credit – instant dismissal from the Shadow Cabinet; but it also catapulted him into national – indeed international – prominence. Before long he seemed to constitute – certainly in the event of Heath losing the next general election – a major threat to Heath's leadership of the Conservative Party. One method of reducing the size of this threat which Heath could, and did, adopt was to minimize the differences between Powell and himself on economic policy. Heath's economic policies were not as far to the right as Powell's, but they were far enough to the right to cover his flank.

The details of Heath's new policies were hammered out during the later 1960s,[2] and the package was pulled into its final shape at a much publicized conference at the Selsdon Park Hotel near Croydon early in 1970, thus enabling Wilson to conjure up – which he did often, and always with relish – the sinister spectre of 'Selsdon Man'.

Although economic policy was not the sole preoccupation of Selsdon Man – he was also keen on more law and order, and an expanded police force to provide it – it was certainly his main concern. In general, he wanted to see a much more competitive climate established – entry into the EEC (quite openly) and a permanently higher level of unemployment than had obtained in the 1950s and early 1960s (rather more discreetly) being among the methods of securing this. He intended to reform industrial relations by law – Labour's cowardice in abandoning *In Place of Strife* being much condemned. He wanted to reduce direct taxes on both companies and individuals, in order to foster enterprise and encourage saving. To some extent the lost revenue would be made good by shifting the burden on to indirect taxation, but in the main it would be offset by cutting public expenditure. Investment grants, for example, would be abolished and replaced once again by investment allowances – one advantage of these latter being that they only go to firms which are making profits, and Selsdon Man tended to equate profitability with efficiency and virtue.[3] Subsidies to the national-

[1] Quoted in Rhodes James, 1972, p. 184.

[2] Altogether some thirty-six advisory groups were active at this time (Rhodes James, 1972, p. 112).

[3] Investment allowances also have the purely presentational attraction that they do not involve higher government expenditure, as investment grants do, but lower government revenue. To those interested in the total amount of public expenditure, rather than the extent to which it is covered by tax revenue, this point is important.

ized industries would be eliminated: these industries would have to pay their way, just as they would if they were still – as in an ideal world they would be – in the private sector. Public expenditure would also be cut by making social service benefits more 'selective', concentrating them on those who really needed them; and by making greater use of charges, for example in the health service. Moreover, Selsdon Man was determined to reduce state interference in the economy generally. Taxes and subsidies which 'distorted' the workings of the economy – like SET and REP – would be abolished. There would be no statutory prices and incomes policy. Public money would no longer be used to assist 'lame ducks', and the IRC would be 'stripped of its power'. A review of the little Neddies would be conducted to determine which of them could be wound up.

Thus Selsdon Man, whatever else might be said about him, at least knew where he stood. To some he looked like a saviour, come to free Britain from the shackles of state interference and excessive taxation, and to release the country's energies and skills for an exciting new era of expansion and achievement. To others, he simply looked like a throwback to the nineteenth century. Others again, while not denying that he had the odd redeeming feature, may have wondered whether he was not an illegitimate creature to have been spawned by those who until a few years before had themselves experienced the responsibility of high office; who knew that the world of government is a world not of blacks and whites but of greys; and who knew – or ought to have known – that Britain is a country that responds best not to dramatic new departures or to the setting of one group against another, but to tactful nudges along a road on which each may have an opportunity to proceed at his own pace, but where those who lag behind are helped to keep up, and all are travelling in broadly the same direction.

THE 1970 GENERAL ELECTION

If ever a Party looked like losing the next election, it was Labour in 1968 and 1969. It lagged far behind the Conservatives in the opinion polls; it lost large numbers of seats in local elections; and it suffered horrific swings, rarely under 10 per cent, and often more than 15 per cent, to the Conservatives in by-elections.[1]

Nevertheless, defeat was by no means inevitable. Labour could

[1] A good many Labour seats were lost in these by-elections: by the time of the dissolution in 1970 Labour's original overall majority of 97 had fallen to 65.

draw comfort from looking back to the late 1950s, when Conservative demoralization and unpopularity in the wake of the Suez fiasco had seemed to many to spell sure electoral doom: yet in October 1959 they had increased their majority from 58 to 100. Sure enough, early in 1970, the tide began to turn – or seemed to. At a by-election in South Ayrshire in March the swing to the Conservatives was only 2.9 per cent. In April, the opinion polls began to show Labour ahead of the Conservatives for the first time for three years. And in the local elections in May, Labour, for the first time since 1964, gained seats from the Conservatives instead of losing them. Wilson decided to take the tide at the flood. With – by his own account – the virtually unanimous agreement of his cabinet and parliamentary colleagues, he announced on 18 May that a general election would be held on 18 June.[1]

The economic background to the 1970 election campaign was a mixed one. In important respects the economy was in a strong position. The balance of payments on current account was very healthy: the surplus for 1970 as a whole would turn out to be some £735 million – the biggest figure (at any rate in money terms) ever recorded. The Government had brought public expenditure under control, and in the financial year 1969–70 had achieved an overall public sector surplus of over £500 million. On the other hand unemployment was still at the relatively high level of 2½ per cent – over half a million people – and, if anything, edging upwards. And the wage explosion which had got under way in the autumn of 1969, with certain groups in the public sector getting increases of 12–15 per cent or even more, was beginning to show up in price increases.

In spite of the level of unemployment, in spite of the fact that an election must be in the offing, and in spite of demands from the NIESR and other economic commentators that the Government should take some reflationary action, the Budget which Roy Jenkins introduced in April gave only a very modest stimulus to the economy. From an economic point of view this was probably justified. The forecasts available to the Chancellor suggested that demand was likely to grow fairly rapidly anyway, because of the effect on consumption of the fairly rapid rise in real wages, and this seemed sufficient to bring about a slow fall in unemployment, without

[1] Wilson, 1971, p. 983. In a television interview at the time, Wilson stated, poker-faced, that so far from making a snap decision to take advantage of the sudden increase in Labour's popularity, he had actually decided the date of the 1970 election four years earlier. Veteran Wilson-watchers felt that their man was on good form.

jeopardizing the hard-won balance of payments surplus or strong public sector financial position, and without doing anything to boost the already quickening pace of wage increases. If the expansionary forces in the economy proved weaker than expected, other steps to increase demand could be taken later. Meanwhile, as Jenkins stressed, it was better to err on the side of caution.

On a purely party-political calculation, the wisdom of the Budget was much more questionable. Some votes may have been – and certainly ought to have been – won by the spectacle (which Jenkins himself was by no means unwilling to present) of a stern, unbending Chancellor, determined at all costs to do what was right for the nation and to have no truck with the kind of give-away pre-election Budgets brought in by the Tories in 1955, 1959 and 1963. But more votes than this were probably lost among those who felt cheated at getting so little out of the Budget, and among those more cynical observers who felt that the very absence of a Budget bonanza was evidence that the economic recovery must be much more fragile than the Government claimed. What is certain is that the Jenkins Budget was subsequently blamed by many Labour supporters for their Party's defeat in the 1970 election, and this was one reason – though by no means the only one – for Jenkins' subsequent unpopularity with the mass of the Labour movement.

The 1970 election campaign was a slightly unusual one, with the Conservatives promising – rather as Labour had in 1964 – faster growth, various reforms and, in general, a new style of government; and Labour assuring the nation – rather as the Conservatives had in 1959 – that everything in the garden was lovely, the only thing that could ruin it being a change of government.

The Conservative manifesto, *A Better Tomorrow,* was very much the work of Selsdon Man. Government expenditure would be cut, and so would income tax; saving would be encouraged; a new Industrial Relations Bill would be introduced, providing for collective agreements to be binding on both unions and employers, and for a secret ballot and a sixty-day cooling-off period in the case of serious industrial disputes; and social security benefits would be concentrated on those who needed them. Rather ominously, in the eyes of those who place a high value on social cohesion, the Conservatives promised to deal with the 'shirkers and scroungers' who 'abused' the social security system, to strengthen the police force, to restore the prison-building programme, and to speed up court procedures for dealing with 'violent offences concerned with public order'. Although the manifesto asserted briskly that 'we will give overriding priority to bringing the present inflation under control', the only concrete proposal for doing this was to disallow unjustifiable price rises in the public sector – a proposal which, if it meant anything at all, seemed inconsistent with the party's philosophy of reducing subsidies in the public sector and making the nationalized industries pay their way.

Labour's manifesto, by contrast, was rather vague, doing little but promise the mixture as before. The flavour is perfectly conveyed by the main pledge on taxation: 'A Labour government will continue its work to create a fair tax system'. It would also, presumably, continue its work against sin. The absence of any specific pledges on taxation, including the introduction of a wealth tax, for which many in the Party were pressing, was generally ascribed to the stand taken by Jenkins who, after Wilson himself, was by now the most powerful figure in the Government. Overall, the Labour manifesto sounded a distinctly flat note, the most lively thing about it being its awful title – *Now Britain's Strong, Let's Make It Great to Live In* – designed, perhaps, with an eye on the teenage vote.[1]

Although little had been said about rising prices in the two manifestos, they nevertheless became the main issue in the campaign. Conservative condemnations of Labour's record on this issue were assisted by the announcement on 20 May that in April alone retail prices had risen (albeit largely due to seasonal factors) by 1½ per cent, to a level 5½ per cent higher than a year before. After the election a myth developed – sedulously fostered by Wilson himself – that the Conservatives had got in on a false prospectus by promising – and subsequently failing – to 'reduce prices at a stroke'. What was in fact promised was that the *rise* in prices would be reduced at a stroke by reducing 'those taxes which bear directly on prices and costs, such as Selective Employment Tax'. While it might be disputed whether SET had raised prices, and therefore whether its abolition would reduce them, this was a perfectly legitimate promise. More meretricious was the Conservatives' pledge to give overriding priority to the defeat of inflation while promising not to introduce a statutory incomes policy.[2] They seem to have benefited from promising no wage controls, without suffering for having no credible prices policy.

[1] Under the Representation of the People Act, 1969, the minimum voting age had been brought down from twenty-one to eighteen.

[2] The manifesto said that 'Labour's compulsory wage control was a failure and we will not repeat it'.

In addition to the specific issue of prices, economic questions generally dominated the election campaign. This was not surprising, in view of the absence of any big perceived ideological differences between the two parties. Labour was not proposing any bold leap forward towards socialism which would divide the nation; and although the Conservatives *were* in fact inviting the country to follow a distinctly different road, it seems probable that this point was not widely appreciated. By most people the Conservatives were seen as offering lower income tax and a tougher line with the unions; it seems unlikely that the full implications of moving to the kind of economy and society envisaged by Selsdon Man were generally understood. And so attention tended to fasten, as it had done in 1964, on the question of who would run the economy better. On this issue – though its own Budget had not helped – Labour's image was dented by some rather bad luck. On 1 June Wilson's old *bête noire,* the former Governor of the Bank of England, Lord Cromer, said on television that any incoming government would find 'a very much more difficult financial situation than the new Labour Government found in 1964'. The most charitable thing that can be said about this absurd judgment is that it may have been actuated by ignorance as much as malice: Cromer's grasp of macroeconomic policy had never been of the strongest. Nevertheless the remark made a considerable impression. On 15 June the May trade figures were published, showing a deficit of £31 million. It was bad luck that this quirky figure (owing much to the delivery of two jumbo jets) should be published three days before polling day, for it strengthened many people's impression that the economy was weaker than the Government claimed. In reality, one thing that was definitely *not* wrong with the British economy in the summer of 1970 was the balance of payments. The first quarter figures, published on 10 June, showed a current surplus of £200 million; but by another piece of bad luck for Labour the impact of these favourable figures (and, incidentally, some very acerbic exchanges between Heath and Powell) was muffled by a newspaper strike. By 16 June, the number of people expecting a new economic crisis had risen substantially, as had the number of people who wanted the Conservatives to handle it.[1]

In retrospect, the result of the 1970 election – an overall Conservative majority of thirty-one – is not particularly surprising. What made it extremely surprising at the time was the fact that, with one

[1] Butler and Pinto-Duschinsky, 1971, p. 167.

exception, the opinion polls had unanimously predicted a Labour victory[1] What went wrong has never been satisfactorily resolved. One theory – supported by the fact that ORC, the only poll to predict the result correctly, had gone on polling later than the others – was that in the last few days of the campaign there had been a decisive swing to the Conservatives. Another theory was that the polls had not allowed sufficiently for 'differential turnout' – the observed tendency of Labour supporters to be less conscientious about actually voting than Conservative ones. Certainly the abstention of Labour voters seems to have been a major factor behind the election result. At 72 per cent, turnout was the lowest for thirty-five years, and the actual number of Labour votes fell by 900,000, or 7 per cent, compared with 1966. At the same time it seems likely that a good many people, particularly skilled manual workers, switched their vote from Labour to Conservative, and that this played some part, together with the return to the fold of Conservative voters who had abstained or even voted Labour in 1966, in raising the Conservative vote by 1.7 million, or 15 per cent.

Underlying this swing from Labour to Conservative was the profound dissatisfaction felt by many people, including large numbers of Labour's traditional supporters, with the result of the Government's economic policies, particularly during the two years following devaluation. During 1968 and 1969 real consumption per head, curbed by statutory controls over wages and by increases in various taxes and charges, had been flat. Public expenditure, too, had been held tightly in check. That this was necessary in order to transform the balance of payments from a big deficit to an even bigger surplus is an intellectual proposition that can hardly be disputed; but it cut little ice with the man in the street. Nor was his reaction entirely unjust. The centrepiece of Labour's promises in 1964 had been faster growth, achieved by national planning, harnessing the white heat of the technological revolution, and all that. But in practice growth had not been given overriding priority; until November 1967 preservation of the existing exchange rate had. As a result the real GDP, so far from rising by 3.8 per cent a year, as envisaged by the National Plan, had risen at a rate of only 2.2 per cent – slower even than the 2.7 per cent rate achieved, on average, by the Tories between 1951 and

[1] Some of the most respected polls came the biggest croppers. On the day before the election, a Marplan Survey published in *The Times* gave Labour an 8.7 per cent lead – enough to give it an overall majority of over 100; and on polling day itself a Gallup Poll published in the *Daily Telegraph* gave Labour a 7 per cent lead.

1964. (And of course, though this was not Labour's fault, some of the rise in output was needed to improve the balance of payments, and therefore not available for use at home.)

The original, essentially arbitrary, decision of Labour's top triumvirate to give preservation of the existing exchange rate priority over all else, and the obstinate determination to stick to this decision until, three years later, it became literally insupportable, lay at the heart of Labour's failure. It was a mistake with harsh economic consequences. It was not entirely unjust that for Labour its political consequences should have been harsh as well.

Chapter 5
PRIDE AND PREJUDICE
June 1970-February 1974

A NEW STYLE OF GOVERNMENT

A new style of government was what the Conservatives had offered, and what they now set out to provide. The first manifestation of this came within a few weeks of the election, when half a dozen prominent businessmen were drafted into the Civil Service Department to recommend improvements in the Government's decision-making techniques. This contrasted markedly with the early days of the 1964–70 Labour Government, when a large number of academics (mainly economists) had been brought into Whitehall.[1] The contrast was not accidental: the Labour Party has for long had stronger links with the academic world than the Conservatives, and the absence of any movement towards the Conservatives in university opinion in the late 1960s – indeed a certain growth of anti-intellectualism in the Conservative Party – was noticed by at least one observer.[2] Among Conservatives there is an inclination to believe that knotty economic problems will evaporate in the face of a more businesslike approach.

A more significant indication that this was a new government with new ideas came in an October White Paper announcing various changes in the machinery of government.[3] These changes were on

[1] In October 1964 there had been only twenty economists in the whole of Whitehall, nearly all of them in the Treasury. When Labour left office in June 1970 there were about 200 economists scattered throughout the Civil Service, some departments (such as the Ministry of Overseas Development and the Ministry of Transport) having built up particularly strong economic units. Growth continued during the first half of the 1970s, though at a much slower pace: the number of economists in the Government Economic Service in 1975 was about 300.

[2] Rhodes James, 1972.

[3] HMG, 1970 (i). One of the sections of this White Paper was actually entitled 'A new style of Government'. Among the most important changes were the creation of the Department of the Environment by adding to the already amalgamated Ministries of Housing and Local Government, and Transport, the Ministry of Public Building and Works; the merging of the Ministry of Technology and the Board of Trade into the Department of Trade and Industry; the transfer of the Ministry of Overseas Development to the Foreign and Commonwealth Office; and the establishment of a central capability unit in the Cabinet Office. This body, subsequently known as the Central Policy Review Staff (CPRS), or Think Tank (there were less complimentary nicknames, too), was responsible for providing the Cabinet with an independent view on major policy issues.

the whole non-partisan, and indeed some of them merely carried to a logical conclusion reforms introduced by Labour;[1] but they were also designed to symbolize the fact that things were different now. Changes in the machinery of government, however, are largely for Westminster-Whitehall consumption; nobody else takes much notice. The first indication to the general public that life really was going to be different under the Conservatives came on 27 October, when Mr Anthony Barber, the new Chancellor of the Exchequer, made a lengthy statement in the House of Commons.[2] The measures he announced fell under three broad headings. First, there was to be a wholesale massacre of the various interventionist bodies and devices established by Labour. In addition to the promised abolition of the Prices and Incomes Board and Selective Employment Tax,[3] the Industrial Reorganization Corporation and the Land Commission were to be wound up, the Regional Employment Premium was to expire in September 1974, as soon as its initial seven-year period came to an end, and investment grants were to be scrapped and replaced by investment allowances. Secondly, there were to be cuts in public expenditure totalling £330 million in 1971–72, rising to some £900 million in 1974–75.[4] The result was to reduce the average growth of public expenditure over this three-year period from 3.5 per cent a year (at constant prices) to 2.8 per cent a year. Various grants – such as those to London area commuter services and to the Consumer Council – were to be stopped; deficiency payments to agriculture were to be replaced by import levies; charges for medical prescriptions, spectacles and dental treatment were all to be increased, as were the charges for school meals; and free school

[1] The changes made by Labour had been considerably more sweeping. 1964 had seen the creation of a number of new departments: the Department of Economic Affairs, the Ministry of Technology, the Ministry of Land and Natural Resources, the Ministry of Overseas Development, and the Welsh Department. Subsequently the Department of Health and Social Security was created out of the two social service ministries, and the Commonwealth Relations Office, having absorbed the Colonial Office, was merged with the Foreign Office. In 1969 Wilson abolished the DEA, and put bits of it, along with Transport and Housing, into the new Ministry of Local Government and Regional Planning.

[2] Barber had succeeded Iain Macleod as Chancellor when the latter died suddenly after less than a month in office. Macleod's death was widely regarded as a tragedy for the Conservative Government, a view which subsequent events did nothing to dispel.

[3] The PIB was officially dissolved in March 1971. SET was halved in July 1971 and eliminated altogether in April 1973.

[4] Both figures are at 1970–71 estimated outturn prices, and exclude investment grants. The details are given in HMG, 1970 (ii).

milk for children over seven was to be abolished. Finally, taxes were to be cut, income tax by 6d. (six old pence) in the pound, and corporation tax from 45 to 42.5 per cent.

The philosophy behind this three-pronged approach was spelled out by Mr Barber. The state should intervene less, concentrating its activities and expenditure on those tasks that it alone could perform; the social services should be more selective, with benefits confined as far as possible to those 'in need'; and direct taxes should be reduced, so as to give people a greater incentive to increase their earnings. The result would be a more efficient allocation of resources, a release of initiative and energy, and a faster rate of growth.

Critics were not slow to point out the drawbacks in this essentially Selsdon approach to the economy. It is a moot point, for example, whether lower direct taxes assist the growth rate by encouraging people to work harder or move to higher-paying and more responsible jobs, because each hour's work now yields higher net pay. It may be the other way round: people may do less work because fewer hours' work will now yield the same net income as before.[1] The evidence is inconclusive. Similarly, a determination to concentrate social security benefits on those most in need, instead of distributing them indiscriminately to everyone regardless of their circumstances, seems no more than common sense. The problem is how to do it? It is true that 'universal' benefits like retirement pensions and family allowances go to many people who do not need them; though the fact that they are taxable means that for wealthy people the net receipts are small. But these universal benefits do have the great virtue that they go to everyone who qualifies, automatically and of right. With 'selective' benefits, on the other hand, which only go to those in need, there is the problem of identifying those in need.

This problem was neatly illustrated by the story of the Family Income Supplement (FIS). This was the one reform announced by Mr Barber on 27 October which might have been expected to have a favourable rather than an unfavourable effect on the distribution of income. It was a supplement to be paid to low-income families where the man was in full-time employment (and therefore did not qualify for Supplementary Benefits). For each pound by which a family's income fell below a certain level, it would receive a weekly supple-

[1] In technical language, the income effect may outweigh the substitution effect. For evidence of the relative strength of these two effects in Britain, see Break, 1957 and Fields and Stanbury, 1971.

ment of 50p.[1] The snag was that in order to receive the benefit, families had to claim it – there was no other way in which they could be identified. And either through a natural reluctance to come forward and try to prove that they were poor enough to qualify or, more probably, because they had not heard of FIS or did not understand what it meant or how to go about applying for it, a great many families failed to claim it: even two years after its introduction, it was calculated that a third of the families eligible for supplements were not receiving them.[2] Compared with the obvious alternative way of relieving family poverty – increasing family allowances – FIS had the virtue of not giving help where it was not needed,[3] and not being politically unpopular. But it had the serious disadvantage of not going to a large proportion of those who needed it.[4]

MUSEUM CHARGES

One proposal which Mr Barber made, though in itself of negligible economic importance, perfectly distilled the essence of the new Conservative Government's economic philosophy: that museums and art galleries should start charging for admission.

From a political point of view this was an odd proposal. Admission to many of Britain's major museums and art galleries has always been free, and few others have charged for admission since 1939. Thus the Conservatives were seeking to change a fairly long-established status quo. There was no money in the proposal: net revenue, after allowing for the administrative costs involved in charging for admission, was estimated at no more than £1 million. Nor can there have been any votes in it; indeed a small but influential segment of centre and centre-right opinion was thoroughly alienated by the proposal, while those who had always regarded the Conserva-

[1] The initial make-up level, when the scheme came into operation in August 1971, was £18 a week for a family with one child, plus £2 for each additional child. Thus a family with two children and total income of £14 would receive a supplement of £3. (The maximum supplement payable was £4 a week.)

[2] *Hansard*, vol. 894, col. 273, 30 June 1975.

[3] By an ingenious adjustment of income tax child allowances, the increase in family allowances introduced by the Labour Government in 1968 had in fact been 'clawed back' from the better-off taxpayers, thus effectively turning a universal benefit into a selective one with 100 per cent take-up. But there was a limit to how far this could be done.

[4] A further irony about FIS was that it was inconsistent with the tax-cutting strand in Conservative philosophy, since its effect, over the relevant range, was to reduce the state benefit by 50p for each extra pound a low-paid worker earned; in other words it meant a marginal rate of tax of 50 per cent – enough, on Tory arguments, to constitute a severe disincentive to extra effort.

tives as philistines seemed to have their views endorsed. In spite of all this, the proposal was not merely introduced, but adhered to through thick and thin for the next three years, when many other far more important policies were abandoned. Charges finally came into operation at the beginning of 1974, though they were abolished two months later by the incoming Labour Government.

The reflationary packages of 1971 and 1972 (see pp. 131–43), which pumped many hundreds of millions of pounds into the economy, provided the culture-loving Mr Heath with ample opportunity to drop a proposal which had the whole cultural establishment arrayed against it; yet he persistently refused to take it. Perhaps this was partly because, as a keen – and paying – concert-goer, he felt it unfair that people whose leaning was towards the visual arts should get in free. If so, he overlooked a crucial difference between the performing and visual arts: actors and musicians still have to earn their living; while on the whole those who created the works that fill the museums and galleries do not.

But it stemmed from something deeper than that. Museum charges, Heath and other Conservatives reiterated, were 'right in principle': those who enjoyed the services provided by museums and art galleries 'ought' to contribute to the cost of providing these services. This principle – if indeed it is a principle and not merely an expression of taste – clearly derives from the classical economic theory of the nineteenth century. According to this, if the economic system is to work efficiently, the price that people pay for goods and services must reflect the cost of producing them. If this is *not* the case, and price is either above or below cost, then the welfare of society cannot be maximized, in the sense of resources being used in the way that people most want; for the prices in the shops, on the basis of which consumers decide how to spend their money, will not reflect the real cost to the economy of producing the goods involved. On the basis of this theory, then, to say that prices 'ought' to reflect costs, or that people 'ought' to pay to get into museums, is not to express a value judgment, but merely to make a factual statement about the conditions that must obtain if the welfare of society is to be maximized. On this basis, museum charges are 'right in principle'.

Unfortunately for the marvellous simplicity of this guiding principle, economic theory has moved on during the past hundred years. Most economists would now agree that the conclusions of the classical theory are only correct if at least three conditions are met: if the existing distribution of income is acceptable; if there are no divergences between social and private benefits and costs; and if people are sufficiently well-informed to be the best judges of their own interests. In the world that actually surrounds us the first two of these conditions are manifestly not met, and the third can at least be argued about. The proposition that people 'ought' to pay for admission to museums is therefore seen to be not an inescapable imperative of the iron laws of economics, but merely a statement of preference or taste. It is hardly to be wondered at that such a taste should have been attacked as mean and short-sighted. Museum charges, while raising a derisory amount of revenue, were bound to reduce visits to museums and art galleries,[1] and it would be the poor rather than the rich who would be put off by admission charges. It might also be regarded as a pity, in a society permeated by the commercial ethos, and in which much time and money is spent in persuading people to buy – or to covet – more and better material goods, to deter people, however marginally, from communing with past civilizations and gazing at man's supreme artistic achievements.

THE INDUSTRIAL RELATIONS ACT

Museum charges, however indicative of the Heath Government's approach to the economy, were merely a sideshow; the real action was taking place elsewhere – and nowhere more than in the field of industrial relations. The Conservatives had had a high old time in 1969 denouncing the cowardice of Harold Wilson and the Labour Government in surrendering to the unions over *In Place of Strife*, and by a natural momentum these denunications were translated into pledges in the 1970 Conservative manifesto. The idea that the forces which had defeated Labour might also defeat the Conservatives did not seem to cross anyone's mind: Labour, after all – Conservatives seem to have assured each other – was the creature of the unions, and had to do the unions' bidding, whereas the Conservatives were a national party, with the responsibility for preventing any particular section of the community – particularly if it happened to be organized labour – from getting too big for its boots. And the unions had grown out of their boots long ago. So the 1970 manifesto pledged that a Conservative government would introduce 'a comprehensive Industrial Relations Bill', which would provide

[1] A survey conducted in December 1970 by *National Heritage* indicated that between one and two million visits a year might be aborted.

> some deterrent against irresponsible action by unofficial minorities . . . create conditions in which strikes become the means of last resort, not of first resort . . . lay down what is lawful and what is not lawful in the conduct of industrial disputes . . . provide for agreements to be binding on both unions and employers. A new Registrar of Trades Unions and Employers' Associations will ensure that their rules are fair, just, democratic, and not in conflict with the public interest. In the case of a dispute which would seriously endanger the national interest, our Act will provide for the holding of a secret ballot and for a 'cooling-off period' of not less than sixty days.

In short, the Conservatives would pass a law to reduce the power of the unions.

To a great many people, reducing the power of the unions seemed a good idea – just as it had the previous year when Labour proposed to do almost the same thing. The power of the unions, and of many small militant groups within the unions, had grown very great; and this power was sometimes used in a socially irresponsible way. There was much to be said for trying to reduce it and to channel it in more creative directions. What seemed doubtful was that such power could be effectively curbed by passing a law. The Conservatives might argue that the only thing that had gone wrong in 1969 was that Labour's resolve had collapsed in the face of threats from its paymasters; a more detached view might have been that the intensity of union objections to legislation by a Labour government would be doubled in the case of legislation by a Conservative government. For a deep and abiding part of union folklore is that the ruling class in general, and Conservative governments in particular, have done their best down the years to defeat the attempts of working men to band together to improve their conditions. It was the Tories who had passed the notorious Combination Acts of 1799–1800, which made it illegal for working men to combine together to demand higher wages or shorter hours. It was a potent symbol of the Establishment – a High Court judge – who in the Taff Vale case of 1901 had decreed that the Amalgamated Society of Railway Servants should pay heavy damages to the railway company because of the activities of some individual members of the union – a judgment which much weakened the position of the unions. It was another High Court judge who, in the Osborne case of 1909, had decreed that union funds could not be used for political purposes. And it was another Conservative government which had passed the 1927 Trade Disputes Act, which outlawed both sympathetic strikes and strikes 'designed or calculated to coerce the government', and substituted 'contracting in' for 'contracting out' of the political levy.[1] So it seemed likely that trade union opposition to the proposed legislation would be intense. Despite this, the Conservatives – and Heath in particular – took the view that legislation was essential, that public opinion was behind them, and that if they were sufficiently determined they would win through in the end.

Opposition started early. Even before the Bill had been published, the TUC called for a countrywide 'day of protest'; and between December 1970 and March 1971 national one-day strikes were held in a number of industries. In Parliament, most of the hundred-odd union-sponsored Labour MPs, and many others besides, were implacably opposed to the Bill. This, combined with the usual exigencies of party political warfare, not to mention the need to be restored to a state of grace in the eyes of the unions after the unhappy experiences of 1969, made it inevitable that the Shadow Cabinet would decide to fight the measure every inch of the way – whatever some individual members of it may have thought privately.[2] The committee stage of the Bill in the House of Commons was the longest (apart from finance Bills) since 1945, and was only ended by Government use of the guillotine before 100 of the Bill's 150 clauses had been debated; the number of divisions on the report stage – fifty-seven, taking over eleven hours – was the highest on record; the House of Lords had the longest sitting at committee stage since the beginning of the century; the five days allocated in the Commons for consideration of the Lords' amendments was the longest such period in the history of Parliament; and even this debate had to be guillotined. Nobody could say that Labour had not tried. All the same, the Bill became law on 5 August 1971, and the trouble really began.

[1] An Act passed by the Liberal Government in 1913 had permitted a certain part of union funds to be used for political purposes provided that union members could contract *out* of this part of their subscription if they wished. The 1927 Act reversed this, requiring union members to take the positive step of contracting *in*. The immediate effect – such is the importance of lethargy in human affairs – was to reduce the Labour Party's income by more than a third (Taylor, 1965, p. 251). Not surprisingly, one of the first steps taken by the 1945 Labour Government was to repeal the 1927 Act.

[2] Particularly piquant, and the source of much innocent amusement among the Conservatives, was the position of Barbara Castle who, as Shadow Employment Secretary, had to condemn a Bill which was not all that different from the one she had introduced in 1969. It was noticeable that in two articles she published at this time in the *New Statesman* (5 and 26 Feb. 1971) she concentrated her attack on a few specific proposals and not on the philosophy of the Bill as a whole. It was also of some interest that Lord Donovan, who had been chairman of the 1965–68 Royal Commission (see p. 92), expressed certain reservations about the Bill, but took pains to avoid condemning it (House of Lords, 5 April 1971).

The basic – and perfectly legal – tactic adopted by the TUC in the face of this legislation came as a surprise to the Government. Under the leadership of Vic Feather, its General Secretary, it instructed unions not to register under the Act. Refusal to register meant that both a union itself, and its individual members and officials, were deprived of the protection they had enjoyed since the Trade Disputes Act of 1906.[1] In consequence, any strike or other industrial action designed to induce people to break a contract would constitute what the new Act defined as an 'unfair industrial practice' and would lay union or individual open to unlimited damages. Some unions, more alarmed at the thought of these dire possibilities than of the wrath of their colleagues, registered; but the great majority, including nearly all the most important ones, did not. And once it became clear that the most powerful unions were not going to register, it was very difficult to see how – except in some totally transformed political context – the Act was going to be workable.

What followed is best regarded as a farce in three acts. In the first act, a transport firm on Merseyside complained to the new National Industrial Relations Court in March 1972 that dockers belonging to the Transport and General Workers' Union, but acting unofficially and at the instigation of their shop stewards, were refusing to handle the firm's containers. This, they contended, was an unfair industrial practice within the meaning of the new Act. The NIRC, under its president, Sir John Donaldson, agreed.[2] The TGWU was told to stop blacking the containers. The blacking continued, despite the efforts of TGWU officials to get it called off, and the union was fined £5,000 for contempt of court. This fine was not paid, the blacking still continued, and the union was fined a further £50,000. On TUC advice, the union then paid the fines, but took the matter to the Court of Appeal, which on 13 June overruled the NIRC and set the fines aside on the grounds that the TGWU could not be held responsible for the unauthorized actions of its shop stewards. Further appeal was then made to the House of Lords. The House of Lords did not reach a decision until 26 July, just in time to

[1] This Act, passed by the then Liberal Government, had effectively been drafted by the trade unions (Ensor, 1936, p. 392). It undid the effect of the Taff Vale decision, and exempted unions from all actions for tort.

[2] A High Court judge, Donaldson had a personality which did nothing to allay the unions' suspicions that the NIRC was a device whereby the upper classes could keep the lower classes in order. Some people must have been irresistibly reminded of prosecuting counsel in the *Lady Chatterley* case, who demanded of a puzzled jury of twelve honest men and true whether they would permit their servants to read the book.

provide the whole play with an appropriate ending (see p. 129). In the meantime, as the first act ended, any observers who were not totally bemused must have been left with two predominant impressions. One was that the Industrial Relations Act was based on a pretence – the pretence that unions can always control their more militant members, whereas in fact they cannot. The other was that the play might be a source of fascination and enrichment to lawyers, but was not much use to anyone else.

The second act, as befits a farce, was played crisply, and with impeccable timing. In April 1972, the rail unions rejected a final British Rail offer of a 12½ per cent wage increase, and began a nationwide go-slow. The NIRC ordered them to call off the go-slow for a fourteen-day cooling-off period. The unions agreed. At the end of the cooling-off period, the go-slow was resumed. The NIRC demanded a strike ballot. The unions agreed. The strike ballot showed overwhelming support for the unions' demands. The go-slow was resumed. Finally the unions were offered, and accepted, an increase almost identical with what they had been refused two months earlier. The moral of act two seemed clear: Donovan had been quite right to reject strike ballots and cooling-off periods. Judged by this example, they were irrelevant at best and harmful at worst.

Act three was much the most dramatic. The leading actors were again dockers and the theme was again the refusal to handle containers, though the scene had shifted from Liverpool to London, and the events took place in June and July. A group of dockers, engaged in picketing a container handling depot, was instructed by the NIRC to desist, and refused to do so. Three of the dockers were thereupon committed to prison for contempt of court. To those whose horizons are bounded by the law courts, this may have seemed a proper, even an inevitable proceeding. To millions of workers, uninterested in legal niceties, it was an outrage: men were to be imprisoned for engaging in a perfectly normal and legitimate union activity. A large number of dockers immediately decided to go on indefinite unofficial strike, an action which was prevented only by the dramatic intervention of a character no one had ever heard of, but who was undoubtedly the hero of the hour, if not indeed the whole play: the Official Solicitor. Unbeknown to the three dockers, this shadowy figure applied to the Appeal Court for the NIRC's verdict to be set aside on the grounds of insufficient evidence; and the Appeal Court obligingly agreed. The prison sentences were rescinded. A week later the container firm and the dockers reached a compromise agreement, and picketing ceased. However another firm, whose cold storage depot had been picketed for some time, now appealed to the NIRC, which again took the view that the men concerned were picketing in support of an unfair industrial practice, and issued an injunction restraining them from doing so. The Court order was again ignored and on 21 July five dockers (two of whom had been among the three involved in the previous case) were sent to prison. This time the Official Solicitor could think of no reason for taking the matter to the Appeal Court. Union response was immediate. The ports of London, Liverpool and Hull came to a standstill; for four days there were no national newspapers; sympathetic strikes were called in a number of industries, including mining, the motor industry, and road transport; and on 26 July the TUC called for a one-day general strike.

On this same day, however, the House of Lords delivered its verdict on the case which had been appealed to it in act one. It decided that the Court of Appeal had been wrong, and Donaldson had been right: a union *could* be held responsible for the actions of its shop stewards. This judgment undoubtedly confirmed what had been the intention of the Industrial Relations Act: that *unions* (which can only be fined) should be held accountable for breaches of the law; *individuals* (who can be imprisoned) should not. And so the TGWU had to pay its £55,000 fines. But the five dockers were released from prison. The threatened confrontation between government and unions receded.

With the release of the imprisoned dockers, the farce was over, and the final curtain fell. It must have been obvious to even the most pedantically legal-minded that the attempt to reduce the power of the unions by passing a law had failed. The firms which had put their faith in the law were left to pick up the pieces as best they might: some surrendered to the shop stewards, some patched up a compromise agreement, some fought on until defeated. The Act's epitaph was spoken in February 1974, when Campbell Adamson, Director-General of the CBI said – shortly before the General Election in which its perpetrators lost office – that he thought it had been a mistake; and finally chiselled in stone when the Conservatives subsequently announced that they would not oppose its repeal by the incoming Labour Government.

THE DEMON BARBER

On 30 March 1971, only a week after the acrimonious conclusion of the report stage of the Industrial Relations Bill, Mr Barber introduced his first Budget. From a macroeconomic demand management point of view it was fairly uncontroversial: most informed opinion was calling for mild expansion, to ensure that the growth of demand did not lag behind the growth of capacity,[1] and Mr Barber duly obliged. The welcome given to the particular measures by which he proposed to do this, however, was less unanimous, for it soon became apparent that the Chancellor was engaged in the time-honoured political pastime of rewarding his friends and punishing his enemies.

Stripped of all irrelevance, the main theme of the budget was a reduction in income tax – and the higher your income, the more your income tax bill was going to be reduced. In addition to the cut of six old pence (2½p) in the standard rate of income tax he had announced the previous October, Mr Barber now increased income tax child allowances by £40. This benefited the large number of income taxpayers who had children, but of course did not benefit families whose incomes were too low to pay income tax. However the real goodies lay in three other proposals. One was the replacement of the one-ninth earned income relief between £4,005 and £9,945 by 15 per cent relief on earned income without upper limit; this had the effect of reducing the tax paid by everybody earning more than £4,005 a year and, in particular, of bringing down the top rate of combined income and surtax[2] on earned income from 88.75 per cent to 75.4 per cent. Another was the proposal that a wife could elect to have her earnings taxed separately; where husband and wife were both high earners this would mean a substantial reduction in their combined tax burden. The third was the abolition of the provision that children's investment income must be aggregated for tax purposes with that of their parents.[3] The benefit of these three concessions, which were estimated to cost the Exchequer £65 million in a full year (in contrast to FIS, which was estimated to cost less than £9 million), accrued almost entirely to those in the top 5 per

[1] See for example NIER, February 1971.

[2] One of Mr Barber's less contentious proposals was the amalgamation of income tax and surtax into a single graduated personal tax.

[3] This provision had been introduced by Roy Jenkins in his 1968 Budget; he calculated it would save £25 million in a full year.

cent of the income distribution; and a very large fraction of it accrued to those within the top 1 per cent.

Mr Barber, a fairly good example of Selsdon Man, might argue, as he did, that by the standards of other Western countries British income tax rates were very high, and that reducing them was a necessary – perhaps even a sufficient – condition of unleashing the energies that would set the British economy back on its feet and enable it to start growing at a rate more in line with its neighbours. No doubt many people agreed with him. But there were also a great many who disagreed, arguing not only that the incentive effects of lower rates of income tax were far from proven, but also that big tax concessions to the richest handful of the population sat in uneasy contrast with the cuts in welfare services and the increased charges for school meals and prescriptions foreshadowed the previous October. Coming as it did against the background of the Government's implacable resolve to get the Industrial Relations Bill on to the statute book, Mr Barber's first budget was a gift to those who were seeking to persuade the working class that it was under lethal attack from a capitalist Tory government. Even to more moderate opinion it appeared, at the least, partisan and short-sighted.

SOME REFLATION

In his Budget speech Mr Barber had said that if, after his mildly reflationary measures had been allowed a reasonable time to have their effect, a further stimulus appeared to be needed, he would apply it. In fact he applied it less than four months later, before the March measures could possibly have had any significant effect. One reason for this was the discovery by the Treasury economists that during the first half of 1971 the level of output was more than 1 per cent lower than had been assumed at the time of the Budget – a classic example of the forecaster's traditional complaint that the most difficult part of the exercise is not guessing what is going to happen in the future, but knowing where you are now.[1] The discovery that the economy was starting from a lower level than previously supposed was taken as justifying a faster growth in demand: whereas in March the Chancellor had been aiming at a 3 per cent growth of demand over the next year, in July he announced that he was aiming at a rate of 4–4½ per cent.

[1] This problem is discussed more fully on p. 146 below.

More compelling than these forecasters' metaphysics were the unemployment figures. In December 1970 unemployment[1] had been below 600,000 (2.6 per cent); by July 1971 it was nearing 800,000 (3.5 per cent), and still climbing rapidly. The economy was clearly heading towards the highest unemployment figure since the War. Most compelling of all, perhaps, was the Government's electoral performance. In local elections held in May Labour made spectacular gains at the expense of the Conservatives, and in two by-elections the same month the swing from Conservative to Labour was around 10 per cent – rising to 16 per cent in another by-election the following month.

And so Mr Barber came forward on 19 July with a reflationary package. Although he announced a temporary stimulus to investment,[2] and pointed to a series of small steps the Government was taking to reduce regional unemployment, the package overwhelmingly took the form of a stimulus to consumption: purchase tax was reduced by approximately 20 per cent, and all hire purchase controls were abolished. These measures, he reckoned, would have the desired effect of increasing the level of national output by 4–4½ per cent between the first half of 1971 and the first half of 1972.

Although the package – and particularly the action on hire purchase – was very much in line with what the NIESR had been calling for in its May *Economic Review,* it was far from being without its critics. The main criticism fastened on the high probability of Mr Barber's consumption-led boom following the same path as all previous consumption-led booms, leading before long to a big rise in imports, a slackening-off of exports, a balance of payments crisis and a savage deflation.[3] In short, we were back to stop-go. While conceding the NIESR argument that private industrial investment could not be stimulated directly – however desirable that would be – the critics rejected the corollary that consumption must be stimulated in the hope that this would induce a rise in investment later on. The answer, they claimed – not for the first time – was

[1] Taking the figure for Great Britain, excluding school-leavers and adult students, seasonally adjusted.

[2] The measure was somewhat similar to that introduced by Labour in 1966 (see pp. 80–1). The first-year allowance on investment in plant and machinery was increased from 60 per cent to 80 per cent for all expenditure incurred before 1 August 1973.

[3] For example Samuel Brittan, Economics Editor of the *Financial Times,* predicted that as a result of the Chancellor's actions a balance of payments crisis would probably occur between mid-1972 and mid-1973 (22 July 1971).

export-led growth. A rapid rise in exports could bring the economy back to full employment over a period of two or three years – more slowly perhaps than by stimulating consumption, but infinitely more safely, because the balance of payments problem would be solved by the very process that was restoring full employment.

The intellectual case for export-led growth was strengthened at about this time by an influential argument propounded by Professor Kaldor,[1] which gave a new twist to the conventional interpretation of the Keynesian analysis of unemployment. In the Keynesian model, there are three possible leakages, or reasons for effective demand falling below full employment level: an excess of saving over investment; an excess of government revenue over government expenditure; and an excess of imports over exports. Any of these leakages – if not offset elsewhere – will mean that a country's full employment income is not all being spent on domestic production, and will cause a decline in output and employment. According to Kaldor, post-war policy-makers in Britain had paid too much attention to the saving-investment relationship, and too little to the import-export relationship. An excess of ex-ante saving over ex-ante investment[2] – which had been the leakage Keynes had been mainly concerned with – posed the main deflationary threat in an economy, like the United States, with a very small foreign trade sector, and had indeed been a problem in Britain in the 1930s, when investment collapsed. But in general the problem for Britain – a very open economy – had lain in another leakage: the tendency for imports to exceed exports.

The emphasis of Keynesian stabilization policy during the post-war period had, according to Kaldor, been misplaced: instead of concentrating on keeping up consumption, in order to avoid an excess of saving over investment, it should have concentrated on keeping up exports, in order to avoid the excess of imports over exports that has been such a monotonous feature of the post-war scene. In other words, exports should have been the main target variable, to be influenced by the instrument of the exchange rate, instead of consumption, to be influenced by the instruments of fiscal and monetary policy. Not only would this have avoided balance of payments crises and stop-go and thus led to a steadier, and probably

[1] Kaldor, 1971. This piece of analysis was the genesis of the approach adopted a few years later by the so-called 'New Cambridge School' (see pp. 194–8 below).

[2] i.e. a situation in which the amount that people *wanted* to save was greater than the amount that businesses *wanted* to invest.

faster, growth path; it would also have led to faster growth for a quite different reason. Because 70 per cent of Britain's exports consist of manufactured goods, compared with only 30 per cent of her consumption expenditure, a strategy which relied on a rapid growth of exports would induce more manufacturing investment than a strategy which relied on maintaining full employment by manipulating consumption. This, combined with the dynamic economies of scale which can be reaped from a rapid increase in industrial output, could have enabled Britain to establish itself on the kind of virtuous circle enjoyed by Germany and Japan.[1]

One need not accept every nuance of this argument; some economists would not accept any of it. Nevertheless, there is a strong case for saying that what Mr Barber should have done in 1971 was to float the pound. An outright devaluation might have been resisted, or retaliated against, by other countries: unlike the situation in 1967, the current account was running a big surplus, and to a superficial eye the case for devaluation might have seemed weak. But the balance of payments surplus was misleading, reflecting as it did the competitiveness of sterling a year or two before. The truth was that the wage explosion which got under way in 1969 had more than eroded the competitive advantage Britain had gained from the November 1967 devaluation: between 1968 and 1971 Britain's export prices, in dollar terms, rose by 23 per cent, compared with a rise of 16 per cent for manufacturing countries as a whole (NIER, May 1972, table 19). A floating pound in 1971 would soon – not perhaps immediately – have fallen enough in relation to other currencies to give a major boost to exports; and there was enough spare capacity in the economy to meet the export orders that would have flooded in. As it was, Mr Barber not only failed to provide a stimulus to exports; he set about increasing domestic demand in a way that would soon pre-empt export capacity.

LAME DUCKS AND ROOSTING CHICKENS

A key strand in the philosophy of the new Conservative Government was the insistence that the State must not go on propping up ailing industries. A more rigorous competitive climate must be created, in which the less efficient firms and industries would go under, releasing capital and labour to flow into the efficient, expanding firms and

[1] The argument is an extension of the original Verdoorn argument (see p. 45).

industries on which economic growth and competitiveness in world markets depended. The point was well summarized in a Commons debate on 4 November 1970 by Mr John Davies, the newly-appointed Secretary of State for Trade and Industry, who said that the country's essential need was 'to gear its policies to the great majority of people, who are not lame ducks, who do not need a hand, who are quite capable of looking after their own interests and only demand to be allowed to do so'. The vast majority, he added, in case anyone had missed the point, 'lives and thrives in a bracing climate, and not in a soft, sodden morass of subsidized incompetence'. This was all stirring stuff. But when the chips were down, would the Government really withhold help from a big company in trouble?

The matter was soon put to the test. The two most dramatic cases were shipbuilding, an industry with a past, and aero engines, an industry with, perhaps, a future. In 1949, nearly half the ships launched throughout the world were built in Britain; twenty years later, the figure had collapsed to 5 per cent. Nowhere were the problems associated with this decline more acute than on the upper Clyde. Late in 1967 the Labour Government had attempted to salvage the situation by amalgamating five firms into Upper Clyde Shipbuilders, and by the time it left office in June 1970 had poured in some £20 million of aid.[1] This was precisely the kind of lame duck John Davies had in his sights, and in October he made a decision that was not so much a shot between the eyes as a blow below the belt: no further government credits would be provided to shipowners wanting ships built at UCS. These credits were in fact restored in February 1971,[2] but in the meantime fatal damage had been done – admittedly to a patient already in a fairly critical condition – and in June the company went into liquidation. Unfortunately the workers did not quietly redeploy themselves into more efficient industries, as the Conservative script had demanded, but occupied the shipyards and refused to budge. Out of a confused situation came a new company – Govan Shipbuilders – backed by much larger sums of public money than had been injected into the industry by the Labour Government. And just visible in the distance, as the smoke of battle lifted, could be discerned the figure of Mr Davies in full, though well-dissembled, retreat.

[1] For a full account of the UCS affair, see Buchan, 1972.

[2] According to some observers (e.g. Macpherson, 1971) this sudden change of heart was to avoid two companies crashing in the same week – see p. 136.

It was not only from an unsuccessful attempt at euthanasia in the shipbuilding industry that Mr Davies was retreating. The case of Rolls-Royce had inflicted just as heavy a defeat on his robustly *simpliste* doctrines. In 1968 Rolls-Royce, effectively the only British manufacturer of aero engines, had snatched from under the noses of the world's big two – the American firms General Electric and Pratt and Whitney – a tremendous contract to supply engines for the Lockheed TriStar. The homecoming negotiating team was greeted with general rejoicing, not to mention knighthoods and lunches at Buckingham Palace. Alas, it turned out that the contract was at fixed prices – a sure recipe for disaster in an age of mounting inflation. By 1970 the company had acute cash-flow difficulties, and in November the Conservative Government felt there was no option but to bale it out, offering £42 million of public money. But the baling-out proved short-lived, and in February 1971 the firm crashed into bankruptcy. However the matter could not be left there, as the Government recognized when it woke up and thought about the problem. Rolls-Royce was one of the few British firms in the vanguard of world technology; it employed, directly and indirectly, many tens of thousands of people; it represented a large chunk of the nation's export effort; it had contracts to service thousands of engines in use all over the world; and it was integrated deep into the West's defence arrangements. It could not be allowed to disappear as if it were a corner shop. And so the Government did what it had said in its manifesto it would never do: it nationalized the major part of it; and then put up £130 million of public money in order to make it viable.[1] Even Mr Davies had to recognize in the end that Rolls-Royce was a lame duck that had to go on flying.

Two factors lay behind the Government's decision to abandon its previous stance and provide support for UCS and Rolls-Royce. One was the political pressure exerted by rising unemployment. Although Conservatives had often talked – usually in discreet euphemisms – about the need for a somewhat higher level of unemployment in

[1] Staunch Conservative supporters could, however, take comfort from the fact that the act of nationalizing Rolls-Royce was accompanied by two acts of *de*-nationalization. One covered the travel firm of Thomas Cook, which had come into the public sector through an accident of war, to prevent legal control of the firm falling into the hands of the Germans. The other related to 200 pubs and one brewery in Carlisle, which had been taken into public ownership in 1916 in a no doubt unsuccessful effort to reduce drunkenness in an area considered vital to the war effort. One imagines that Aneurin Bevan, who used to call for nationalization of the 'commanding heights' of the economy, would not have been displeased with the swap.

order to provide a more bracing, competitive climate in which resources would flow to where they showed the highest return, the experience of 1970–72 demonstrated that the opposite was true: a time of high and rising unemployment was a time when people clung tenaciously to their jobs, using every possible weapon to resist redundancy, whatever slide-rule calculations of profit and loss might show. The second factor was the dawning recognition by the Government that in a modern economy capital and labour are not, as classical theory predicates, homogeneous and infinitely divisible factors of production which, if released from one employment, will flow effortlessly into another. The uncertainties and rigidities in the system are much too great for that. In the end, it took an act of faith greater than all but the most diehard Conservative Ministers could summon up to imagine that if Rolls-Royce were allowed to collapse, the resources released would flow into some other sector, producing equal or higher output and exports.

The U-turn on industrial policy performed by the Conservative Government between 1970 and 1972 was even greater than the *ad hoc* interventions in the case of UCS, Rolls-Royce and a few others might suggest. Early in 1971, when its actions were still being determined by the Hyde-like attitudes into which it had fallen in opposition, the Government had abolished the IRC and repealed key sectors of Labour's 1968 Industrial Expansion Act. By the following year, the personality of Dr Jekyll had got the upper hand. Reversing themselves completely, the Conservatives passed an Industry Act that give the Secretary of State sweeping powers to intervene in industry, by providing any form of financial assistance to any industry or any firm, in any case where he thought that this assistance would be of benefit to the economy of the U.K. or any part of it.[1] So sweeping were these powers, indeed, that they proved more than adequate to the needs of the interventionist-minded Labour Government which took office in March 1974: Mr Benn's much-criticized forays into the hinterland of British industry in 1974 and 1975 all took place under

[1] Industry Act, 1972, Section 8. Announcing the proposals, Mr John Davies said blandly that 'I certainly am not nor ever have been an advocate of abandoning to their fate major sectors of British industry whose long-term success lies at the very heart of our industrial resurgence. In a new and rapidly changing world industrial and commercial environment, the Government cannot stand aside when situations arise which industry and the financial institutions cannot meet alone.' (House of Commons, 22 March 1972.) There had been nothing like it – as Harold Wilson once observed about the conversion of the Conservative front bench on another issue – since the Emperor of China baptised his army with a hose.

the imprimatur of Conservative legislation (see pp. 217–18). If 1971 and 1972 were good years for lame ducks, 1974 was the year when the chickens came home to roost.

A LOT MORE REFLATION

Throughout 1971 unemployment mounted rapidly, in spite of the March Budget, which assumed that demand would increase enough to prevent much further rise in unemployment, and in spite of the July mini-Budget, which slashed purchase tax and abolished hire purchase controls. The percentage rate of unemployment,[1] which had been stable at 2.5 per cent during 1970, rose to 2.8 per cent in the first quarter of 1971; 3.2 per cent in the second; 3.5 per cent in the third; and 3.7 per cent in the fourth. By January 1972, when the rate was 3.8 per cent, and the crude figure 918,000,[2] the spectre of a million unemployed was near, and a million unemployed had long been regarded as a critical figure which would provoke strong adverse reaction in the trade unions and indeed the electorate as a whole. Experienced fine-tuners would – or should – have been cautious at this point, recognizing that the time-lags in the system were such that there was no conceivable way in which the March tax cuts, let alone the July measures, could have had much impact on unemployment before the end of 1971; that quite strong expansionary forces were probably already getting under way in the economy; and that any further reflation should be a modest and limited one.[3] But the Government had learned nothing from the experience of the previous twenty years. In the autumn of 1971 it panicked, and started pulling every reflationary lever in sight.

The first of these levers was monetary policy. Bank Rate, which had been 7 per cent at the beginning of 1971, was cut to 6 per cent in April and 5 per cent in September. Much more significant, though coming a little later, was a rise in the money supply that was moderate or very big according to the definition taken.[4] To some

[1] For Great Britain, excluding school-leavers and adult students, seasonally adjusted.

[2] Before seasonal adjustment.

[3] This was, broadly speaking, the line taken by the NIESR in its November 1971 *Economic Review*.

[4] The narrow definition of the money supply (M_1) covers only current private bank accounts and notes and coins in circulation. The broad definition (M_3) covers various other kinds of deposits as well, notably private deposit accounts, deposits by the public sector, and all deposits by residents in non-sterling currencies. (M_3 is two to three times as big as M_1.) M_1 rose by 14 per cent in 1972 and 7 per cent in 1973. M_3 rose by 28 per cent in 1972 and 29 per cent in 1973 (*Economic Trends*, Annual Supplement 1975, pp. 107–8).

extent this increase in the money supply reflected a rising public sector borrowing requirement (PSBR).[1] But a large part of it was the result of an explosion of bank lending to the private sector: bank advances rose by 48 per cent during 1972 and 43 per cent during 1973. It was this enormous injection of credit into the private sector of the economy that, more than anything else, fuelled what came to be known as 'the Barber boom'.

Although the Government certainly intended bank lending to the private sector to rise, in order to stimulate consumption and, with luck, investment, the sheer magnitude of the creation of credit which occurred seems to have taken it by surprise. The main reason for this lay in a new set of ground rules that it had laid down for the banking sector in 1971.[2] In line with the *laissez-faire* element in Conservative philosophy, the clearing banks, which had for many years maintained as solid a front on deposit and lending rates as any text-book cartel, were to be encouraged to compete with each other in the terms and services they offered to the public. But if they were to do this, there would have to be a change in the existing method of controlling bank credit, which took the rather haphazard form of requiring the banks to maintain an 8 per cent ratio of cash, and a 28 per cent ratio of liquid assets, to liabilities, and supplemented this from time to time by imposing a ceiling on bank advances: it would be difficult for the banks to compete with each other if the total amount each could lend was restricted by an arbitrary ceiling based on what it had lent in the past. And so the Government introduced a new method of credit control: a 12½ per cent minimum reserve asset ratio. Provided a bank ensured that its holdings of certain approved assets represented at least 12½ per cent of its deposit liabilities, it could lend as much as it liked.[3] And in order – so it was supposed – to give the Government greater control over the volume of credit and thus of the money supply, the same minimum asset requirements, with minor modifications, were applied to a host of fringe banks and

1 The PSBR, which had been negative in 1969 and 1970, was £1.4 billion in 1971, £2.1 billion in 1972, and £4.2 billion in 1973. The rise in M_3 during 1972 and 1973 (£12.5 billion) was thus twice as big as the PSBR for these two years.

2 Bank of England, 1971 (i) and (ii).

3 Approved assets were balances with the Bank of England, Treasury Bills, company tax reserve certificates, money at call with the London money market, British government stocks with a year or less to maturity, rediscountable local authority bills and (up to 2 per cent of deposits) rediscountable commercial bills. One of the criticisms made at the time was that it was inappropriate to include call money and commercial bills in the list, since experience had shown that the quantity of these assets was not under the control of the Bank of England.

financial intermediaries which had sprung up, partly because they were not subject to the old controls. But someone had blundered. The imposition of the new 12½ per cent minimum reserve asset ratio on the clearing banks had the effect of reducing the old 28 per cent liquidity ratio to only 15–20 per cent;[1] in other words they suddenly became free to expand their lending very substantially. Now that they were on their mettle to compete with each other, they wasted no time in doing so, and between mid-1971 and mid-1973 bank advances doubled. There being no way in which such a large increase in demand could be translated into a rise in output, most of it was translated into a rise in price – mainly of existing assets. A huge property boom got under way, not unconnected with the fact that between mid-1971 and mid-1973 bank advances to the financial sector rose from £1.3 billion to £4.8 billion; and over the same two-year period the price of houses rose by about 70 per cent.

The second reflationary lever the Chancellor pulled was public expenditure, and the scale on which decisions were taken in 1971 and 1972 to increase public expenditure bore testimony to the extent to which the Government had taken fright. Although there are severe limitations on how far public expenditure can be used as an instrument of short-term stabilization policy if intolerable waste and inefficiency is not to result,[2] there are some kinds of expenditure which can be altered at short notice. It would have been perfectly reasonable for Mr Barber, in the course of 1971, to take decisions which had the effect of increasing public expenditure by perhaps £50 million in 1971–72 and £100–150 million in 1972–73: this would have helped to lift the economy out of recession in the short run, without raising public expenditure above the planned level in 1973–74 or 1974–75, when the economy was likely to be operating at full capacity again. Although this may have been Mr Barber's intention in the summer of 1971, the scale on which the intention was subverted by the actual course of events was spectacular. This can be seen by focusing on the public expenditure planned for 1974–75. The public expenditure White Paper published in January 1971, putting into effect the cuts Mr Barber had announced in October 1970,[3] showed that expenditure in 1974–75 would be some £950 million lower

[1] See *The Economist*, 22 May 1971 for a full discussion of this point.

[2] These limitations had been stressed in the Plowden report of 1961 (HMG, 1961), and were stressed again in a report of the House of Commons Expenditure Committee early in 1972 (HC, 1972).

[3] See p. 120.

than previously planned.[1] So far, so good: the Conservatives, true to their election pledges, were holding down the growth of public expenditure much more firmly than Labour would have. But then the picture began to change: by the time the next White Paper was published, in November 1971, planned expenditure for 1974–75 had been raised by nearly £500 million above the January projection. In fact the November White Paper was out of date before it was published, since two days earlier Mr Barber announced in the House of Commons substantial further increases in public expenditure which were not included in the White Paper. Further announcements of increased expenditure followed. The net result was that by the time the next annual White Paper was published, in December 1972, planned public expenditure in 1974–75 had been increased, compared with the November 1971 White Paper, by a further £1,200 million, or 4 per cent.

Thus Mr Barber's actions in late 1971 and early 1972 went far beyond authorizing the kind of quick-acting and short-lived increases in public expenditure that could make a useful reflationary contribution in 1972–73. They put in motion increases in public expenditure which were very substantial, but which would only show up in the medium term – in 1973–74 and 1974–75, when it seemed likely that the pressure of demand in the economy would once again be intense.[2] Mr Barber's actions flew in the face of both Conservative philosophy and the principles of sound economic management.

Much more in line with traditional Conservative philosophy was the third reflationary lever the Chancellor pulled. In March 1972 he introduced a budget which it was estimated would reduce net revenue by £1.2 billion in 1972–73, four-fifths of the reduction resulting from a cut in income tax,[3] most of the rest from cuts in the higher rates of purchase tax. The effect, according to Mr Barber, would be to raise the short-term rate of growth of the economy from

[1] All the figures for 1974–75 quoted in this paragraph are at 1972 Survey prices, and are taken from HC, 1973, p. viii.

[2] This danger had been explicitly stressed to the Expenditure Committee in early 1972 by Wynne Godley, Director of the Department of Applied Economics at Cambridge (HC, 1973, p. vi).

[3] The single person's allowance was raised from £325 to £460 and the married allowance from £465 to £600. This (in sharp contrast with the changes in the 1971 Budget) was an egalitarian step, in that the effect was to reduce income tax by about £1 a week for everybody, regardless of how high their income was. On the other hand a number of concessions on estate duty, surtax and tax relief on interest payments, including abolition of the higher rate of tax on the first £2,000 of investment income, only benefited the better-off.

3 per cent to 5 per cent. It was arguably the most expansionary Budget ever introduced.

The Barber boom has been much criticized, and with justice. Effective demand was increased much faster between 1971 and 1973 than could possibly be matched by a rise in output. The result was inevitable and, indeed, familiar: imports rose rapidly, and so did prices. By October 1973, before a cent had been put on the price of oil, inflation in Britain was proceeding at a rate of about 10 per cent, and the balance of payments current account was in deficit at a rate of £800 million a year. Nevertheless, there were three features of the situation which, if they did not mitigate Mr Barber's expansionary policy, at least provided a partial excuse for it. First, it did at least represent an attempt to restore full employment and achieve a faster rate of growth. These two objectives had been neglected for too long: unemployment had been over 2 per cent since the end of 1966, and over 3 per cent, and rising rapidly, since early 1971; and since 1966 total output had been growing by little more than 2 per cent a year. Secondly, there was – with some honourable exceptions[1] – little criticism of Mr Barber at the time. The only major criticism of the 1972 Budget made by the *Financial Times*, for example, was that proposed new regional incentives would favour capital-intensive rather than labour-intensive investment.[2] *The Times* doubted whether Mr Barber had gone far enough, and hoped that he would 'respond flexibly and speedily to any evidence that too little has again been done too late'.[3] The Labour Opposition, which had been capitalizing heavily on the unemployment issue, could think of little to say: Harold Wilson was reduced to criticising minutiae about share options. And in a considered view in its May 1972 *Economic Review* the NIESR stuck to the line it had taken in February[4] – that what was needed was tax cuts of £2,500 million, and that the Budget had been insufficiently expansionary. Although there was some concern

[1] These exceptions included some monetarists, whose main concern was not with the total size and effects of Mr Barber's various reflationary measures, but simply with the size of the likely increase in the money supply, and the implications of this for inflation. The monetarist analysis is discussed on pp. 159–64.

[2] *Financial Times* leader, 22 March 1972.

[3] *Times* leader, 22 March 1972. The Economics Editor of *The Times*, Peter Jay, was however more cautious, expressing concern about the medium-term implications for inflation and the balance of payments.

[4] Which was itself a reversal of the line taken in November 1971 (see p. 138 and footnote). The NIESR seems to have lost its head later than the Government, but lost it more completely. It was still calling for a further stimulus to the economy as late as November 1972.

about the possible effect of the Budget on inflation and the balance of payments, it was fairly muted: the general view was that rapid expansion of output would have a favourable effect on prices and international competitiveness by reducing unit costs. As if to endorse this opinion, the *Financial Times* ordinary share index rose eleven points during Budget day to a new record level of 521.[1]

Thirdly, the speed with which the economy ran into bottlenecks came as an unpleasant surprise to a great many observers. It had been widely assumed that, with the slow growth of output over the previous few years, the economy at the beginning of 1972 had a great deal of spare capacity. In fact, as output started to expand faster, shortages of capacity and skilled labour began to appear quite quickly. The abandonment of the National Plan, which was supposed to foresee and forestall such bottlenecks, and the years of low investment and inadequate training and re-training programmes, were taking their toll.

The main trouble with the Barber boom – as is clear at any rate in hindsight – was not that it took place, but that it was too rapid and took the wrong form. Had it been exports and productive investment that were stimulated, rather than consumption and public expenditure, and had the pace of expansion been slower, allowing extra demand to be met by domestic production instead of rising prices and rising imports, the outlook for the economy would have been much more favourable.

DOUBTS ABOUT FINE TUNING

Those who criticized Mr Barber for stimulating consumption instead of going for export-led growth were still operating within the framework of conventional post-war demand management policies, albeit twisting the framework into a new shape. In the meantime, a number of people had begun to question whether the framework was an appropriate one.

Since the War – indeed since the Kingsley Wood budget of 1941, which saw the first practical application of Keynesian theory – macroeconomic policy-making had consisted of forecasting the growth in the economy's productive potential over the next year or two; forecasting the likely change in effective demand over the same

[1] The index peaked two months later at an all-time high of 543 – a level which had not been nearly regained even four years later.

period; and taking steps to bring the latter into line with the former. Some parts of this operation were easier than others. Productive potential, compounded of the increase in the labour force and the increase in the average level of productivity, was reckoned to grow at a fairly steady rate of about 3 per cent a year, and in short-term forecasts this figure was generally taken as fixed, even though the object of much policy (for example of the National Plan) was to increase the figure in the longer run, and even though the export-led growth enthusiasts thought that if their policies were adopted the underlying rate of growth would automatically rise.[1] Much trickier was the forecasting of effective demand, and particularly those components of it, such as exports and private investment, which were regarded as being, at least in the short run, exogenous, i.e. outside the Government's ability to influence. Nevertheless, as time went on the forecasting process became increasingly elaborate and – it was hoped – accurate: forecasts were made on a quarterly basis, and not just for whole years; efforts were made to reconcile forecasts arrived at in different ways; research threw new light on key economic relationships; and increasing use was made of computerized economic models. Similarly, the instruments used to bring the forecast path of output and employment into line with the desired path became more flexible and sophisticated – examples being the introduction of the regulator in 1961, the use of import deposits in 1968–70, and the temporary stimulus to investment announced in 1966 and again in 1971.

But there were some who were unimpressed. The whole procedure of constructing forecasts three times a year and making minor adjustments every few months if the economy seemed to be moving off course – a procedure designated as 'fine-tuning' – came under attack. One blow was struck by Matthews (1968), who argued that if government intervention had been responsible for full employment since the war one would have expected to see a chronic budget deficit, as successive governments followed the Keynesian prescription of cutting taxes or raising public expenditure in order to sustain effective demand. In fact, he pointed out, there had been a chronic budget surplus. The factor which had maintained full employment was not government policy, but a high level of exports and private

[1] See p. 43 above. An argument for taking the rate of growth of productive potential as a variable rather than a constant even in the relatively short-term was put forward by Bray, 1970 and 1971, who advocated Box-Jenkins methods of forecasting. However Bray's methods do not purport to identify relationships describing economic behaviour, and have so far found little favour among economists.

investment. The implication was that the whole of post-war demand management policy had been an unnecessary charade. As was emphasized by various commentators,[1] Matthews' argument is not entirely convincing because it makes the implausible assumption that exports and private investment would still have been what they were if the Government had *not* been pledged to intervene in order to maintain full employment. Nevertheless, Matthews' argument could not, of its nature, be disproved, and it undoubtedly played a part in the revival in the early 1970s of the notion underlying nineteenth-century classical economics, that the economy would get on perfectly all right if the Government confined itself to balancing its own budget, and kept its nose out of other people's business.

Even unkinder than the charge that government intervention had been unnecessary was the charge that it had been positively destabilizing, and had actually made things worse. According to Dow (1964), successive governments had waited too long before acting, and had then underestimated the time-lags in the system. When belated expansionary or deflationary measures failed to show quick results, further measures were taken. By the time all these measures started to affect the economy the underlying situation had changed, so that expansionary measures came through at a time when a boom was already well under way, and deflationary measures hit the economy on the head after it had already turned down. In short, intervention had taken the form of 'too much, too late', and had aggravated instead of smoothing out the economic cycle. Dow's charge was supported by Hansen (1969), who not only agreed that Britain's macroeconomic policies had been destabilizing, but went on to observe that Britain was the only one of seven OECD countries studied of which this was true. Since Britain had attached more importance to stabilization policy than any other OECD country with the possible exception of Sweden, this was the unkindest cut of all.

Neither Dow nor Hansen was without his critics. Dow was taken to task by Little (1964), who emphasized the difficulty of assessing what would have happened in the complete absence of discretionary intervention. Similarly, there seems little doubt that Hansen's technique of assessing the effects of stabilization policy, based on a static model and certain simplifying assumptions, was doubly unfavourable to Britain. British policy was blamed for aggravating fluctuations in employment, without getting credit for the fact that these fluctua-

[1] For example Armstrong, 1968 and Stafford, 1970.

tions took place much closer to full employment than in most other countries; and no account was taken of the fact that in Britain government intervention at the macro level, including changes in government expenditure and public investment, had often been taken for economic or social reasons other than achieving a high and stable level of employment – for example in order to cope with a balance of payments crisis and a run on sterling. Nevertheless, despite these criticisms, and despite the fact that subsequent studies (Bristow, 1968 and Artis, 1972) suggested that intervention had not been significantly destabilizing, the suspicion grew that government intervention had done more harm than good; a suspicion particularly welcome, of course, to those temperamentally or ideologically opposed to government intervention in the economy.

Just where the truth lies is exceedingly difficult to say. It might, for example, seem a simple matter to decide whether a forecast was right or wrong; but it is not. One problem is that data relating to the past, on the basis of which forecasters make their projections, are often revised, sometimes substantially.[1] What is it that constitutes accuracy in a short-term forecast – correctly predicting the level of a particular variable eighteen months ahead, or correctly predicting its rate of growth between now and then? When the value of the variable at the base date is revised, it is impossible for both predictions to be correct. Another problem is that forecasts are necessarily made on the basis of 'present policies'. If the picture presented by the forecasts is unacceptable, the policies will be changed and – unless policies are totally ineffective – so will what actually happens. But unless one knows the exact effect of the policy changes – and this is one of the factors most in doubt – one will not know how far the actual outcome reflects the accuracy or inaccuracy of the forecast and how far it reflects the effectiveness or ineffectiveness of the policy change.

Nevertheless, a series of attempts has been made to evaluate the accuracy of the forecasts. One of the first of these (Kennedy, 1969) concluded that forecasts of GDP between 1959 and 1967 had been relatively accurate, but that this was largely a matter of luck, considerable errors in some of the components happening to offset each other.[2] Various assessments of the balance of payments forecasts

[1] The often startling extent of these revisions over the period 1953–70 is documented by Balacs, 1972.

[2] More formally, Kennedy found that the difference between the forecast and the most recent actual change in GDP was in the same direction as the difference between the two actual values for eight out of nine forecasts. No formal forecasts were published by the Treasury until 1968, and Kennedy based his assessment on NIESR forecasts.

were also rather discouraging: inspection of the errors in the forecasts in crucial years like 1960, 1967 and 1968 caused a number of observers to wonder whether balance of payments forecasting, either short or medium term, was really a possible or worthwhile exercise; and Major and Surrey (1970), studying the NIESR February forecasts, found an average error of £250 million over the period 1963–69 – approximately equal to the error of a 'naive' forecast which simply extrapolated the past into the future. The most elaborate and technically sophisticated assessment of forecasts so far attempted (Ash and Smyth, 1974) examined the forecasts made by five different organizations, though focusing mainly on those of the Treasury and NIESR.[1] Like Kennedy, the authors found that errors in different variables were in large part offset in aggregation. They also found that over the period 1951–71 the Treasury's forecasts were more accurate than any of four different 'naive' models for every variable except investment in stocks; and that for the period 1963–71 the NIESR forecasts tended to be better than the Treasury's. Even so, the errors in the forecasts of particular variables were considerable, sometimes surprisingly so: one of the variables the Treasury was worst at forecasting, for example, was public authorities' current expenditure, which it is supposed to control; and both organizations were bad at forecasting gross fixed investment, half of which is supposed to be controlled by the government and the other half of which is covered by exhaustive surveys of investment intentions. More generally, both organizations, but particularly the Treasury, had a disappointing record in predicting turning points, which is really what forecasting is all about: between 1951 and 1971 33 per cent of the turning points predicted by the Treasury were not realized, and 28 per cent of the actual turning points which occurred were not predicted.

To the catalogue of inaccuracy revealed by these investigations, one can reply that poor forecasts are better than no forecasts, and that they can be, and should be, further improved. There is still plenty of scope for raising the quality and extending the range of the data above past developments on which forecasters have to work; for doing more research on the key functional relationships in the economy; and for making greater allowances for the systematic biases shown by existing forecasting techniques. In a way it is en-

[1] The other forecasts were those made by OECD, the London Business School and the *Sunday Telegraph*. For the years from 1951 to 1968 Ash and Smyth calculated Treasury forecasts by applying their own and others' quantification to information contained in the annual *Economic Survey* and the Budget speech.

couraging, rather than the opposite, that – as all the assessments of forecasts have demonstrated – many of the forecasting errors of the past two decades should have been due to a systematic underestimate of imports: this is a problem that can be taken care of (in the forecasting sense; the real world implications are more disturbing). Similarly, there is no reason why the forecasting of intentions should not be improved: the problem here is largely one of timely reporting of decisions already made. More generally, a point brought out by Ash and Smyth is that the Dutch forecast their economy considerably better than the British do. The Netherlands is, of course, a smaller economy than the British, but it is also considerably more open, with a foreign trade sector accounting for some 45 per cent of the GDP. There seems no good reason why British forecasting should not approach more closely in accuracy that of the Dutch, by paying more attention to the dynamic structure of models and making more extensive but at the same time more selective use of econometric techniques.[1] And in any case – those who are in favour of fine-tuning would argue – even in the present state of the art it is better to forecast and then act on the forecasts, even though this process can sometimes go wrong, than not to forecast at all. On this view the instability in the economy over the past twenty years 'has been a predominantly planned phenomenon and technical errors due to poor forecasts have played a relatively minor role'.[2] In other words, despite the errors in forecasting particular components of demand, stop-go was not an accident, but the result of periodic lurches in government policy from one priority to another, and the experience of the last twenty years provides no case for abandoning the practice of forecasting and fine-tuning.

[1] A more elaborate economic model does not, contrary to what many people imagine, guarantee better forecasts, since the more explanatory variables one introduces, the more variables one needs to predict (Hey, 1975). (As with an aeroplane, the more moving parts it contains, the more things can go wrong.) There is also the problem that the more elaborate the model, the less anyone understands it, and the more likely is it that the laymen who always make the ultimate decisions will revert to back-of-envelope calculations or hunch. It is said, for example, that the forecast which emerged from the Treasury computer in the early spring of 1970 looked 'too low' to the top brass, because the savings ratio involved looked 'much too high', which implied that the rise in consumption was being underestimated. In consequence the forecast rise in the GDP between 1970 and 1971 was raised to 3.3 per cent, and Roy Jenkins brought in a neutral Budget. The actual rise was only 1.4 per cent – hence the spot in which Mr Barber found himself in 1971.

[2] Kennedy, 1973, p. 83. According to Kennedy's estimates, the only two occasions between 1953 and 1972 when the forecasts had gone badly wrong were 1959, when the strength of the boom was underestimated, and 1961–62, when the strength of the recession was underestimated.

The alternative line is that forecasts are so inaccurate, time-lags between action and response in the economy so long and so variable, and our understanding of the effects of particular actions so imprecise that fine-tuning is a hopeless exercise, likely to do more harm than good. This line is adopted particularly, though not exclusively, by the monetarists. According to the monetarists, changes in the money supply have a predominant influence in determining changes in the national income (and not, as some people would argue, the other way round).[1] But although this is true 'over any considerable period of years', one cannot predict the relationship at all accurately 'month to month, quarter to quarter, or even year to year'.[2] It follows that any attempt to use monetary policy (or, for that matter, fiscal or any other policy) as a short-term precision instrument is as likely to destabilize the economy as to stabilize it. The moral is that the government should abandon any attempt to fine-tune, and simply increase the money supply at a steady rate from quarter to quarter and year to year, and balance its own budget.

Like all marvellously simple remedies, this one has its attractions, but also its drawbacks. One is its implausibility in economic terms. It rests – as did the classical theory of the nineteenth century – on the assumption that the economy, if left to itself, and not thrown off course by mismanagement of the money supply, is self-balancing at full employment level. But the history of the last 150 years and the interpretation put on this by Keynes's *General Theory,* suggest that this is not so, and that a hands-off approach by government will result in considerable cyclical instability and, quite possibly, prolonged periods of stagnation and high unemployment. Even if a blind eye is turned to the waste of human and material resources represented by heavy unemployment, there is a second drawback to the monetarist remedy: no government which allows heavy unemployment to develop and persist is likely to retain office beyond the next election. The importance of this political constraint is amply attested by the actions of Mr Barber in 1971 and 1972. Although Conservative philosophy had flirted with monetarism in the late 1960s, the doctrine was now completely rejected in the face of rising unemployment. In the same way the Nixon administration in the United States, which had taken office at the beginning of 1969 on a staunchly monetarist and budget-balancing platform, turned its back on Friedmanite ideas in the face of mounting unemployment in

[1] Monetarism, mainly in the context of inflation, is discussed more fully on pp. 159–64.

[2] Friedman, 1959, p. 144.

1970–71, Nixon himself actually going to the lengths of publicly declaring that 'I am now a Keynesian'. The leader of the more conservative party in the most conservative of Western democracies had opted for Keynes and not for Friedman.

FLOATING

Something in Mr Barber's 1972 Budget speech which had attracted widespread attention was his statement that 'it is neither necessary nor desirable to distort domestic economies to an unacceptable extent in order to maintain unrealistic exchange rates'. This was generally taken to mean that if a conflict developed between the existing exchange rate and a faster rate of growth, it would be the exchange rate that would be sacrificed. This decision was partly a reflection of lessons taught by the past: the Conservatives were not going to repeat Labour's critical mistake. But it also reflected changes in the international monetary field. Since the mid-1960s, the system of fixed exchange rates established at Bretton Woods in 1944 had been showing increasing signs of strain. With different trends in money incomes and productivity in different countries, internal price levels diverged; and as price levels diverged, so some currencies became overvalued and some became undervalued. But countries were reluctant, mainly for domestic political reasons, to devalue or revalue as the Bretton Woods rules required. So exchange rate adjustments were delayed until they were disruptively large; and speculators were on a one-way option. In consequence, and particularly after the sadly belated sterling devaluation of November 1967, there had been increasing interest in the idea of smaller and more frequent changes in exchange rates (such as the 'crawling peg' system), and in floating. Although the Canadian dollar had floated throughout the 1950s, this was regarded as an isolated eccentricity, particularly in view of its relatively small fluctuations in relation to the U.S. dollar, and it was not until 1969, when the deutschmark was floated for a short time that the first crack in the Bretton Woods structure began to appear. In May 1971, when the deutschmark was floated again, together with the Dutch guilder, the crack widened.

Closely tied up with the question of exchange rate adjustments, and how best to achieve them, was the problem of the dollar. For many years after the end of the War the dollar had been the world's predominant currency, and the value of most other currencies was expressed in terms of it; thus the British devaluations of 1949 and 1967 took the form of a change in the number of dollars to the pound. However, sluggish growth in the U.S. and rapid growth in Europe and Japan meant that during the 1960s the dollar became increasingly overvalued – particularly after November 1967. If the newly-strong currencies – notably the German deutschmark and the Japanese yen – had been revalued upwards enough in relation to the dollar, all might have been well; but they were not. The only way the Americans could achieve a *de facto* devaluation of the dollar in relation to other currencies was by increasing the price of gold and hoping that other currencies would stay pegged to gold rather than to the dollar. For many years such a devaluation of the dollar in terms of gold was deemed to be ruled out by its unpopularity with the voters; but in August 1971, after a considerable period of sharply deteriorating trade figures, President Nixon took the plunge and announced that the U.S. Treasury would cease to buy or sell gold. The immediate result of severing the link between the dollar and gold was that the dollar floated in relation to other currencies; other currencies, too, floated in relation to each other. Before very long significant adjustments had taken place, with the dollar being devalued in relation to the other major currencies by amounts which varied between 2 and 10 per cent.

However, there was considerable nervousness about a system of generally floating rates; the spirit of Bretton Woods was not easily exorcised. In December 1971, at a meeting of the Group of Ten in the Smithsonian Institute in Washington, a new set of fixed exchange rates, validating the new parities which had emerged from the experience of floating, and including a rise in the official price of gold from $35 to $38, was agreed upon. These new exchange rates, though they could vary within wider margins than before, were very much an updated version of Bretton Woods. Nevertheless, it was an open question how long a fixed exchange rate regime could now survive. In an era of increasing inflation, price levels in different countries were more than ever likely to diverge, and exchange rates to get out of line; a system of fixed exchange rates which would only be changed at infrequent intervals looked increasingly unrealistic. This was particularly true now that floating rates had been tried, albeit for a limited period, and found to work reasonably well. Provided floating was accompanied by a fair amount of judicious intervention, to prevent wild fluctuations of the kind that private speculation could lead to, it looked like a sensible way of enabling currencies to move in relation to each other as economic circumstances required.[1]

It was against this international background, of official support for a fixed exchange rate system but increasing scepticism about its viability, that the Treasury, on 23 June 1972, announced the floating of the pound. Although the float was described as temporary, the pound has in fact floated ever since.[2] The immediate cause of the decision to float was a massive outflow of short-term capital, in part a response to the troubles in the docks sparked off by the Industrial Relations Act, and to Britain's relatively high inflation rate. But although Mr Barber – taking a leaf from the book Mr Wilson had brandished so often in the 1960s – claimed that there was no objective justification for these short-term capital flows, others saw it differently. Figures published early in June showed a very sharp deterioration in the balance of payments; and there was growing realization that Britain's projected entry into the EEC would cause her balance of payments to worsen even further – a point underlined on 19 June by Denis Healey, Labour's Shadow Chancellor.[3]

Thus the 1972 downward float, so far from being the key to export-led growth that it might have been a year earlier, was forced by factors not very different from those which forced the 1967 devaluation. But there were two marked differences. The 1967 devaluation had been accompanied and followed by a series of stringent measures to cut back public expenditure and private consumption in order to make room for higher exports and more import substitution. The 1972 float was not accompanied by such measures, Mr Barber arguing – quite wrongly – that there was plenty of spare capacity in the economy and that rising personal and public expenditure would not inhibit higher exports. Secondly, whereas the 1967

[1] There were those, mainly monetarists, who took the view that exchange rates should be allowed to float freely, without any official intervention, on the grounds that private speculation would iron out fluctuations, and official intervention would be destabilizing. This view neglected the fact that most financial markets have very short time-horizons, and although they may in theory lead to the correct exchange rate in the long run, in the short run they can accentuate fluctuations, with disruptive effects on exports and import prices. (For a discussion of this point in the context of the early 1970s, see Hirsch and Higham, 1974.)

[2] To be precise – for 'floating' could hardly be a more inapposite word – it has *sunk* ever since. By the middle of 1976 it had sunk by about 40 per cent in relation to the weighted average of the currencies of Britain's trading partners at the time of the Smithsonian agreement.

[3] In a speech that could be viewed as anything from realism to sabotage, Healey said that he did not see devaluation being delayed beyond July or August. (House of Commons debate, 19 June 1972.)

change of parity had been to a new fixed rate which everyone knew had to be held, the 1972 change was much more insidious, for there was no particular exchange rate at which the nation had to stand and fight. If inflation proceeded faster in Britain than in other countries, there was no need to worry about the balance of payments going into deficit – so it was said – for the exchange rate would fall a bit further, exports would stay competitive, and all would be well. But all would not necessarily be well, for a falling exchange rate meant rising import prices, feeding through the system and speeding up inflation. As inflation speeded up, the exchange rate would fall further, import prices would rise further, and a vicious circle would be established. By removing the discipline imposed on the rate of inflation by the need to maintain a fixed exchange rate, floating could start the nation off on a very slippery slope.

This is not to say that floating exchange rates are a bad idea; on the contrary, in a world in which the rate of inflation in different countries is very different, they are a sensible mechanism for ensuring that particular countries do not run increasing balance of payments surpluses or deficits. But floating is a bit like alcohol: while initially it may be a stimulus, it can easily become a refuge from reality. Under a regime of fixed exchange rates, an above-average inflation rate soon results in a balance of payments deficit which concentrates the mind wonderfully. With floating rates, it is easier to postpone the day of reckoning, as rapid inflation is accommodated, apparently painlessly, by a falling exchange rate. But in the end – as events in 1976 were to demonstrate – a falling exchange rate would bring a cut in living standards which was all the fiercer for having been so long delayed.

EEC: THIRD TIME LUCKY?

The objective to which the Heath Government attached most importance during its first two years of office was not cutting taxation and public expenditure, leaving lame ducks to their fate, or even reforming industrial relations; it was getting Britain into the EEC. The resignation of President de Gaulle in April 1969 had weakened, though by no means eliminated, French resistance to British entry, and before long the Labour Government had started manoeuvring carefully towards new negotiations. By June 1970, when the Conservatives took office, these new negotiations were just about to start. Mr Heath – in contrast to the turnabout in policy on many other fronts – took over where Mr Wilson had left off. The main negotiations were effectively completed a year later, after a successful summit meeting in May 1972 between Heath and the new French President, M. Pompidou. A six-day debate (the longest since the war) took place on the issue in the House of Commons in October. In the ensuing vote thirty-nine Conservative MPs voted against the Government on a free vote; but sixty-nine Labour MPs defied a three-line whip to vote for Mr Heath's motion. The result was a Government majority of 112. Although there were to be some nasty moments during the passage through Parliament of the European Communities Bill which ratified the Treaty of Accession (at one point the Government's majority fell to eight), the issue, as far as the Conservatives were concerned, was satisfactorily settled: the U.K. was to enter the EEC on 1 January 1973.

But as far as Labour was concerned, the issue was very far from being settled. Within a year of the 1970 election, the Party's basically pro-Common Market stance, into which it had been led by Harold Wilson and George Brown in 1966, had been reversed. A special conference of the Labour Party held in July 1971, taking its tone from a television broadcast by Wilson a week before, expressed hostility to joining the EEC on the terms negotiated by the Government. Adverse votes were recorded later in July by the Labour Party's National Executive Committee and by the TUC General Council; and the clincher came in October, when the Party's annual conference voted against entry on the proposed terms by a majority of five to one. Accordingly, on the last day of the six-day Commons debate, Wilson, arguing – with some justification – that Heath had no mandate from the British people to enter the EEC, said that the next Labour government would re-negotiate the terms of entry, the implication being – though Wilson worded his statement very carefully, being unwilling to incur the charge of threatening to break a Treaty – that if these re-negotiations were unsuccessful, Britain would pull out.

For those who favoured British entry into the EEC the uncertainty caused by this announcement was bad enough; but worse was to come. In March 1972, prompted perhaps by the surprising decision of President Pompidou to hold a referendum in France on whether Britain should be allowed to join, the Shadow Cabinet decided to support a referendum on the question of British entry. In protest against this decision, Roy Jenkins, Labour's leading pro-marketeer, resigned as Deputy Leader of the Party and Shadow

Chancellor of the Exchequer; two other members of the Shadow Cabinet, and a number of other Shadow Ministers, resigned as well. The Shadow Cabinet's decision was subsequently endorsed, albeit by a slender margin of only thirty-three, by the Parliamentary Labour Party. In October the Party's annual conference, observing that the Norwegians, in a referendum the previous month, had voted *against* entry into the EEC by a margin of 53.5 per cent to 46.5 per cent, endorsed a referendum by a two to one majority. The final result was that the Labour Party's 1974 election manifesto promised 'a fundamental renegotiation', the results of the negotiation being submitted to the British people for approval at either a referendum or another general election.

The strange behaviour of the Labour Party between June 1970, when the Labour Government was about to start new negotiations for entry into the EEC, and June 1975, when the electorate finally validated EEC membership by a referendum vote of two to one, is susceptible of two entirely different interpretations. According to the first, Harold Wilson's opportunism was a way of life, and Labour's *volte-face* on the EEC in the early 1970s was a particularly disgraceful example of the cynical jockeying for political position which has so bedevilled British economic policy since the mid-1960s. On this view, once Wilson had recovered from the shock of losing the 1970 general election,[1] he seized on the latent nationalist and internationalist opposition to the EEC which existed in the Labour Party (nationalist on the part of those who did not want to be messed about by a lot of foreigners, internationalist on the part of those who saw the EEC as a selfish, inward-looking rich man's club) to confirm his position as leader, and to cash in on the unpopularity of the EEC in the nation at large – an unpopularity occasioned by the fact that the one thing about entering the EEC that everyone had grasped was that it would mean higher food prices. Opportunism by its nature requiring a cloak of respectability, Wilson argued that while he was of course still in favour of entering the EEC on the *right* terms, the terms negotiated by the Conservative Government were the *wrong* terms, and it was his duty to draw this fact to the attention of the

[1] No one who saw Wilson in the months after 18 June 1970 doubted that the shock was considerable. Many were convinced that his days as Leader of the Party were numbered – a conviction strengthened by his action in shutting himself up for five months and writing – at enormous length – the story of the 1964–70 Labour Government. For a *future* Prime Minister to write in such a way was unprecedented, and observers drew their own – entirely erroneous – conclusions.

nation. Pro-marketeers regarded this as a particularly objectionable piece of hypocrisy, since both George Thomson, the Labour Government's chief Common Market negotiator, and Roy Jenkins claimed at the special conference in July 1971 that a Labour Cabinet would have accepted the terms negotiated by the Conservatives – a claim which seemed plausible to most objective opinion. Only when the electoral dividends from opposition to the EEC had played their part, and Wilson was safely back in Number 10 – the critics averred – did Wilson, recognizing the appalling implications for Britain's tottering economy of a decision to withdraw from the EEC, set himself, with as much disregard for principle as ever, to persuade the electorate that the marginal improvements in the terms secured by renegotiation made all the difference and that people should, after all, vote to stay in.

The alternative interpretation is much more charitable. According to this, Wilson realized that irreconcilable differences over the Common Market could split the Labour Party, rendering it impotent for a decade and perhaps destroying it altogether; that his duty not only to the ideals of the Labour movement but to the continuation of a stable two-party system was to prevent this from happening, outweighing in importance the question of whether Britain entered the EEC or not;[1] and that even if, on balance, one decided that membership would be beneficial to Britain, the only way of reconciling the large minority hostile to it was to hold a referendum which would settle the matter once and for all. On this view, Wilson's conduct of the whole operation was masterly, and triumphantly vindicated by the course of events.

The truth may lie somewhere between these two opposing interpretations – or contain elements of each. It seems highly likely that, after his unhappy experiences over *In Place of Strife,* Wilson decided to place himself at the head of the growing opposition to the Common Market in the Labour Party. Similarly, he took good care not to be outflanked on the left on the issue by potential rivals, of whom Tony Benn was beginning to look the most threatening; and he may have welcomed the chance to make life difficult for the ex-Gaitskellites in the Party – notably Roy Jenkins, the vociferous support for whom in the media Wilson found a source of perennial

[1] No attempt has been made here to rehearse the lengthy economic arguments for and against entry. The position is best summarized by two letters in *The Times* on 22 October 1971. One, signed by 142 economists, said that entry was a good idea; the other, signed by 154 economists, said that it was a bad idea.

irritation. And the apparent unpopularity of the EEC in the nation at large must have been an irresistible temptation. Nevertheless, underlying all these personal and tactical considerations, there may have been a strategy, according to which the nation would be allowed to decide and, following the advice tendered by a Labour government which had negotiated somewhat better terms, would decide to stay in. And if the strategy paid off, and history regarded Wilson rather than Heath as the man finally responsible for securing Britain's adhesion to the Common Market, that would be an agreeable bonus, and a fitting tribute to a superlative politician.

INFLATION AND THE EVANESCENT PHILLIPS CURVE

By about the end of 1971, the vigour with which the Conservatives had pursued many of their major policies had produced some tangible results: income tax had been cut and welfare charges increased; the House of Commons had voted for entry into the EEC on the terms the Government had negotiated; and the Industrial Relations Act was on the statute book. But there was one glaring omission in the record. If there was one single pledge on which the Conservatives had been elected in 1970 it was the pledge to get on top of inflation. Yet at the end of 1971 retail prices were 9 per cent higher than a year before – compared with a rise of 8 per cent during 1970 and only 5 per cent during 1969. What had gone wrong?

The Government's incomes policy, in so far as it had one, consisted of two strands. One was its determination to 'stand firm' on the pay claims in the public sector for which it had direct or indirect responsibility. Indeed the idea was to stand a little firmer as time went on, slightly reducing the size of each successive settlement: hence the policy's nickname of 'N minus 1'. The other strand was an aspect of the 'lame duck' policy: firms in the private sector, knowing that they would not be baled out by the Government in an increasingly competitive climate, particularly if their difficulties arose from granting excessive wage claims, would have a strong reason for standing firm too. By itself, this policy cannot have seemed very plausible: something like it had been tried before, notably by the Conservatives in 1956–57, without any marked success. But underlying the Government's confidence in the policy this time lay one of the most dazzling magic keys in the history of economics: the Phillips curve.

The idea that there is an inverse relationship between unemployment and the size of wage increases – that the higher the level of unemployment, the lower the size of wage increases – is intuitively plausible, and has a long history in economic theory. What Professor Phillips (1958) discovered was that for the past 100 years the relationship, as far as Britain was concerned, had been a remarkably precise and stable one: any particular unemployment rate was associated pretty invariably with a particular rate of wage increases. Phillips, later backed up by Professor Paish, predicted that at an unemployment rate of 2½ per cent, wages would increase at about the same annual rate as productivity – 3 per cent or so – and the price level would therefore be stable (Paish and Hennessy, 1964). Although a substantial body of professional economic opinion argued strongly that past relationships could not be used for prediction in this extremely naive way, the beautiful simplicity of the Phillips curve had an irresistible fascination for laymen, and indeed for many economists. As a result, much discussion in the early 1960s had focused on whether an unemployment rate of 2½ per cent (compared with a post-war average of about 1¾ per cent) was a sacrifice worth making in order to eliminate inflation; the Right, broadly speaking, saying yes and the Left saying no.

Although faith in the Phillips-Paish theorem might have been expected to be dented a little by the experience of the later 1960s, when unemployment had averaged almost 2½ per cent while inflation, so far from disappearing, had speeded up, this seems to have been explained away by special factors, such as the effects of devaluation, the distortions introduced by the operation of the incomes policy, and the fact that some of Labour's legislation had probably had the effect of raising the level of unemployment associated with a given pressure of demand.[1] There seems little doubt that during their first year in office the Conservatives were relying on an unemployment rate which was high by post-war standards, but apparently not so high as to be politically unacceptable, to play a major part in keeping down the size of wage increases. Hence Mr Barber's neutral 1971 Budget, designed to keep unemploy-

[1] Both the Redundancy Payments Act, which came into effect in 1965, and earnings-related unemployment benefits, which began in 1966, had the effect of giving an unemployed worker more time than before to decide on a new job. For a given pressure of demand in the economy (as measured, for example, by vacancy figures) this would lead to higher unemployment figures. As against this it was sometimes argued that greater awareness of hiring and firing costs might lead employers to be slower than before to make workers redundant: this would work in the opposite direction.

ment at around the 3 per cent level: it was only when it became clear that unemployment was rising rapidly towards 4 per cent that the Government lost its nerve. Yet, in spite of this high and rising level of unemployment the increase in wage rates, so far from falling to a figure of 3 per cent or less, continued throughout 1971 at an annual rate of about 12 per cent, and in 1972 – the year which saw the highest unemployment figure for thirty years – actually rose to 16 per cent. The Phillips curve, like the Cheshire cat, had vanished into thin air, leaving behind it not so much an enigmatic smile as a sickly grin.

The Phillips curve explanation of inflation was essentially a Keynesian one. Keynesian theory said that too low a level of demand in the economy led to unemployment, and too high a level to inflation, and that it was the job of demand management to get the level right, thus avoiding both unemployment and inflation. Where Paish and others went wrong in the 1960s was in supposing that avoiding excessive demand was a sufficient condition, as well as a necessary condition, of avoiding inflation. The breakdown of the Phillips curve came as no great surprise to that other group of Keynesians which had long argued that avoiding excess demand was not a sufficient condition of price stability, and that one could have 'cost-push' inflation at a time when by no stretch of the imagination could demand be described as excessive. In short, the experience of the late 1960s and early 1970s seemed to vindicate what might be called the neo-Keynesians, who believed in demand management *plus* an incomes policy, rather than the orthodox Keynesians who believed in demand management alone. But that was far from the end of the story, for by this time the Keynesian account of the causes and cure of inflation was beginning to be vigorously challenged by the monetarists.

THE MONETARIST SOLUTION

The best way to understand the monetarist position is to start with the *quantity equation.* This states that

$$MV = PQ,$$

where M is the quantity of money, V the average velocity at which it circulates, Q the number of physical transactions in the economy in a year, and P the average price at which these transactions take place. The quantity equation is an identity, not an explanatory equation; it is necessarily the case that the number of transactions in the economy, multiplied by their price, is equal to the supply of money, multiplied by the number of times it circulates. The quantity *theory* of money, on which monetarism is based, injects causality into this equation, asserting that MV determines PQ. Since in practice V is fairly stable, and Q increases relatively slowly over time, in line with the productive capacity of the economy, it follows that M determines P. In other words, changes in the money supply determine changes in the price level. Hence the basic monetarist argument that inflation is caused by an excessive increase in the money supply, and that to defeat inflation one need only control the money supply. It is not in dispute that – in the long run at least – there is quite a good correlation between the money supply and the price level. What is in dispute is the nature of the relationship. Do increases in the money supply cause prices to rise? Or are rising prices the cause of increases in the money supply?

Put at its simplest, the monetarist explanation of Britain's post-war inflation goes as follows. For prices to be stable, the money supply should only increase in line with the productive potential of the economy – in Britain's case about 3 per cent a year. (In the terminology of the quantity equation, if Q rises by 3 per cent a year and V is stable, then for P to be stable, M can only rise by 3 per cent a year.) Unfortunately whenever, during the downswing of the stop-go cycle, unemployment has reached 2½ or 3 per cent, the government has reacted by increasing the money supply by considerably more than 3 per cent in order to expand the economy and bring unemployment down again. It has done this both by directly encouraging or enabling the commercial banks to lend more to private customers by way of advances and overdrafts, and by itself running a Budget deficit and financing this by short-term borrowing from the banking system. In the short run, this rapid increase in the money supply has brought unemployment down, but in doing so has pushed it below its 'natural rate' (which is determined by the structure of the labour market – the extent to which there is mobility of labour between different occupations, regions and so on). With unemployment below its natural rate, inflationary strains have developed which have pulled up wages and prices.

This simple monetarist story suffers from two defects. First, in attributing inflation to excess demand in the labour and product markets, it gives a less plausible account of how this comes about than the Phillips-Paish school of Keynesians. The Keynesians attribute excess demand to the impact on the economy of the sum total of many different kinds of expenditure – investment, exports, consumers' expenditure, public expenditure – which are financed in a variety of ways, of which borrowing from the banking system is only one. If the sum of these expenditures exceeds the capacity of the economy, then there will be excess demand, and prices will rise. This seems more convincing than the monetarists' argument, that whether or not there is excess demand, and hence rising prices, will be determined by one single factor – whether or not the money supply has been rising too fast.

The second defect in the basic monetarist position – and in the Phillips-Paish version of Keynesianism – is that it is very difficult to reconcile with the observed fact that nowadays powerful unions can, and in 1971 and 1972 did, secure large wage increases when in no reasonable sense is there excess demand in the economy. In response to this criticism, the monetarists somewhat shifted their position in the early 1970s, by placing more emphasis on *expectations.* The rate of inflation, they now argued, is determined not only by the pressure of demand, but also by the rate at which inflation is *expected* to proceed; and the expected rate of inflation is determined by the past rate of inflation. This explains how the rate of inflation can be quite high at a time when the pressure of demand is low. But the same thing is wrong with this explanation of inflation as with the earlier monetarist explanation: it attempts to explain – and predict – a highly complex phenomenon in terms of only two explanatory variables (one of which – the expected rate of inflation – is in any case exceedingly difficult to measure). The explanation offered by the neo-Keynesians – those who believe in demand management plus an incomes policy – is more plausible: it fully recognizes that wage increases are likely to be influenced by the size of past wage and price increases, and expectations of future wage and price increases, but argues that there are many other factors involved as well – the size of profits, the militancy of the union rank-and-file, the policies of the government on the social services and the distribution of income, and quite arbitrary factors like a change in union leadership or a small shift in the political balance on a union executive.

The implausible nature of the monetarist explanation of inflation can be traced back to one simple fact: the monetarists have put the cart before the horse. In terms of the quantity equation, it is not changes in M that determine changes in P. It is changes in P that determine changes in M. What happens is that powerful unions, motivated by a variety of unpredictable factors, secure big wage increases, and these are soon passed on by employers in higher prices. This rise in the money value of output (PQ) puts a strain on liquidity in the economy (V rises), threatening to cause a sharp contraction in credit and a steep rise in interest rates, leading in due course to bankruptcies and unemployment. To prevent this from happening the Bank of England permits an increase in the money supply (M rises to accommodate the rise in PQ). In short, an excessive increase in the money supply is not the cause of inflation; it is the effect.

In response to this argument, and the econometric case that can be made out for it,[1] monetarists have recently shifted their ground somewhat further. The blame which is attached to the behaviour of the monetary authorities – the Treasury and the Bank of England – now takes a rather different form. The emphasis is less on their having actively over-expanded the money supply in order to get unemployment down; it is more on their having passively permitted the money supply to be over-expanded in order to prevent big wage increases from leading to unemployment. In the terminology of the quantity equation, the government has failed to stand firm on MV, letting increases in P be offset by a fall in Q; it has instead allowed M to rise as fast as was necessary to accommodate whatever rise was taking place in P without jeopardising Q. Thus the monetarists have to a considerable extent accepted the argument that – whatever the pressure of demand, or even the past rate of inflation – strong unions can negotiate themselves excessively big wage increases. Where the authorities have failed, they now claim, is in allowing these wage increases, and the price increases to which they usually lead, to be validated by excessively increasing the money supply. If the supply of money was kept under proper control – i.e. allowed to increase by only 3 per cent a year – these big wage increases would lead to an increase in unemployment, among either the workers concerned or other workers. Unions – the story goes – would soon learn that by insisting on big wage increases they were pricing themselves out of jobs, and would come to accept wage increases that were not inflationary.

However, even this more sophisticated version of the monetarist thesis suffers from two fatal drawbacks. One lies in its assumption that the monetary authorities can in fact control the money supply. The trouble is that, within quite broad limits, they cannot; or rather,

[1] See Bispham, 1975 for a useful critique of the monetarist position.

that what they can control is not what they need to control if monetarism is to work. Money is an elusive concept. In the most literal sense it consists of notes and coins. But a current bank account is a virtually perfect substitute for money in the form of cash, as is acknowledged every time a payment is made by cheque; so, up to a point, is a credit card. A deposit account, which can be liquidated at seven days' notice, is a near-perfect substitute; so, to a lesser degree, are building society deposits, shares, even houses. That this is not a fanciful point is demonstrated by the existence of the two separate definitions of the money supply – M_1 and M_3 – both of which are always quoted together. The reason for this is that monetarists cannot agree on which is the more relevant one to control. Yet, because of the difference in their coverage, it is possible – indeed likely – that if one of them were to rise at a rate that some monetarists regarded as acceptable, the other would be rising at a rate which other monetarists regarded as unacceptable.[1] Other evidence of the Protean nature of the money supply lies in the way that attempts by successive governments over the past twenty years to control bank credit, by imposing ceilings or demanding special deposits, have been undermined by the growth of the fringe banking sector. Until 1971 the fringe banks were not subject to the rules governing the clearing banks, and in effect frustrated governments' attempts to control the money supply by creating extra liquidity which was not included in the definition of the money supply that the governments were trying to control. And the changes introduced in 1971 altered the appearance of the problem rather than the substance.

The second drawback of the sophisticated monetarist argument is political rather than economic. The argument relies – via tight credit, high interest rates, and bankruptcies – on higher unemployment as the mechanism which will bring down wage increases to a non-inflationary level.[2] But the problem is that nobody knows how far unemployment would have to rise, or how long it would have to stay there, to bring about the desired result (though Milton Friedman, the founding father of modern monetarism, has been known to speculate

[1] This happened in 1972 and 1973; see p. 138.

[2] The same mechanism was implied in the earlier version of the monetarist case, which attributed inflation to the pressure of demand and the expected rate of inflation. Since the expected rate of inflation was determined by the past rate of inflation (which was indeed used as a proxy for it in the monetarists' econometric models), and nothing could be done about the past rate of inflation, it followed that inflation could only be eliminated by reducing the pressure of demand – i.e. increasing unemployment.

about a transitional period of up to ten years). But it seems highly likely that the intensity and duration of unemployment required is one which no democratically-elected government would be able to tolerate; certainly none has tried.[1]

The monetarist solution is a mirage. The money supply cannot be controlled with the precision claimed, and even if it could, the political repercussions of a policy which relied on indirectly discouraging inflationary wage increases by high and long-lasting unemployment would make such a policy untenable. An essential condition of a policy for defeating inflation is a policy which influences prices and wages at source: an incomes policy.

BACK TO A STATUTORY INCOMES POLICY

Despite the demise of the Phillips curve, the N minus 1 policy seemed, for a while, to be working. It had emerged from its first real test relatively unscathed. In October 1970, manual workers in the electricity supply industry – who probably have their knife closer to the nation's jugular vein than any other group of workers[2] – had put forward a 25–30 per cent wage claim, to which the Electricity Council had responded with an offer of 10 per cent. Early in December the men started an overtime ban and a work-to-rule, but this was called off a week later when a Court of Inquiry was set up under Lord Wilberforce. The Court evidently accepted the validity of the N minus 1 policy, as urged on it by the Treasury, and made an award, accepted by the union, which the Government reckoned to amount to 11 per cent, though Barbara Castle claimed it was 12½ per cent. Whatever the precise truth, it was apparent that the power workers had settled for little more than they had originally been offered, and less than half what they had asked for. The same story was repeated a month later, when postal workers, after a seven-week strike in support of their claim for an increase of 15–20 per cent, went back to work for a 9 per cent increase – only 1 per cent more than they had originally been offered. Moreover, a few months later,

[1] This thought has prompted the suggestion that a *deus ex machina* should be constructed in the form of a permanent, unsackable Currency Commission, independent of government, which would regulate the money supply come hell or high water (Jay, 1976). Unfortunately, or perhaps fortunately, democracy does not work like that either.

[2] It was the closing down of the power stations by the loyalists in Ulster in May 1974 that defeated the Government's attempts to introduce power-sharing: modern power stations are apparently too sophisticated to be operated by the army (Fisk, 1975). Nowadays an industrial society literally cannot exist for very long if its electricity is cut off.

in July 1971, the Government persuaded the CBI to ask its members to co-operate in a voluntary agreement to limit price increases over the next twelve months to 5 per cent. As many as 179 out of the country's 200 leading firms agreed to do so. But any rejoicing was premature. The Government had reckoned without the miners.

At its annual conference in July 1971 the National Union of Mineworkers made two decisions. One was to press for wage increases of 35–47 per cent. This was widely regarded as ridiculous. The other was to reduce from 66⅔ to 55 the percentage majority required in an industry-wide ballot to authorize a national strike. The significance of this was less widely appreciated. In the autumn the National Coal Board responded to the miners' demand by following the logic of the N minus 1 policy and offering an increase of 7½ per cent. Since for some years miners' earnings had been falling behind the earnings of other workers in less arduous and dangerous jobs, this was also regarded as rather ridiculous, though less so than the claim. The NUM, however, saw no humour in the situation, and started an overtime ban at the beginning of November. Since this did not appear to be producing results, the executive balloted the membership on whether it was willing to authorize strike action; 58.8 per cent – too few under the old rules, but more than enough under the new ones – said yes, and a full-scale national strike – the first of its kind since 1926 – began on 9 January 1972.[1]

A national miners' strike does not bring the country to a standstill as quickly as would a national power workers' strike, but the process is no less sure – particularly if, as on this occasion, it is backed up by aggressive picketing of power stations and coal depots. Within three weeks, voltage reductions began; within five weeks a State of Emergency had been declared, prolonged power cuts were a regular feature of life, most of industry was on a three-day week, and at any given moment 1½–2 million workers were unemployed. The trusty Lord Wilberforce was again summoned to the rescue and a week later, on 18 February, recommended increases which worked out at around 30 per cent. Sufficiently satisfied, at least for the moment, though perhaps not failing to observe that the moderates in the union leadership, who had not wanted a strike, had been proved wrong and the militants right, the miners went back to work.

[1] By an unfortunate coincidence the Top Salaries Review Body had announced a 38 per cent increase in pay for Ministers and MPs on 6 December, while the strike ballot was taking place. Since they had had no pay increase for seven years, this represented an *annual* rate of increase of only about 5 per cent; but not everyone took this point.

The Government, meanwhile, was left to lick its wounds. One of these was the implication for its policy of making nationalized industries pay their way. Although coal prices were put up by 7½ per cent (in technical breach of the CBI's voluntary agreement, to which the nationalized industries had also subscribed), this was not enough to cover the cost of the settlement, and the industry's deficit grew. Other nationalized industries – notably the railways and the Post Office – told the same sad story. Exchequer grants to the nationalized industries, so far from being eliminated, had to be increased. The Government was discovering that one of Selsdon Man's most cherished principles was easier to preach than to practise. This, however, was something of a side issue. The main problem was that the N minus 1 policy lay in ruins. However loudly the Government proclaimed that the miners were a 'wholly exceptional' case, and however wide the apparent public acceptance of this, the importance of traditional differentials in British collective bargaining made it highly unlikely that other unions would settle for 7 or 8 per cent now that the miners had got 30 per cent. Sterling was already looking groggy. The Conservatives were committed to bringing down the rate of inflation. What was to be done?

One answer was to do what the monetarists recommended: get a grip on the money supply and hold on to it through thick and thin – thick being continuously rising unemployment and thin being, in all probability, regular by-election losses. But the Cabinet had no stomach for the fight, the only full-blooded monetarist of national stature – Enoch Powell – having been uncharitably left on the back benches by Heath, and others later associated with monetarism – such as Sir Keith Joseph and, perhaps, Margaret Thatcher – having apparently become wise only safely after the event. The common sense element in the Cabinet recognized that monetarism offered no answer to a powerful union determined to extract a massive wage increase. There was only one answer: an incomes policy. It could not be a statutory incomes policy, because the 1970 manifesto had categorically rejected such a possibility. So in the following month, March 1972, talks on a voluntary incomes policy began.

But such a policy has to be supported by the unions. And the unions were in no mood to support any initiative of a government which had virtually refused to talk to them for the last year and a half; which had cut taxes on the rich and increased social charges on the poor; which had presided over a rise in unemployment to the highest level since the 1930s; and which had passed the detested

Industrial Relations Act, that even now was resulting in massive fines and the threat of jail sentences for time-honoured union activities. As the unions saw it, the Heath Government had started the policy of confrontation, and was now stuck with it. So adamant were they in their indignation that they apparently failed to appreciate, as spring turned into summer, and summer into autumn, and as the venue of the talks moved from Downing Street to Chequers, and from Chequers back to Downing Street, the full extent of the sinner's repentance. By the time the talks finally broke down, at the beginning of November, Mr Heath was no less desperate than a car salesman throwing in a free radio and six months' free petrol. He was offering, among other things, the promise of 5 per cent growth for at least two years, a rapid fall in unemployment, strict control over a wide range of prices, subsidies for nationalized industries, possible amendment of the Industrial Relations Act, a new body to help the lower-paid, and a norm for pay increases which was much more egalitarian than anything Labour had ever proposed: a £2 a week increase in wage rates for everybody.

It was not enough. The TUC had set the price of its agreement at repeal of the Industrial Relations Act, 6 per cent growth, a higher norm for wage increases, the abandonment of proposals for council house rent increases, the effective reversal of the Conservatives' tax handouts, a wealth tax, a surcharge on capital gains tax, and much else besides. And so came the most dramatic transformation of Mr Hyde into Dr Jekyll: on 6 November Mr Heath announced the introduction of a statutory prices and incomes policy, starting with a ninety-day freeze. Meanwhile the Labour Party, which in government six years before had introduced a statutory incomes policy, starting with a 180-day freeze, turned into Mr Hyde, denouncing the Government's Counter-Inflation (Temporary Provisions) Bill and accusing the Government of responsibility for the failure of talks on a voluntary policy. It received some support in the division lobbies from Enoch Powell. Turning a blind eye on Labour's apostasy, he told Mr Heath in the Commons on 6 November 1972 that it was 'fatal for any government or party or person to seek to govern in direct opposition to the principles on which they were entrusted with the right to govern', and went on to enquire whether he had 'taken leave of his senses'.

In spite of the indignation of Mr Powell and the Labour Party, the Counter-Inflation (Temporary Provisions) Bill was enacted on 30 November, and the official ninety-day freeze (extendible by up to sixty days) began. But what would happen when this period was up? Freezes are easy; it is thaws that cause the trouble. The Government came to exactly the same conclusion that the Labour Government had come to in the mid-1960s: there had to be a norm for pay and price increases, and there had to be an umpire to say whether or not particular proposals for pay or price increases were in accordance with the norm. The pay norm the Government announced in January 1973 was a weekly increase of £1 plus 4 per cent, with a maximum annual increase of £250. This would amount to an increase of 7–8 per cent for the average worker, but was redistributive in that lower-paid wage and salary earners would do better than the average, and better-paid ones would do worse.[1] On prices, the rule was basically that only unavoidable costs could be passed on in higher prices – and pay increases outside the norm were emphatically not unavoidable. As far as an umpire was concerned, what the Government needed – as its more candid members would admit – was the Prices and Incomes Board. This, however, was no longer available, having been formally killed off in March 1971. So a new body was set up with virtually identical functions though, to avoid everybody embarrassment, it actually took the form of two separate bodies, one called the Pay Board and the other called the Price Commission.[2] These two bodies would have the job of applying pay and price codes prepared by the Treasury, and approved by Parliament. On the basis of these proposals, Stage Two of the prices and incomes policy was to come into operation in April 1973, and last until the autumn.

Although the Conservatives were now treading in Labour's footsteps, Labour would have none of it. The trade unions did not like what was happening; neither, therefore, did the Labour Party. In January 1973, the TUC decided not to co-operate with the Government over Stage Two, and not to nominate members for the Pay Board or the Price Commission. In January, too, the Labour Opposi-

[1] The fact that the norm implied an average increase in wages of 7–8 per cent meant that (unlike the norms in Labour's incomes policies) the policy was merely aiming to slow down the rate of inflation, not to stop it. This may have been a psychological mistake, as is argued by Sewill in his perceptive account of the Conservative Government's economic policy (Harris and Sewill, 1975).

[2] Thus Mr Heath continued uncannily to follow the path mapped out by President Nixon. Nixon took office a devotee of reducing state intervention and letting market forces work; so did Heath. Nixon explicitly repudiated incomes policies; so did Heath. Two and a half years after taking office, Nixon introduced a ninety-day freeze on pay and prices; so did Heath. To cope with the resulting problems, Nixon set up a Pay Board and a Price Commission; so did Heath. Happily for Heath, the circumstances in which they both lost office in 1974 were very different.

tion voted against the Government on the rather flimsy grounds that the proposals did not adequately control the price of food (although it knew perfectly well that no government can control the price of many foodstuffs, which are determined on a day-to-day and week-to-week basis by fluctuations in supply and demand), and that it was regrettable that Parliament would have no opportunity to amend the Pay and Price Codes. In March, Labour divided the House on the grounds that 'the problems of inflation now require the adoption of Socialist policies democratically controlled by Parliament'. In May the TUC organized a fairly effective national one-day stoppage of work in protest against statutory controls on wages while food prices continued to rise. Of most significance, however, was a joint TUC-Labour Party document issued on 28 February. Not unjustifiably, this castigated the Conservatives for their policies during their first two years in office – the cuts in food subsidies, the increases in rents, fares and prescription charges, the redistribution of income to the wealthier sections of the community, and the confrontation entered into with the trade unions. Much less justifiably, and much more dangerously, it argued that rising wages had little to do with inflation, since over the previous decade British wages had risen less than the average for industrial countries, and that the fault lay mainly with profits, rents, taxes and import prices. Out of this highly questionable analysis came a series of prescriptions: rents, fares, and food prices must be controlled, by subsidies where necessary; direct taxes must be made more progressive; there must be a tax on wealth; charges for social services must be phased out as soon as possible, with prescription charges being the first to go; pensions must be increased; industrial democracy must be promoted; new investment must be undertaken by new public enterprise; defence expenditure – of course – must be cut; and much alse besides. Some of this was admirable; much of it was nonsense. Underlying it was the philosophy expressed by Norman Atkinson in December 1969 (see p. 106 above): control prices, but leave wages alone. Labour had given the nation notice of what it would do if re-elected; the seeds of the farcical first stage of the social contract of 1974–75 had been sown, in full view of those who had eyes to see.

1973 – ANNUS HORRIBILIS

Although Mr Heath's offer of 5 per cent growth and various other goodies in return for a voluntary incomes policy had been rejected by the unions, this rejection did not mean that the Government abandoned the 5 per cent growth target. On the contrary: it seemed likely that a statutory incomes policy would be workable only against the background of an expanding economy, with falling unemployment and rising living standards. And so throughout late 1972, and well into 1973, the commitment to 5 per cent growth remained the central feature of the Government's economic policy. Although Mr Barber did not take the advice of the NIESR, which as late as November 1972 was calling for a further stimulus to the economy, he made little move to restrain the growth of demand, and in March 1973 brought in a neutral Budget, affirming that the Government was expecting output to go on growing at an annual rate of 5 per cent until at least the first half of 1974, and that this was just what it wanted.

However by the beginning of 1973 some observers had started to take a different view.[1] No evidence indicated that there had been any acceleration in Britain's growth of productive potential; if anything, indeed, the sluggish growth of investment in plant and machinery during the late 1960s, and the actual decline since 1970, suggested that Britain's already slow underlying growth rate might have slowed still further. Thus perhaps as much as half the 5 per cent growth of which the Government kept on talking would have to come from taking up slack. But how much slack was there left? By early 1973 the reflationary measures on which Mr Barber had embarked in July 1971 had already had a major effect: total output was 5 or 6 per cent higher than a year before, and unemployment had fallen rapidly throughout 1972, after peaking in the first quarter. Although the unemployment rate was still relatively high in the first quarter of 1973, at 2.9 per cent, it was by no means certain, when allowance was made for the changed relationship between the unemployment rate and the pressure of demand (see footnote, p. 158), that a lot of slack still remained. These doubts were strengthened by the figures of unfilled vacancies, which by the first quarter of 1973 were already higher than in any year since 1966, and rising rapidly. It seemed possible, therefore, that the Government's policy would lead not to an effortless 5 per cent growth in domestic output but – as so often before – to increasing production bottlenecks and labour

[1] For one example of such a view, largely borne out by events, see Godley and Cripps, 1973. For a highly critical view of the steps the Government had taken to expand public expenditure – subscribed to by Conservative as well as Labour backbenchers – see the report of the House of Commons Expenditure Committee published in February 1973 (HC, 1973).

shortages, and increasing imports. The incomes policy would be jeopardized by the wage drift which characterizes any period of intensive demand for skilled labour.[1] And the balance of payments would deteriorate because – this being a consumption and not an export-led boom – rising imports would be nothing like matched by rising exports.

In the event these fears proved amply justified. Domestic output rose by only 2 per cent during 1973, unemployment fell sharply, unfilled vacancies rose to much higher levels than those in the mid-1960s, and imports rocketed. The best idea of what went wrong can probably be obtained by comparing the full year 1973 with the full year 1971: this covers the whole period of the Barber boom, while avoiding the effects of temporary fluctuations. At constant prices, consumers' expenditure rose by 11 per cent between 1971 and 1973, and public authorities' current expenditure by 8 per cent. But GDP rose by only 7 per cent. Part of the big rise in consumption was at the expense of investment, which rose by only 5 per cent, but most of it was reflected in a worsening in the balance of payments: the volume of imports rose by 27 per cent, whereas the volume of exports rose by only 14 per cent. In short, only about two-thirds of the rapid increase in British living standards over this two-year period was earned by producing more; the other third was financed by borrowing from abroad.

However, the large discrepancy that developed in 1972 and 1973 between the volume of Britain's exports and the volume of its imports was only the beginning; the gods were not going to leave it at that. In the third quarter of 1972 Britain's terms of trade started to deteriorate. A year later, by the third quarter of 1973, they had worsened by 14 per cent, a 13 per cent rise in her export prices being swamped by a 32 per cent rise in her import prices; and there was no sign of this deterioration coming to an end. One consequence of these adverse trends in both volume and price was a marked worsening in the balance of payments. In 1971 the current account had shown a surplus of over £1,000 million. By the third quarter of 1973 it was showing a deficit at an annual rate of something like £750 million. The other consequence was a severe upward pressure on domestic costs and prices, particularly food prices, that posed an

[1] Both the Treasury and the NIESR models at this time appear to have emphasized the *favourable* effects on prices and incomes policy of the fall in unit costs which attends a rapid increase in output. The *unfavourable* effects of a rapidly rising demand for labour seem to have been overlooked, or at any rate underestimated.

increasing threat to the viability of the £2 a week incomes policy.

This rise in import prices was largely due to factors over which Britain had no control. By something of a coincidence – though a common factor could have been the relaxation of the traditional balance of payments discipline on domestic expansion resulting from the generalized system of floating inaugurated by the U.S. measures of August 1971 – nearly all the main industrial countries experienced a boom during 1972 and 1973: the industrial production of the OECD countries rose by 7 per cent in 1972 and 9 per cent in 1973. This meant a rapid rise in the demand for primary commodities which, given relatively inelastic supply, led to some big price rises; and this effect was compounded, in the case of food, by bad harvests in 1972 in both North America and the Soviet Union. The result was that the price of the exports of primary producers rose, in dollar terms, by nearly 70 per cent between 1971 and 1973; and many commodity prices went on rising well into 1974.

However, the balance of payments and inflationary effects of these increases in commodity prices varied greatly from country to country, depending on what happened to their exchange rates in terms of the dollar. The deutschmark, for example, appreciated by 25 per cent in relation to the dollar between 1971 and 1973, with the result that Germany's import prices, in terms of her own currency, rose by far less than 70 per cent. Sterling, on the other hand, showed no great change in relation to the dollar over this period, and thus bore the full brunt of rising commodity prices. Indeed the point can be put less charitably: because inflation in Britain continued throughout 1972 and 1973 at a considerably faster rate than in most other countries, sterling fell[1] by 15 per cent between June 1972, when it was floated, and the third quarter of 1973. In other words, a large proportion of the rising import prices which Britain suffered during 1973 was a reflection of her inability to control inflation as well as other countries.

Although gloomy talk seems to have been the order of the day in top political and civil service circles since at least the beginning of the year,[2] it was not until May that the Chancellor announced rather unconvincingly that it was now time to look beyond the first half of 1974, and that he was accordingly cutting public expenditure in 1974–75 by £500 million; and not until July that the traditional

[1] In relation to a trade-weighted average of other currencies.

[2] At any rate if Cecil King is to be believed; and there seems no reason why he is not (King, 1975).

panic action was taken to raise Minimum Lending Rate, which went up from 7½ per cent to 11½ per cent within the space of a week. But none of this was going to have much effect on either inflation or the balance of payments. To anyone contemplating the short-term future on the morning of 6 October 1973, the outlook was for a continued rise in import prices, a continued worsening in the balance of payments, and a very real doubt over how much longer the statutory incomes policy – now almost a year old – could survive the inexorable rise in the price of food.

THE OIL CRISIS

On 6 October 1973 another Arab-Israeli war broke out. Like its two predecessors in 1956 and 1967, it lasted only a short time; in this case the fighting was stopped within three weeks. But, unlike its predecessors, it left in its wake a world economic crisis worse than anything that had been seen in peacetime since 1929, when the Wall Street Crash ushered in the Great Depression.

Since the beginning of the decade the Organization of Petroleum Exporting Countries (OPEC) had been flexing its muscles with steadily increasing confidence. It accounted for more than half of world oil production (most of the rest coming from the United States and the Soviet Union); and of this half, some 60 per cent was produced by Arab countries. Although the Tehran Agreement, signed in February 1971, purported to fix oil prices for the next five years, it was in fact breached within a year; and 1972 and the first half of 1973 saw increasing pressure from the producing countries for participation in the concessions held in their territories by the oil companies, and for further price increases to take account of western inflation. This pressure became even more acute after the middle of 1973, with Arab producers in particular determined to show their displeasure at American unwillingness to force Israel to give up the territories she had occupied since the Six Day War of 1967 by taking a much tougher line with the oil companies. Accordingly, OPEC decided at a meeting in Vienna in the middle of September to demand a substantial increase in the posted price – this being generally interpreted to mean an increase from $3 to about $4 or $4.20.

Just what connection existed between this decision and the attack launched on Israel by Egypt and Syria three weeks later is impossible to say. But within a fortnight of the outbreak of the war the Arab producers had agreed to start cutting back their output progressively by 5 per cent a month until the Israelis had withdrawn from all the occupied territories and the legal rights of the Palestinians had been restored. In addition, some countries imposed a total embargo on shipments to the United States. Early in November the cutback was stepped up: total production would be 25 per cent below the September figure. The effect was wonderfully to concentrate the minds of the consumer countries, particularly Western Europe and Japan. The EEC countries (Britain, of course, now among them) hastily called on Israel to withdraw from the territories it had occupied since 1967, and declared that any settlement must take account of the 'legitimate rights of the Palestinians'; and Japan soon followed suit, adding that it might have 'to reconsider its policy towards Israel'.

Although it was to be two years before Israel did start to withdraw from the occupied territories, the oil cutbacks were soon modified, and then abandoned altogether. Perhaps the Arabs felt that Israeli withdrawal was now only a matter of time. Perhaps noble political attitudes crumbled away in the face of economic self-interest. Perhaps the Arabs saw that any large and sustained stoppage of the flow of oil to the West might either prompt some desperate military intervention, or lead to a collapse of Western economies which would put the Arabs at the mercy of the Soviet Union. Whatever the reasons, the oil-producers, alerted to the full significance of their power – not least by the abject posture adopted by Europe and Japan – now switched from cutting off supplies to putting up prices. In the middle of October the posted price had been put up by 70 per cent, from \$3 a barrel to \$5; towards the end of December the price was more than doubled, to \$11.65. Waking up on New Year's Day 1974 Britain, like other oil-importing countries, contemplated the scarcely credible fact that oil prices had been almost quadrupled since the beginning of October.

A favourite question in examination papers in applied economics in the summer of 1974 was, 'Is the quadrupling of oil prices inflationary or deflationary?' The highest marks went to candidates who said 'Both'. It was inflationary in the sense that it gave a fierce upward thrust to import prices, and thus to the cost of living, in oil-importing countries. In the case of Britain it was reckoned that the oil price increase would raise the retail price index by over 2 per cent; this was before taking account of any increase in the duty on oil which the Government might impose in an attempt to further reduce the demand for it.[1] At the same time, however, the quadrupling of oil prices was massively deflationary. Consumers in oil-importing countries would now have to pay so much more to heat their houses and run their cars, not to mention to buy the goods which are made out of oil and the foodstuffs which are grown with the assistance of oil-based fertilizers, that they would have much less to spend on other things; there would be a big fall in effective demand. Indeed the effect would be exactly the same as if the government had introduced a savage new indirect tax, without offsetting this by cuts in direct taxes or increases in public expenditure. Of course, in the longer run the resources released in this way would be needed to pay for the higher level of oil prices, in the form of the extra goods that would eventually flow to the oil-producers. But in the short run the absorptive capacity of the oil-producers, particularly the majority of the Arab producers, was limited: there was no way in which they could raise their imports of capital and consumer goods to anything like the extent necessary to fill the hole which the oil price increase had dug in world demand. Or, to look at it the other way round, there was no way in which, in the short run, the oil-producers could spend all their enormously increased incomes; all they could do was to pile up reserves, mainly in the form of bank balances and holdings of dollar, sterling and other securities. By remaining idle, and not being spent on goods and services, these funds would lead to a fall in world output and employment of major dimensions. Looking at the world economy as a whole in the simplest Keynesian terms, there had been a shift in income from those with a high propensity to consume to those with a low propensity to consume; thus world saving was going to increase. And since those doing the extra saving were unable to invest these higher savings in real physical assets which needed to be produced (as opposed to paper assets which might or might not be a title to physical assets which already existed), the result must be a fall in the level of world income to a lower equilibrium.

The irony was that this kind of problem had been solved, on a national basis, by the Keynesian revolution. Had there been a world government, the recession which threatened could have been avoided by Keynesian policies. But with a multitude of sovereign nations pursuing their own self-interest – and a fatal lack of world leadership

[1] Because it was only the posted price of oil which had quadrupled, and not such other items as freight, insurance and refinery costs, it was reckoned that the landed cost of oil in Britain had increased about 2½ times (NIER, Feb. 1974, p. 8).

resulting from the U.S. Administration's absorption in the task of preventing the Watergate scandal from landing half its members in jail – it seemed no more likely that the right antidote to a world recession would be found than that the right antidote to a national recession would emerge from the pursuit of their own self-interest by a multitude of different firms and families. Instead of expanding demand, maintaining the volume of their non-oil imports, and letting their balance of payments remain for several years in heavy deficit, it seemed only too likely that countries – particularly the richer countries of North America, Western Europe and the Pacific – would allow effective demand to fall, in order to cut their imports and keep their payments in balance. This would make the world recession worse – just as individuals within a country, who cut their spending during a recession in an effort to balance their own books, make a national recession worse.

The implications of all this for Britain were appalling. Already struggling to reduce one of the highest inflation rates in the Western world and facing a large and growing balance of payments deficit, the short-term prospect was now of a sharp rise in import prices and a sudden increase, estimated at up to £2.5 billion a year, in the balance of payments deficit. The vulnerable balance of payments situation would make it more difficult for Britain than for the U.S. or West Germany to ride out the coming world recession: unless the country retreated into a siege economy, which would probably mean an even bigger fall in living standards, there was bound to be a big rise in unemployment. All this was in the short run. Things were not much more encouraging in the longer run; for the higher oil price would have to be paid in the form of more goods and services shipped to the oil-producers. For years ahead – until North Sea oil came to the rescue – this would pre-empt a large part of whatever rate of growth the economy was capable of achieving; the rise in living standards would be exceedingly slow. The grim years 1967–70, when the balance of payments had had to be painfully restored, but on a much smaller scale, might come to be looked back on with nostalgia.

Even this was not all. One did not have to be excessively melancholic in temperament to see the quadrupling of the oil price as the tip of an iceberg. Was there any reason to suppose that what had happened to oil could not happen to other minerals, each in their own way just as essential – to copper? to bauxite? to phosphates? If the price of oil could be quadrupled within three months, was there any reason to suppose it could not be, say, doubled again within three years? Was the huge rise in commodity prices in 1973 not just the result of a particularly vigorous upswing of the trade cycle, but a symptom of a permanent shift in the world balance of power? Were the terms of trade beginning to swing irreversibly away from the producers of manufactured goods and in favour of the producers of primary products?

Such questions had been posed from time to time over a period of a century or more, but had always been answered in a way that was satisfactory to the industrialized countries of the West: Britain's terms of trade, for example, were much more favourable in 1970 than they had been in 1900.[1] But by the winter of 1973–74 people were much more receptive to the idea that things might be different now, having been softened up over a period of several years by the arguments of those who described themselves as 'ecologists'. In Britain, the debate really got under way in January 1972, when a monthly periodical entitled *The Ecologist* devoted its whole issue to a document called 'A Blueprint for Survival'. Endorsed in broad terms by thirty-three eminent people, most of them scientists, the Blueprint argued that the rapid growth of world population and industrial production had already brought mankind within sight of disaster from an exhaustion of natural resources, or the effects of pollution, or both; and that drastic steps must be taken if life on the planet was not to cease to exist within the next seventy-five years or so. Underlying this flesh-creeping stuff was a series of models of future world developments worked out by Professor Dennis Meadows and others on a computer at the Massachusetts Institute of Technology.[2] These purported to demonstrate, among other things, that as a result of the continued exponential growth of world population and industrial production per head, non-renewable natural resources, such as minerals and fossil fuels, would before long be exhausted – some within the next fifteen or twenty years, most of the others within the next fifty. In fact, a thorough examination of Meadows's work conducted at Sussex University[3] demonstrated that as it stood it was simply unacceptable: if different but equally plausible assumptions had been fed into the computer, very different results would have been obtained; and Meadows had committed the cardinal methodological error of leaving out of his model the nega-

[1] LCES, 1972, table K.
[2] Meadows *et al.*, 1972.
[3] Cole *et al.*, 1973.

tive feedback loops representing such crucial factors as the way that the economic system responds to changes in relative prices, and the way that the goals and attitudes of individuals, and the policies of governments, change over time in response to the problems that confront them. Nevertheless, the Sussex team were more successful in showing that the Meadows scenario was wrong than that some more optimistic scenario was right. By the end of 1973 a careful follower of the debate might agree that the Meadows model was dead; but he would have argued that the issues raised by it were very much alive. And he might well have seen the effortless quadrupling of the oil price as an ominous pointer.

But the catalogue of woe is not yet quite complete. To anyone warming his hands at a bonfire on Guy Fawkes' night, 1973, contemplating the announcement earlier in the day that the Arabs were going to cut back oil supplies to the West by 25 per cent, conscious of the 70 per cent increase in the oil price that had already taken place, and suspecting that further price increases were to come, one thing that Britain could do without might have seemed to be a miners' overtime ban, followed after a decent interval by a full-scale and prolonged strike. This *coup de grâce,* however, the NUM was about to provide.

THE SECOND MINERS' STRIKE

On 8 October 1973 – two days after the outbreak of the Arab-Israeli war – Mr Heath unveiled the Government's proposals for Stage III of the incomes policy.[1] On the whole, these were intelligent and relevant proposals, and deserved to succeed. Over the next twelve months, the average income could rise either by £2.25 a week, or by 7 per cent, with a maximum increase of £350 a year. On top of this were various other improvements, which could bring the average increase up to about 8 per cent. But there were two other important provisions. One was for 'threshold' increases, an imaginative attempt to dissuade unions from bargaining to protect themselves against *future* price increases, by guaranteeing that beyond a certain threshold such price increases would be automatically compensated by

[1] HMG, 1973 (Oct.).

wage increases.[1] The other was a provision that special increases could be paid to those who worked 'unsocial hours'. This was a crucial element in the Government's pay strategy. The belief of the Yorkshire miners' leader Arthur Scargill that in revenge for 1972 Heath was determined 'to inflict a defeat on the miners' in 1973–74 was the opposite of the truth.[2] Heath had learned through bitter experience of the power of the miners, and he was well aware of the threat posed to his incomes policy by the decision of the NUM's annual conference at the beginning of July to demand increases ranging from 22 to 47 per cent. Stage III, Heath recognized, must provide that the miners be treated as a special case, so that they could get a substantially bigger increase than anybody else, restoring their relative wage position to where it had been immediately after the Wilberforce settlement of February 1972. To this end, Heath arranged a highly secret meeting in the middle of July between himself, Sir William Armstrong, now Head of the Civil Service and Heath's main adviser on counter-inflation policy, and Joe Gormley, President of the NUM.[3] Heath and Armstrong appear to have obtained from Gormley an assurance that if the Stage III limits included an unsocial hours provision which enabled the miners to get a bigger increase than anybody else, then the miners would settle within those limits. Armed with this secret assurance, and confident that with the miners taken care of, Stage III would be a success, Heath went ahead. But Stage III proved to be not a success, but a catastrophe.

One reason for this was that although price control was to be continued in a general way, no attempt was to be made to subsidize food prices. By the last quarter of 1973 food prices – very largely as a result of world price movements – were nearly 20 per cent higher

[1] For every 1 per cent increase in the retail price index beyond a level 7 per cent above that prevailing in October 1973, all employees would be entitled to an increase of 40p a week – 1 per cent on average – in their wage or salary. In effect, the Government was saying that it expected prices to rise by only 7 per cent between October 1973 and October 1974 (i.e. slightly less than average earnings), and that if prices did rise more than that, people would be compensated accordingly. It was unfortunate that the policy was discredited by the effects of the oil price increase, and of Whitehall's mistaken belief that in October 1973 other world commodity prices had already peaked (in sterling terms commodity prices – excluding oil – rose by another 30 per cent or so before levelling out during 1974). By October 1974 retail prices were actually 18 per cent higher than a year before, and eleven threshold payments had therefore been made.

[2] Interview in *The Observer*, 14 September 1975.

[3] The existence of this meeting was only revealed much later, in a carefully-researched reconstruction of the events of late 1973 and early 1974 published in *The Sunday Times* (Fay and Young, 1976).

than a year before, compared with a rise of only 13 per cent in average earnings. This provided a background of resentment to a policy seen by many in the unions as one of 'wage controls', and provided Labour – largely hostile to Britain's newly-achieved membership of the EEC – with an irresistible temptation to blame high food prices on the Community's Common Agricultural Policy. Whether the failure to control food prices would by itself have caused Stage III to break down, however, will never be known, for this mistake soon came to seem small compared with another mistake: it turned out that Mr Heath had not managed to buy off the miners, after all.

The stone that started the avalanche that swept Mr Heath out of office and out of the Tory leadership looked at the time like a mere tactical error. The National Coal Board, in its negotiations with the NUM on 10 October 1973, offered an average increase of 13 per cent; this figure included an amount of about 4½ per cent for unsocial hours, and was thus the maximum the NCB could offer under the Stage III rules: there was no further room for negotiation. But underlying this apparent tactical error lay the real problem: Heath had no idea what made the miners tick. If the moderates on the finely-balanced executive of the NUM were to swing the union behind a 13 per cent increase, it had to be fought for and seemingly wrested from the Government as a reluctant admission that the miners were a special case. This was Gormley's understanding of what had been agreed at the secret July meeting: the extra 4½ per cent for unsocial hours would be brought dramatically out from under the table at a late stage in negotiations, resolving a deadlock. Heath, however, had not seen it like that. To him, an extra payment to miners was justified and indeed inevitable, and so it was announced at the start, in the Green Paper published on 8 October. And that was to be that: no messing about. But the fact that Heath's first offer was also his final offer, however sensible and businesslike it may have seemed to him, made no sense in the context of the internal politics of the NUM. From the time that the NUM rejected the Coal Board offer on 10 October, the writing was on the wall. The confrontation between the Government and the miners which Heath had been so determined to avoid was now unavoidable.

On 12 November the miners started an overtime ban. Although the immediate effects of this were not great, they combined with a number of other factors to give the nation a feeling of mounting crisis. At the beginning of November the power engineers, in pursuit of a pay claim of their own, had started a ban on 'out of hours' working; this meant that a carefully planned system of selective power cuts of the kind successfully operated in 1972 was now impossible. On 12 December ASLEF started a work-to-rule; this meant that any rational policy for moving coal from where it was to where it was needed was now impossible as well. And all this was taking place against the background of the OPEC announcement at the beginning of November that Britain, like other Western countries, would be subjected to a 25 per cent cut in her oil supplies.

By the middle of December the Government was acutely worried by the short-term fuel crisis, particularly as it affected electricity. Perhaps it was also worried by some deeper aspects of the situation; certainly it should have been. Late 1973 and early 1974 saw the opening up of class divisions and the emergence of social antagonisms on a scale probably not witnessed since the General Strike half a century before. What many miners and railwaymen thought they were doing – encouraged by the extravagant language of some of their leaders[1] – was fighting to defend the living standards of the working class against the assault of a ruthless capitalist system, as represented by a ruthless right-wing government. What many other people – not necessarily Conservative voters – thought they were doing was stabbing the country in the back at a time when it was already under attack from an external enemy. What the miners saw as a courageous battle, many others saw as something close to treason. What the railwaymen saw as working-class solidarity, many others saw as a sinister conspiracy.[2]

On 13 December Heath announced that during the second half of the month industry and commerce would only receive five days' electricity, and would move on to a three-day week in the New Year. (To bring the full magnitude of the crisis home to the average Briton, he added that television transmissions would stop at 10.30 p.m.) Four days later Mr Barber introduced a mini-Budget: public expendi-

[1] Throughout the dispute neither Mick McGahey, the vice-president of the NUM and a prominent communist, nor Lawrence Daly, the union's General Secretary, made any secret of the fact that they were out to bring down the Government. Particularly notorious was a speech by McGahey at Aberdeen on 27 January 1974, in which he talked of the miners calling on the troops to help them if they were brought in to move coal.

[2] The conspiracy theory was given a timely boost by a meeting on 13 December between NUM and ASLEF leaders, after which Ray Buckton, the ASLEF General Secretary, obligingly said that they had discussed ways in which the two unions could help each other. It was hardly laid to rest two months later, when ASLEF called off its work-to-rule in response to a personal appeal from Harold Wilson not to harm Labour's chances in the general election by continuing to infuriate commuters in marginal seats.

ture, a football booted so vigorously up the field a couple of years before, was now booted vigorously down again: it was to be cut by £1,200 million in 1974–75. In addition, credit was to be tightened; hire purchase controls were to be reintroduced; development gains on the sale of land and buildings were to be taxed; and a 10 per cent surcharge was to be imposed on 1972–73 surtax bills. The tightening of credit was of some relevance, given the worsening in the terms of trade and the balance of payments: room must be made for higher exports.[1] The taxing of development gains was not; it came too late. A year earlier, when it had become clear that developers were making fortunes out of the property boom, an effective tax might have softened the atmosphere surrounding the early days of the new incomes policy; now it looked a sad case of locking the stable door after the horse had been stolen.

It was on the three-day week that the most acute controversy fastened. The Opposition argued that it was an unnecessary and exceedingly expensive stunt designed to put unfair pressure on the miners and prepare the country for an election on the issue of whether the country was run by the Government or the unions. The Conservative Government retorted that the situation was so critical that the electricity needed to pump sewage, heat old people's homes, run the hospitals and keep other essential services going could only be made available if industry and commerce were put on a three-day week. There was probably some truth on each side; there was also much party political manoeuvring. While these accusations and counter-accusations flew to and fro, increasingly feverish efforts were made by the Government to persuade the miners to settle within the Stage III limits. The miners refused to budge. So did the Government. The irresistible force had come up against the immovable object.

[1] The logic of Mr Barber's deflationary measures was in fact rather complicated, and not entirely coherent. He foresaw the main problem in 1974 as being a fall in *output*, caused by cuts in imported oil supplies (which now accounted for half of Britain's energy) and coal supplies, which would not be equally matched by a fall in *incomes*; there would thus be a tendency for excess demand to develop. This would be partly countered by rising unemployment and short-time working in the private sector, but there would be little such effect in the public sector, and for this reason cuts were concentrated in the public sector. So far, so good. But these cuts must avoid any reduction in employment in the public sector, which would add to the national unemployment problem; they must be devoted to cutting the public sector's direct and indirect demand for energy. Accordingly, most departments were required to reduce their capital expenditure by a fifth and their current expenditure *excluding staff costs* by a tenth. The idea that the public sector should cut down on everything but the number of employees was to look very odd in the light of arguments which developed during the next year or two (see pp. 224–6).

At this point – on 9 January 1974 – came a development of major importance. The TUC, perhaps more genuinely worried about the effects of the three-day week than either the Government or the Opposition, said that if the miners were allowed a settlement above the Stage III limits, other unions would not advance this to support their own wage claims – a pledge almost unanimously endorsed a week later by the leaders of unions affiliated to the TUC. The miners' claim, said the TUC General Secretary, Len Murray, was not only exceptional but unique. Let the miners be given an exceptional rise, said the TUC; let us get the country back to work; the rest of us, though in the nature of things we cannot guarantee it, will at any rate try to abide by the Stage III limits. It was a dazzling ray of sunshine. But it was rapidly extinguished. Mr Barber, in a political mistake of the first magnitude – one which seemed, at any rate to his critics, to epitomize his conduct of affairs at the Treasury – brushed the offer flippantly aside. The Government line continued to be that absolutely no settlements would be permitted outside the Stage III limits.

The Government was given one last chance. On 24 January the Pay Board published a report,[1] which had been under preparation since the middle of 1973, on the problem which is at the heart of any successful incomes policy – relativities and differentials. The report recommended that a Relativities Board be established, which would consider whether any groups of workers were unfairly paid, and should therefore be treated as a special case. Had the Government immediately designated the Pay Board as the Relativities Board, and referred the miners to it as a possible case for exceptional treatment under Stage III, the day might still have been saved. But Ministers thought of the Relativities Board as a piece of permanent machinery needing careful construction, not something to be established overnight to solve a particular dispute, and they let the opportunity pass.[2] Twelve days later, on 5 February, the NUM, backed by a four-to-one majority in a national ballot of the membership, announced that a full-scale strike would start in five days' time.

Meanwhile Heath had come under very heavy pressure from within his own party to hold an early general election. The leading hawks in the Cabinet, including Lord Carrington, the Secretary of State for

[1] Pay Board, 1974 (Jan.).

[2] William Whitelaw, the avuncular and conciliatory figure who – immediately after an exhausting spell in Northern Ireland – had recently taken over the Department of Employment, later admitted that he had 'fluffed it' (Fay and Young, 1976, part 3).

Defence, and James Prior, Lord President of the Council, took the view that the NUM, under the influence of its Communist vice-president Mick McGahey, was out not merely to bring down the Government but to smash the system – a view apparently increasingly shared by Sir William Armstrong, not normally thought of as suffering from the right-wing Tory proclivity for seeing reds under the beds. If the Conservatives went to the country on the issue of 'who runs the country, the government or the unions', it would get overwhelming support, claimed the hawks. But the election must be held quickly – on 31 January or 7 February, before the Government's position started eroding[1] and before the new electoral register, which would help Labour, came into operation on 15 February. But Heath demurred, apparently on the grounds that an election on the 'who runs the country' issue which returned a large Conservative majority would put class differences onto a war footing: as Fay and Young put it, although Heath 'grasped the political arguments for an election, he saw the national arguments against one'. If so, Heath's decision was statesmanlike, not to say quixotic. But the effect was ruined by his soon changing his mind and deciding that he would have an election after all, but on a different issue: the Government would ask the country for a new mandate to deal with the difficult economic problems that would result from the quadrupling of the oil price. This idea of getting a new mandate did not make much sense. If the Government was not going to beat the miners by winning a landslide victory in a 'who runs the country' election, then it would have to settle with them; and since it had a majority of sixteen and a year and a half before its natural term of office ended, there was no reason why a settlement with the miners required an election.

Heath's announcement on 7 February that there would be a general election on 28 February was his last major act as Prime Minister. His destruction at the hands of the miners had about it many of the elements of a Greek tragedy. Heath was an honourable man. He had taken office as an apostle of the free market, a firm opponent of state intervention in the fixing of wages and prices. But he had come to accept – though only after two long and divisive years – that the world was not as he had thought. Some of the

[1] Secret opinion polls commissioned by the Conservatives during January showed that as time went on the proportion of voters who thought there should be an early election was falling, and the proportion who thought that the Government should give the miners what they wanted was rising (Fay and Young, 1976, part 3).

policies he had attacked so vigorously when in opposition – notably an incomes policy backed by statutory powers – were, it transpired, necessary after all, at any rate if worse evils were to be avoided. Having drawn the conclusion, he acted on it. But he had in his eye too much of the fanatic gleam of the new convert. The laws of economics had not been repealed when the prices and incomes law had been enacted, and according to those laws, the quadrupling of the price of oil between October 1973 and January 1974 made coal, and the miners who dug it out of the ground, much more valuable than they had been. Rules about how much miners should be paid which had been laid down before October 1973 – as Stage III had been – simply must be wrong by January 1974. Yet Heath and his Conservative Government would not yield an inch in the face of a proposition on which, if on anything, the whole of Conservative economic philosophy is based: that price must be determined by supply and demand. There was about Heath – more than about Gaitskell, at whom the accusation had originally been levelled – something of the desiccated calculating machine. There was also something of the martinet. The desiccated calculating machine said that what the miners were being offered was fair, and it was right that they should accept it. The martinet said that the miners must obey the rules like anybody else. And so Heath refused to shift from the position he had taken all along: no settlement outside the Stage III limits. It was courageous, and Britain was in need of courage; but it was foolhardy, and Britain could do without foolhardiness. Heath saw himself, perhaps, as a Leonidas, holding the pass at Thermopylae at any cost against the hordes of anarchy and destruction. It might have been better if he had possessed some of the wiles of a Caesar.

THE INCONCLUSIVE ELECTION

The Conservative election campaign of February 1974 suffered from a certain ambivalence, Mr Heath claiming that the issue was not government versus unions, while most active Conservatives in the constituencies were convinced that it was. No such ambivalence blunted Labour's attack: here the personality of Mr Hyde was firmly in control. The miners must be given whatever was necessary to get them back to work, said Labour; whatever the cost of the settlement, it would be tiny compared to the losses being sustained by the nation in consequence of the three-day week. To avoid further provocation to the unions, the statutory incomes policy and the Pay Board would be abolished, and the Industrial Relations Act repealed. These measures, together with strict price controls, food and rent subsidies, and action to redistribute income and wealth, would form a Labour government's contribution to the 'social contract' which – so a somewhat sceptical electorate was assured – had been agreed between the Labour Party and the TUC. And the unions' contribution to the social contract? That was slightly less clear-cut, but was presumed to be voluntary pay restraint, to keep the rise in money incomes in line with the rise in production.

A number of things went wrong for the Conservatives during the campaign. The main one had a double element of poetic justice: it only happened because the Government, having failed to use the relativities report to refer the miners' claim to the Pay Board at the right time, had done so, quite irrationally, the day after Heath had announced an election; and it called to mind a comparable episode when the Labour Government's image had been dented by a statement of Lord Cromer's during the 1970 election campaign (see p. 116). At the Pay Board's hearings of the miners' claim under the new relativities procedure, Derek Robinson, deputy chairman of the Board and as instinctively a Labour supporter as Cromer was a Conservative one, produced statistics which suggested that the Government had got its figures of miners' earnings wrong. The implication was that the miners could have been offered considerably more under the Stage III rules, and that the whole three-day week episode had been unnecessary. Although a furious Heath denied this, a delighted Wilson made the most of it, and casual opinion was left with the impression that the Government had made a bit of a mess of things. This impression was reinforced, in a wider context, when Campbell Adamson, Director-General of the CBI, said a few days later that the Industrial Relations Act had done more harm than good and ought to be repealed.

In spite of these misfortunes, five opinion polls which published their final results on polling day gave the Conservatives a lead over Labour. The polls were, in a sense, right: in the actual voting the Conservatives had a lead of 300,000, or 1 per cent. But votes are not the same thing as seats, and Labour had more seats than the Conservatives, and was the largest single party in the House of Commons. Nevertheless, it was some way off having an overall majority.[1]

[1] There were now 635 seats, so 318 were needed for an overall majority. Labour had 301, the Conservatives (excluding the Speaker) 296. Had the Conservatives received another 576 votes in suitable places they, not Labour, would have formed the largest party, and history might have been different.

This deadlocked result was followed by several days of confusion, while the miners' strike and the three-day week dragged on. It was arguable that Heath's bid to secure a fresh mandate had demonstrably failed, and that it was his duty to advise the Queen to send for Wilson. Heath saw it differently. On most issues he could rely on the votes of the eleven United Ulster Unionists;[1] if he could persuade the fourteen Liberals to enter a coalition with the Conservatives, he would be able to carry on. To this end he seemed prepared to offer the Liberals – understandably frustrated at having received 6 million votes (20 per cent of the total) but only fourteen seats (2 per cent of the total) – what they most wanted: some form of proportional representation. But this plan foundered on a reef which Harold Wilson (who had rejected a similar idea ten years earlier) knew all about: half the Liberals dislike Labour more; the other half dislike the Tories more. Jeremy Thorpe, the Liberal leader, told Heath that he would be prepared to enter an all-party government of national unity, but not a coalition with the Conservatives. Heath's rather undignified bid had failed, and Harold Wilson, probably somewhat to his own surprise, found himself back in 10 Downing Street.

[1] In the past these MPs would, ironically, have counted as Conservative MPs and thus given Heath the biggest party in the Commons. But they had broken with the Government following the Sunningdale Agreement of December 1973, in which Heath had tried to get the Northern Ireland Protestants to agree to the formation of a Council of Ireland.

Chapter 6

DESPERATE REMEDIES

Since February 1974

The economic situation Harold Wilson inherited in 1974 was much worse than that of a decade before. So was the political situation. In Northern Ireland there was anarchy and terror, as Protestants and Catholics slaughtered each other. Within months the attempt – begun by the Conservatives and carried on by Labour – to get the Protestants to share power with the Catholics was to be destroyed by a Protestant general strike which brought the Province to a standstill. In Scotland nationalism had become a major factor, fuelled – surely *le mot juste* – by the prospect of future wealth from the North Sea in the form of what was always referred to north of the border as Scottish oil. The force of this nationalism was attested by the presence at Westminster of seven Scottish National Party MPs, dedicated to securing independence for Scotland. Similarly, there were two Plaid Cymru MPs, dedicated to securing the independence of Wales. Together with the eleven hard-line Ulster MPs, dedicated to maintaining the Protestant ascendancy in Northern Ireland, this must have seemed a formidable collection of fanatics to a government seventeen seats short of an overall majority; though at least it meant that a significant part of the potential opposition was disorganized, ineffective or quirkish – a big help to the Government in getting its measures through.

It was not only within the House of Commons as a whole that things had changed since Labour had left office in 1970. The composition of the Parliamentary Labour Party had changed as well. Between 1964 and 1970 the Tribune group of left-wing MPs had numbered about forty; now it numbered about eighty. Although the much-publicized activities of this group were soon to lead to the formation of a somewhat larger body of centre and right MPs which called itself the Manifesto group, this did not alter the fact – indeed it was in a way a defensive response to the fact – that since 1970 the Labour Party had moved fairly markedly to the left. Many constituency Labour parties had been taken over by people who believed that the Labour Government of 1964–70 had failed because it had not been nearly radical enough; and this was reflected in the choice of Parliamentary candidates, the resolutions forwarded to the Party's annual conference, the election of members of the Party's National Executive Committee and, in somewhat muted form, the Party's election manifesto. What these radicals wanted was a big extension of public ownership and what Tony Benn (who had contrived to put himself at the head of this new surge of socialist feeling) frequently termed 'a fundamental and irreversible shift in the balance of wealth and power in favour of working people and their families'. Although they accounted for less than a third of the PLP, which remained essentially a social democratic rather than socialist body, they commanded a majority on the NEC and at the Party's annual conference. The stage was clearly set for a series of confrontations between the Government and the Party, not least over the question of Britain's membership of the EEC. It seemed likely that Harold Wilson was going to need all of the new-found zest and bounce which, according to the press, he had lately been displaying.

THE ECONOMIC PROBLEM

As far as the miners' strike was concerned, Labour was as good as its word. Morally sustained by the Pay Board's report on the relative pay of miners, which Mr Whitelaw had commissioned on 8 February and which was conveniently available immediately after the election, recommending 'exceptional' payments to the miners, the Government agreed to pay increases ranging from 22 to 32 per cent, and costing in total almost two and a half times what Mr Heath's Stage III offer would have cost. Within a week of the Labour Government's taking office the miners were back at work, the nation was back on a five-day week, and Ministers began to take stock of the economic problems which confronted them.

These were formidable. The first problem was that Britain had become considerably poorer, since higher prices for oil and many other imported commodities meant that much more had to be exported in order to pay for the same quantity of imports.[1] Given

[1] Alternatively, less could now be imported in exchange for the same quantity of exports. Although an argument soon developed about whether the solution to Britain's problems lay in promoting exports or restricting imports (see pp. 231–2 below), the effect on the resources available for use in Britain would be the same.

Britain's already lagging investment rate, resources for higher exports could only rationally be diverted from private and public consumption. The result would be lower living standards. The second problem was how to ensure that these resources, if no longer consumed, *were* actually used to increase exports and close the balance of payments gap – no easy task in view of the recession into which the world was already plunging. Failure to divert resources to exports (or import-saving) would not only lead to the accumulation of huge external debts, but would lead to high levels of unemployment. The third problem was how to stop people trying to maintain or even increase their living standards by securing large money wage increases which would accelerate inflation. This problem was made even more acute by the existence of the threshold agreements, negotiated in quite different economic circumstances in which the rise in commodity prices had been much underestimated and the quadrupling of the oil price not foreseen at all. Threshold agreements were designed to ensure that increases in prices were automatically matched by increases in wages.[1] This was the opposite of what was now needed.

In either a free market economy, in which resources flow in directions dictated by the profit motive, or a command economy, in which they flow in directions dictated by the central government, this complex of problems would, after a fashion, have been fairly simply solved; though historical experience suggests that in each case the solution would have been attended by much inefficiency and injustice. But Britain in early 1974 had long since ceased to be a free market economy, without having become anything like a command economy. Any solution had to be planned and supervised by the Government; yet the lessons of the early 1970s demonstrated how limited was the Government's ability to get people, particularly if they happened to be organized in powerful trade unions, to behave according to the script.

From an economic point of view, by far the most rational policy in March 1974 would have been a tough incomes policy, backed by statutory controls. Whether – like Labour's policy from July to December 1966, or the Conservatives' policy from November 1972 to April 1973 – it was a freeze, or whether – like the periods which immediately succeeded these two freezes – it was merely a period of severe restraint, would not have mattered a great deal. A period of a

[1] Because marginal income tax rates are higher than average rates, a 1 per cent wage rise does not fully compensate for a 1 per cent price rise; but for most workers it compensates to a substantial degree.

year or two[1] in which the rise in money incomes was held well below the rise in prices would have reduced consumption, and freed resources for the balance of payments; it would have reduced imports, and thus helped the balance of payments directly; it would have brought down the rate of inflation – at least in the case of a freeze – to no more than a few per cent a year; it would have greatly increased Britain's competitiveness in world markets, and given British exporters both the ability and the incentive to boost overseas sales at a rapid rate. For a year or two life would have been hard; but by the beginning of 1976 Britain would have been in a strong position, with a low rate of inflation, a relatively low rate of unemployment, a secure balance of payments, and the prospect of a resumption of the rise in living standards at a rate of 2 or 3 per cent a year.

It was not to be. In opposition, in the early 1970s, Labour had succumbed to the same easy temptation as the Conservatives in the late 1960s: 'the Government's unpopular statutory incomes policy is a dreadful thing, and if you vote for us we promise to abolish it.' Just as the Conservatives in 1970 had swept away the vestiges of Labour's incomes policy – already much weakened by their relentless attacks upon it – so now the Labour Government swept away the Conservatives' Stage III – already fatally damaged by Labour's support for the miners. Mr Heath had despatched Mr Wilson's Prices and Incomes Board; now Mr Wilson abolished Mr Heath's Pay Board. Let wages be determined by free collective bargaining, Mr Heath had announced. Exactly so, Mr Wilson now declared. And so Labour was hoist by its own petard. A statutory incomes policy – indeed any interference with collective bargaining – was out. Even to mention it in Labour circles in 1974 was like using a four-letter word in a nineteenth-century drawing-room.

If a statutory incomes policy was out, what was in? There were basically two possibilities. The first was to adopt a thoroughgoing monetarist line, rigorously restricting the growth of the money supply, refusing to subsidize nationalized industries, and thus ensuring, among other things, that large wage increases in the mining industry or other nationalized industries were immediately passed on fully in higher prices, thus reducing demand for the product and for the labour which made it, reducing the real incomes of the rest of the community, and having a generally deflationary effect. But such a

[1] The length of time needed would have depended partly on whether the Government was willing to abrogate the threshold agreements, due to continue until October 1974.

policy – even if one believed the monetarists' assurance that it would defeat inflation in the end – would involve the deliberate creation of a very high level of unemployment, and was simply not an option open to a Labour government in the conditions of early 1974.

The other possible course of action – and the one which the Government in fact adopted – was to try to secure the objectives of a statutory incomes policy by entirely voluntary means. The essence of such a voluntary incomes policy was wage restraint by the unions. But if the unions were to agree to restrain the size of their wage claims, they must be given – so it was argued – all sorts of concessions in return. Any steep rise in unemployment must be avoided. Food prices must be subsidized, as must council house rents and the price of such essential items in working-class budgets as fuel and public transport. Wealth, and the transfer of wealth from one generation to another, must be severely taxed, as must high incomes, whether earned or unearned. Workers must be given more control over the decisions which affected their working lives. Existing legislation which the unions believed interfered with their freedom must be repealed. New legislation which the unions considered essential must be enacted. And so on. This was the 'social contract'. From the point of view of a political party with an avowedly socialist philosophy and an overwhelmingly working-class constituency, largely financed by the unions and dependent in Parliament on a hundred union-sponsored MPs, the social contract made a lot of sense. Taken as a whole, it constituted a large step forward on the road to socialism. It also made some sense to anyone who, contemplating Mr Wilson's defeat by the unions over *In Place of Strife,* and Mr Heath's defeats over the Industrial Relations Act and the miners' pay claim, had concluded that the unions were now so powerful that government could be effectively conducted only with their consent. Yet many felt that the social contract, quite apart from its implausibility as an anti-inflationary strategy, represented an unacceptable surrender to the unions, who were in effect being bribed by the Government not to wreck society.

The Government's first move to implement its side of the social contract came in Denis Healey's first Budget, introduced on 26 March, only three weeks after Labour had assumed office. From the unions' point of view, this was quite a large step in the right direction. Pensions were raised; food subsidies were to be increased in 1974–75 by £500 million, and rent subsidies by £70 million; and local authorities were to be encouraged to build more council houses.

On the other side of the ledger, income tax was to be raised, particularly on unearned incomes and on the highest earned incomes; corporation tax was to be increased, and paid sooner; and gift and wealth taxes were to be introduced.[1]

The redistributive nature of this budget was predictable. What was perhaps less predictable was its overall effect, which was very slightly deflationary: the Chancellor estimated that as a result of his measures, output would by the end of the year be running at about one-third of 1 per cent below what it would otherwise have been. The main instrument of this modest deflation was a series of substantial increases in most nationalized industries' prices, which would reduce the total subsidy bill for these industries in 1974–75 from a potential figure of £1,400 million to one of only £500 million. As a result, there would be a marked fall in the size of the public sector borrowing requirement (PSBR). This was estimated to have been £4.3 billion in 1973–74; Healey calculated that his Budget would bring it down to £2.7 billion in 1974–75. To bring about a sharp reduction in the budget deficit[2] at a time when Britain, and the world as a whole, was about to plunge into much the worst recession for nearly forty years (even though this was probably not fully foreseen) was, on the face of it, an odd thing for a Labour Chancellor to do. Ever since the early 1940s, when the lessons of Keynes' *General Theory* had been absorbed, it had been an axiom of British economic policy-making that to cure or prevent a slump, one increased public expenditure or reduced taxation, thus budgeting for an increased public sector deficit. Yet Healey, while still budgeting for a deficit, was budgeting for a distinctly smaller one than the year before. It seemed more like the action of a Conservative Chancellor of the 1930s than a Labour Chancellor of the 1970s. What was the reason for this apparent paradox? A good deal of the answer was to be

[1] The ball was also returned smartly across the net in the eternal game of ping-pong over tax concessions which do not amount to much in total, but make a lot of difference to people at the top of the income distribution. The aggregation for tax purposes of children's investment income with that of their parents, for example, which Labour had introduced in 1968, had been discontinued by the Conservatives in 1971; Labour now announced that it would be re-introduced. Similarly, tax relief on interest payments on private borrowing had been generally abolished by Labour in 1969, but re-introduced by the Conservatives in 1972. Now Labour abolished it again. As usual, it was lawyers and accountants who did best out of these changes.

[2] The budget deficit, or public sector financial deficit, is not quite the same thing as the public sector borrowing requirement, since the latter also includes funds which are onlent to other public agencies. For the purpose of the broad brush treatment adopted here, however, the differences are unimportant, and the terms are used interchangeably.

found in the influence being exerted at this time by the doctrines of the 'New Cambridge School'.

NEW CAMBRIDGE

The New Cambridge doctrine (so called because it originated in Cambridge, and gave a distinctly new twist to the theories developed in the same city by Keynes forty years earlier) started from one of the simplest Keynesian equations. In an economy in which there is a private sector, a government sector, and trade with the outside world, let it be assumed that the saving of the private sector is equal to its investment, i.e. that the private sector neither lends to, nor borrows from, the government sector or the rest of the world. In this situation the surplus or deficit in the government sector must, according to the rules of national income accounting, be exactly matched by a corresponding surplus or deficit on the balance of payments current account. In the same way, if the private sector regularly has an annual surplus of, say, £1,000 million of saving over investment, and lends this £1,000 million to the public sector, the public sector can run a deficit of £1,000 million a year, and the balance of payments will be in balance. If the government deficit is only £500 million, there will be a balance of payments current account surplus of £500 million; if, on the other hand, there is a public sector deficit of £2,000 million, there will be a balance of payments deficit of £1,000 million. And so on. The arithmetic is easy.

The New Cambridge doctrine did two things. First, it claimed that since the early 1950s the private sector in Britain had had a fairly stable surplus of about £1,000 million a year.[1] Secondly, it argued that the public sector (or Budget) deficit *determined* the balance of payments deficit. In other words, given the stable nature of the private sector's investment and saving behaviour, if there was a large Budget deficit – because government revenue was much lower than government expenditure – there simply had to be a large balance of payments deficit, which would be only £1,000 million smaller than the Budget deficit. Alternatively, if the country was to achieve a

[1] The technical term for private saving was 'net acquisition of financial assets' by the private sector; and after a while this was said to be not 'stable' but 'small and predictable', and not an absolute figure of £1,000 million a year, but a figure related to the money value of the GNP (Cripps, Godley and Fetherston, 1974). But none of this affects the basic argument.

balance of payments surplus of £1,000 million, then the government must balance its budget.

The implications of this doctrine were profound. As summarized by one of its leading exponents (Neild, 1974), they amounted to saying that the Budget should be used to determine the foreign balance and the exchange rate to determine the level of activity; and that the opposite usage of these two instruments had contributed to most of Britain's economic problems since the war. In other words, when faced by a balance of payments deficit the government should not devalue, since this would simply raise the level of output, employment and incomes, and lead to a rise in imports which would cancel out the increase in exports resulting from greater competitiveness in foreign markets, and leave the balance of payments unchanged. What it should do was concentrate on balancing its own budget. Similarly, when faced by unemployment resulting from too low a level of demand, it should not do the orthodox Keynesian thing and go for a budget deficit by reducing taxes or increasing public expenditure, since this would merely lead to a corresponding worsening in the balance of payments. It should instead devalue, raising domestic demand by way of higher exports and greater production of import substitutes.

Part of the attraction of the New Cambridge doctrine lay in its iconoclastic claim that people had been doing things exactly the wrong way round – a claim of the kind (made and substantiated in earlier ages by Copernicus, and by Keynes himself) which always appeals to the irreverent. But part of the attraction was that – like monetarism – it made the conduct of economic policy very much easier. Once employment and balance of payments targets are specified (and that is so easy that economists would be quite happy to leave it to politicians) and once the long-term growth of public expenditure is decided (an issue perhaps more difficult to leave to politicians), the size of the Budget deficit and the amount of tax revenue that will be required are both determined. There is no need to rely on all those fallible short-term forecasts. All the government has to do is to set taxation at the appropriate rates, and then leave things alone. As the New Cambridge exponents said in written evidence to the House of Commons Expenditure Committee in June 1974, 'demand, output and the balance of payments might have been more stable than they were had some simple rule been followed through thick and thin, such as that a tax yield should be sought such as to cover, as nearly as possible, some fixed proportion of public expenditure.'[1] The parallel with the monetarists' doctrine that all that a government needs to do is to keep the money supply expanding by 3 per cent a year, no more and no less, is too close to need labouring. It is the non-monetarists' version of the philosopher's stone.

Before long the New Cambridge doctrine came under heavy fire.[2] Although much of this criticism was technical and detailed, there were two main charges. The first concentrated on the New Cambridge reversal of the traditional targets and instruments – the argument that the balance of payments was determined by the budget balance and the level of domestic activity by the exchange rate, rather than the other way round. A change in the exchange rate, it was contended, manifestly does affect exports and imports, and although the New Cambridge devotees might be right in saying that some of these effects are offset by the consequences of exchange rate changes on employment and incomes, it is far from the case that all of them are. Devaluation, for example, while it will lead to some increase in employment and incomes and thus to a larger volume of imports of food and materials, will also lead to higher exports and lower imports of manufactured goods on competitive grounds, and the latter effect will easily outweigh the former. In other words, devaluation *does* improve the balance of payments, and the Old Cambridge doctrine which asserts this is a better guide to policy than the New Cambridge doctrine which denies it.[3] Similarly, increasing public expenditure or reducing taxation, and thus enlarging the Budget deficit, does have some effect in increasing output, employment and incomes; by no means all of this increased Budget deficit – perhaps only quite a small part of it – is reflected in an increased balance of payments deficit. Here again, it was contended, New Cambridge was a more uncertain guide than the traditional approach.

The second, and more fundamental criticism fastened on the stability of the relationships on which the New Cambridge doctrine placed so much weight, and on the nature and direction of the causality involved in these relationships. The apparent stability of the private sector's net saving over the previous decade or two was not a universal law – it had no satisfactory theoretical underpinning – but something of a fluke, and certainly too fragile a relationship on

[1] Cripps, Godley and Fetherston, 1974, para. 2.

[2] See particularly Kahn and Posner (1974), Worswick (1974) and Bispham (1975).

[3] This improvement in the balance of payments will, of course, be accompanied by a corresponding rise in the surplus – or fall in the deficit – of the private sector. Kahn and Posner, 1974 (i) provide a detailed account of the ways in which this might happen.

which to decide what the budget balance ought to be if a certain balance of payments outcome was desired. More critically still, it was contended, the relationship between the budget deficit and the balance of payments deficit was an *ex-post* one and not an *ex-ante* one.[1] In other words, at the end of the day these two variables had to stand in a certain relationship to each other, given whatever, at the end of the day, the relationship between private saving and investment was; but this did not mean that one could start off by deciding what the Budget surplus or deficit was going to be, and thus attain, indirectly, a certain balance of payments figure. The Budget surplus or deficit is not an operational variable that can be fixed in advance. It is the net result of the out-turn of a vast number of factors on both the revenue and the expenditure side of the balance sheet. The government must, of course, try to control the size of the Budget deficit, but if it is to do this it must forecast the factors on both the revenue and expenditure sides which will affect it, and then take appropriate action to bring the forecast result into line with the desired result. But in order to forecast both the revenue and the expenditure of the entire public sector, which in any modern economy accounts for a third to a half of the national income, there is no way it can avoid producing forecasts of all the other variables in the economy in exactly the same way as it does at the moment. So the New Cambridge claim to have discovered a method of regulating the economy without having to rely on short-term forecasts was fallacious.

These criticisms did not for long remain purely academic: the New Cambridge equation performed hopelessly badly in 1974. Despite Mr Healey's good intentions and best endeavours, both 1974 and 1975 showed enormous budget deficits, and although this was not the fault of the New Cambridge doctrine, it dramatically illustrated how far the budget deficit was from being an operational variable under the control of the government. The charge which could be levelled at the New Cambridge doctrine was the total failure of the balance of payments in each of these two years to behave in the way the equation predicted: in each case the current account deficit was very much smaller than it 'ought' to have been.[2] Underlying this

[1] As one critic put it, the New Cambridge argument was based on 'an identity masquerading as a strategic equation' (Balogh, 1974).

[2] According to Bispham (1975), in calendar 1974, given the size of the Budget deficit, the balance of payments deficit ought to have been £11 billion on the basis of the New Cambridge equation; in fact it was only £3¾ billion.

failure was a far bigger increase in private saving than was consistent with the New Cambridge doctrine. But whether – as the critics averred – the cornerstone of the New Cambridge edifice had collapsed, or whether – as the New Cambridge School claimed (CEPG, 1976, ch. 6) – it merely required a little repositioning, remained to be seen.

ANOTHER BUDGET, ANOTHER ELECTION

Part of the keenness Mr Healey displayed in his March budget to reduce the public sector borrowing requirement stemmed from a flirtation with the New Cambridge thesis that this was a necessary condition of reducing the potentially huge balance of payments deficit. Part of it, on the other hand (for intellectually this was a somewhat eclectic budget) seems to have stemmed from a qualified acceptance of the monetarist argument that a large budget deficit leads to a large increase in the money supply, which in turn leads to inflation. That Mr Healey's conversion to these two heresies was only partial, however, was demonstrated by his promise to introduce another budget in the autumn – a strong objection to this kind of fine-tuning being one of the things that monetarism and the New Cambridge doctrine had in common. Mr Healey did indeed introduce another budget in the autumn, but it turned out to be the next but one; the next one was in July.

There had been no particularly dramatic turn of events in the meantime; just an increasing concern about inflation. Despite the large expansion of food and rent subsidies announced in the March budget, and the extension and tightening up of price controls by Labour's new Department of Prices and Consumer Protection, prices continued to rise rapidly. In May the retail price index rose enough to trigger off no fewer than three threshold payments of 40p a week; in June it rose again, to a level 16½ per cent higher than a year before, triggering off another two threshold payments. Things seemed to be getting out of hand, particularly as the dismantling of the Conservatives' statutory incomes policy and the abolition of what Labour publicity described as the 'oppressive Tory Pay Board' had naturally encouraged unions – whatever lip service was paid to the social contract – to put in demands for wage increases of 30 per cent or more. The basic objective of the mini-budget introduced by Healey on 22 July was, as he put it, to 'attack inflation at its source', by which he meant – somewhat to the surprise of those who believed that now that world commodity prices had reached a peak and started to fall back, the main engine of inflation had become huge wage increases – action to reduce prices. The rate of VAT was reduced from 10 per cent to 8 per cent, and subsidies were made available to keep down the rise in the domestic rate on housing. The immediate effect of this would be to bring down the retail price index by about 1½ per cent. In addition – a concession to the free market philosophy – dividend controls were relaxed, supposedly in order to help raise funds in the capital market for new investment; and the Regional Employment Premium was doubled in order to restore the competitiveness of the assisted areas to something like what it had been when the scheme was first introduced. This latest instalment in Labour's counter-inflationary strategy did not look particularly convincing, especially since it was followed two days later by the announcement that workers in one of Britain's most overmanned industries – the railways – were to get a wage increase of 30 per cent. But, given that both massive unemployment and a statutory incomes policy were regarded by the Government as unthinkable, it was probably about the best that could be done. And although it was estimated that these various measures would add some £340 million to the borrowing requirement in 1974–75, this did not seem to concern the Treasury overmuch.

The period between March and October 1974, like the period between October 1964 and March 1966, was one in which no economic decision was taken without at least one eye on its political implications. It was more than forty years since Britain had had a government without an overall majority in the House of Commons, and although in many ways things worked out better than most observers had expected, there was a general assumption that before long Wilson would have to go to the country in an attempt to secure a workable majority. Part of the objective of economic – and other – policy was to avoid any disastrous turn of events which would put Labour on the defensive in this forthcoming election. By September, somewhat miraculously, the ice on which Labour had been skating, though thin, was still intact. The oil-producers, though voicing occasional displeasure at loose talk in Britain about the desirability of letting sterling float down in order to keep exports competitive, had continued to place a sufficient proportion of their rocketing balance of payments surpluses in London to finance Britain's yawning balance of payments deficit. And the TUC obligingly rallied round by overwhelmingly endorsing, at their annual Congress early in

September, a document which pledged co-operation in implementing the social contract. Close scrutiny of the document, which spelt out the guidelines which the TUC felt that unions should follow in formulating wage claims – basically that wages should rise no more than was necessary to compensate for the rise in the cost of living – revealed that at the crucial points it was so vague that virtually any union could argue that virtually any wage claim was consistent with the social contract. This was not, however, a tactful point to make to Labour politicians. Nor was the price of union co-operation negligible: the left wing of the trade union movement got it on record that in return for its co-operation it would expect a large-scale redistribution of income and wealth, a massive increase in house-building, a wide-ranging and permanent system of price control, vastly improved social services, a substantial increase in public ownership and, of course, substantial cuts in defence expenditure.

What the net effect of all this was on the election which Harold Wilson called for 10 October one does not know. But he must have been disappointed by the result: an overall majority of three. At least this gave Labour the crucial advantage of a majority on all the standing committees of the House of Commons which do the detailed work on legislation; but it was not nearly enough to give the Government a clear prospect of four or five years in which to make some fundamental changes.

THE DISINTEGRATING SOCIAL CONTRACT

Despite its minuscule majority, the new Labour Government came back in October 1974 determined to press on towards socialism. According to the Queen's speech opening the new Parliament, estate duty was to be replaced by a much more foolproof capital transfer tax; a select committee was to be set up to recommend the best form of wealth tax; industrial democracy was to be introduced into the national health service; the Government was to press ahead with completion of a fully comprehensive system of secondary education; development land was to be taken into public ownership; a National Enterprise Board and a system of planning agreements were to be established; a British National Oil Corporation was to give the state a key role in North Sea oil; and the shipbuilding and aircraft industries were to be nationalized. Although one or two items in this programme had not made much headway a year and a half later,[1] a great

[1] Notably the wealth tax, the select committee on which, amid some confusion, had brought out no fewer than five minority reports.

deal of it had. Moderate opinion was somewhat divided about its wisdom, some saying it was necessary in order to get union co-operation with the social contract, others arguing that it was irrelevant to the country's acute economic problems. A more sombre view was that it was radical enough to antagonize the country's political centre without being radical enough to satisfy the Left, including those elements of the Left which at this time wielded critical influence in many key unions. But that has always been the essential dilemma of social democratic politics.

In October, the results of the social contract so far could not be said to be encouraging. Retail prices were 18 per cent higher than a year before; but weekly wage rates were 26 per cent higher, and on top of this most wage and salary earners were now receiving eleven threshold payments, totalling £4.40 a week. As a result, real personal disposable income in the fourth quarter of 1974 was in fact 2½ per cent higher than a year before – an absurd situation, given the 10 per cent worsening in the terms of trade over the same period, and one made possible only by a large increase in the balance of payments deficit.[1] The sensible method of dealing with this situation would have been a statutory incomes policy, which would simultaneously have reduced real incomes, slowed down inflation and improved the balance of payments. But this was still ruled out on the grounds that the unions would simply not accept it.

Nevertheless, the Chancellor was by now taking a more realistic view of the situation, having moved some way from the approach adopted in both his March and July Budgets. In his third Budget, introduced in November, he said that earnings, not import prices, had now become the main engine of inflation, and that if the unions were not willing to abide by the TUC guidelines, he would be forced to tighten demand, which would inevitably result in higher unemployment. In line with this tougher approach he announced the phasing-out of subsidies to the nationalized industries, and sharply raised the price of petrol – the effect of these measures being, ironically enough, to increase the retail price index by about as much as his July measures had lowered it. The less well-off were to be afforded some protection against these measures, and against inflation generally, by another increase in pensions, to take effect only eight months after the last one; and – for the first time since Labour

[1] In the fourth quarter of 1973 – according to the June 1976 *Economic Trends* – the current account deficit had been running at an annual rate of £1.5 billion. In the fourth quarter of 1974 the figure was £3.8 billion.

had last increased them in 1968 – family allowances were raised. More realism than in March was also apparent in the Chancellor's treatment of the company sector: to ease the acute pressures on corporate liquidity, resulting from a combination of rapid cost increases and price controls, there was some relaxation of the Price Code, and abnormal stock appreciation was relieved of Corporation tax. The total effect was to improve the company sector's liquidity position by about £1.5 billion.

The most talked-about aspect of Mr Healey's November Budget, however, was not its effect on prices or corporate liquidity, but its new forecast of the public sector borrowing requirement for 1974–75. Put at £2.7 billion in the March Budget, the estimate had now shot up to £6.3 billion, £800 million of the increase resulting from the November measures, another £340 million from the July measures. This still left over £2.4 billion of the rise unaccounted for. This seemed to many people rather alarming, and at about this time the claim began to be heard that public expenditure was 'out of control'.[1] Nevertheless, most of the increase in the estimate of the PSBR between March and November was the result of the effect on public expenditure of the large increase in wages and salaries in the public sector during 1974, and of the big rise in housing and food subsidies that arose from the Government's policy decisions.

From an orthodox Keynesian point of view, a large budget deficit was perfectly in order in the circumstances of late 1974. Unemployment was approaching the 3 per cent level, and still rising; even after the Budget, the Chancellor expected it to go on rising slowly, though he reckoned it would stop well short of a million, or approximately 4 per cent. Cuts in public expenditure or increases in taxation of the kind required to reduce the budget deficit would lead to an even higher level of unemployment; and – quite apart from the danger that this might make it more difficult for union leaders to keep their rank and file behind the social contract – the prevention of a high level of unemployment was what the Keynesian revolution was all about. More surprising, perhaps, than the fact that the budget deficit was in line with Keynesian orthodoxy was the fact that it could not easily be faulted on either New Cambridge or monetarist lines. The New Cambridge school accepted that for some time to come there would have to be a sizeable deficit on the balance of payments

[1] This claim is discussed on pp. 221–7 below.

current account,[1] and the counterpart of this would be a large PSBR – particularly since a sizeable fraction of this would reflect the surplus in the company sector resulting from the November measures. Similarly, since it was planned to finance most of the budget deficit by borrowing either from the non-bank public or from abroad, the large PSBR need not lead to much increase in the money supply, and the monetarists could not protest too much.

The fact that the Chancellor was unwilling to take drastic action to reduce the size of the budget deficit did not, however, mean that he was indifferent to the rate at which public expenditure was apparently rising. In his Budget speech he stressed – as had all his predecessors for the last thirty years – the need to increase investment and exports, and promised that public expenditure, as well as private consumption, would be held back in order that this might be done: over the next four years public expenditure would be allowed to increase, in real terms, by only 2¾ per cent a year. To what extent the hard decisions necessary to restrain the growth of public expenditure would actually be taken remained to be seen. But the basic problem, as always, was how to ensure that lower demand for public or private consumption would indeed lead to higher exports and higher investment, and not just lower output and higher unemployment.

So much for the Budget of November 1974. Three months later preparations were in full swing for the next Budget, to be introduced in April 1975. Once again, the economic outlook had deteriorated. It was becoming apparent that the world recession was deeper than expected, and that the volume of British exports had peaked in the third quarter of 1974, and was now declining. On the wages front, things could hardly be worse. All sorts of worthy people – nurses, teachers, local authority workers, bakers – had been given wage increases, publicly defended as being in line with the social contract, of 25–30 per cent. It seemed unlikely that unions with far more industrial muscle were going to settle for any less. By February wage rates were about 30 per cent higher than a year before, and it was clear from the simplest arithmetical calculation that the rate of inflation – already at the unprecedented figure of 20 per cent – was bound to rise even further. The Government issued periodic warnings

[1] Indeed it appeared to contemplate with equanimity a balance of payments deficit of about £2.5 billion a year until 1978 (CEPG, 1975), a prospect that filled more orthodox commentators with horror: the cumulative deficit involved – if it could be financed – would have mortgaged much of the balance of payments benefits of North Sea oil.

about the consequences of these enormous wage increases, but did little else.[1]

In considering what he ought to do about all this, the Chancellor was not short of advice. Within the PLP, the Tribune group called for an increase in public expenditure, to reduce unemployment, and import controls, to improve the balance of payments. In the latter appeal (thought not in the former) they received the intellectual backing of the New Cambridge School, which had decided, on convincing grounds which never quite seemed to square with their basic position, that Britain's exports would never rise fast enough to provide full employment and an adequate balance of payments, and therefore the nation had better concentrate on keeping out imports.[2] As against this, the Manifesto group of middle-of-the-road Labour MPs called for a tightening of the social contract and repudiated import controls, being backed in the latter stance by a number of Oxford economists who argued that suitable changes in the exchange rate could do all that import controls could do, and more besides.[3] Meanwhile the serious press, the commanding heights of which (notably *The Times* and the *Financial Times*) were occupied by economic commentators of a monetarist cast of mind, continued to deplore the social contract as being not only unworkable but also undesirable, distorting differentials, misallocating resources, choking off enterprise, and diverting attention from the need to eliminate the budget deficit and get an unshakeable grip on the money supply.

On the whole, the Chancellor managed to resist some of these siren voices without being totally seduced by others. He could hardly turn a deaf ear to the fact that the PSBR for 1974–75, estimated at £6.3 billion as recently as the previous November, had actually turned out to be £7.6 billion, mainly because wage increases in the public sector had continued to be higher than expected, and housing

[1] The flavour of the situation was nicely captured by a spoof news item in *Private Eye* (21 March 1975):

WAGES

Wilson Warns

By our Political Team

In a shock warning last night the Prime Minister Mr Harold Wilson gave his strongest warning yet.

He warned: 'Make no mistake. If wages continue to rise, people will take home more money. That is the consequence of continued wage rises.'

In what was clearly intended as a warning to the Unions, Mr Wilson warned: 'You have been warned'.

[2] CEPG, 1975.

[3] Corden, Little and Scott, 1975.

and other subsidies had continued to mount. Still less could he ignore the fact that in the coming financial year (1975–76) the PSBR, on present policies, was estimated at over £10 billion, or some 11 per cent of the GDP. Without going all the way with either the monetarist or the New Cambridge School, Healey accepted that this figure must be cut. Although plans were in hand to phase out nationalized industry subsidies completely by April 1976, he recognized that no significant cuts could be made in public expenditure – at any rate without disproportionate disruption – until 1976–77.[1] So in the short run the burden had to fall mainly on higher taxes. Accordingly, rates of income tax were increased (though the effect of this was much modified by raising personal allowances and thus actually reducing the tax paid by a third of all taxpayers); duties on alcohol and tobacco were increased; and VAT on various consumer durable and electrical goods was raised from 8 per cent to 25 per cent. In consequence, the PSBR for 1975–76 would be brought down to about £9 billion.

The net effect of all this, Healey acknowledged, would be to slow down the rise in demand and output, and lead to unemployment rising to perhaps a million, or 4 per cent, by the end of the year; but until the inflationary pressure eased, he argued, he had no option. This line of argument was remarkably calmly received, with no outcry against it from any major trade union leader – the first clear gain to the Government from the social contract. This contrasted with the panic into which the Conservatives had been thrown by trade union warnings only three years earlier, at a time when unemployment was still well under a million. The policy left a good deal to be desired, nonetheless. Most of those who were due to become unemployed were not the militant workers in the mines, the power stations or the docks – or even the hospitals or the bakeries – whose pay demands were fuelling inflation. They were the old, the slow, the unskilled, the school-leavers. No doubt rising unemployment among these relatively disadvantaged groups would have some effect on the vigour with which powerful unions demanded wage increases; by early 1975 some economists were claiming to discern such an effect. But it was an inefficient and unjust way of doing the job. Although Mr Healey also announced in his Budget that more would be spent on training and re-training, and subsidies made available to prevent some redundancies, such measures – overdue in the first case and irrational

[1] Cynics argued that on past form it was doubtful whether they could be made at all.

in the second – could make little impact in a situation in which macroeconomic policy was intentionally deflationary. What was needed was an anti-inflationary strategy which went to the heart of the matter, and brought wage increases down from the stratosphere to something closer to the 3 per cent a year rise in the nation's productivity.

THATCHER REPLACES HEATH

While Labour grappled with the economy, the Conservatives, now back in the wilderness, could indulge in the luxury of grappling with each other. This they proceeded to do with their customary gentlemanly ferocity. Much rank-and-file Conservative opinion had been shocked and demoralized by Heath's U-turns on industrial policy and incomes policy, which seemed a betrayal of the spirit of Selsdon, and a repudiation of the tough policies to promote competition and efficiency which Heath had been elected Leader of the Party to carry out. The realities of power may have transformed Mr Heath from Hyde to Jekyll after two years in office; it had failed to have a similar effect on many of his backbenchers. This would not have mattered so much if the Conservatives had been re-elected; but by the middle of October 1974 Heath – as Harold Wilson kept on helpfully pointing out – had lost three of the last four elections. The Conservatives, always readier than Labour to defer to successful leaders, give shorter shrift to unsuccessful ones. Heath resisted to the last the idea that there should be an election for the leadership, apparently taking the view that, like the Queen, the job was his for as long as he wanted it. But the pressure from Conservative MPs was too strong, and Heath was forced to ask Sir Alec Douglas-Home (who a decade before had been eased out to make way for Heath) to draft new rules for regular election of the Conservative leader.

The chief beneficiary of the Tory backlash against Heath and his later policies seemed likely to be Sir Keith Joseph, a right-wing intellectual and successful businessman who epitomized the spirit of Selsdon. Sir Keith had been a member of the Cabinet throughout the period of Conservative government; whatever misgivings he may have felt about the *volte-face* on policy, they were evidently not severe enough to prompt his resignation. But after the Conservatives had lost the February 1974 election, he soon became the best-known and most articulate exponent of the view that the Conservative Government had failed because it had abandoned the principles on which it had fought, and been elected, in 1970. *Mea culpa,* exclaimed Sir Keith, hoping no doubt to get Conservative policies back on the right lines and also, perhaps, that there would be enough rejoicing in the Tory ranks over the sinner that repented to propel him into the leadership.

Sir Keith's economic message was simple, and by no means unfamiliar.[1] The Conservatives should have concentrated harder on cutting public expenditure. They should have intervened less, and given market forces far more scope. Above all, they should not have tried to maintain an unrealistically low level of unemployment by running budget deficits and pumping far too much money into the system. Attempts to keep unemployment below the 'natural rate' had been responsible for inflation ever since the war.[2] Of course, efforts should be made, by increasing labour mobility and expanding training and re-training facilities, to reduce the natural rate of unemployment. But the key to the problem of restoring what he called 'sound money' was not an incomes policy, which stultified the efficient working of the economy. It was to control the money supply, come what may, so that it increased by no more than a small and regular amount each year. Only in this way could one have stable prices, a reasonable growth rate, and as full a level of employment as the attitudes and institutional arrangements of the country permitted. It was, in fact, the basic monetarist argument, with all its superficial attractions and fundamental weaknesses.

Sir Keith himself soon came a cropper, appearing to argue in another speech that compulsory birth control should be imposed on families of low intelligence;[3] overnight he ceased to look a viable

[1] It was set out in detail in a speech at Preston in September 1974, and carried in full by *The Times* on 6 September.

[2] Sir Keith argued that the great majority of the registered unemployed were not really unemployed in an 'involuntary' or 'Keynesian' sense, being either briefly between jobs, physically or mentally unsuitable for most jobs, scroungers, or actually employed and therefore on the register fraudulently. If these categories were excluded, claimed Sir Keith, the number of genuinely unemployed since the war had been typically in the range 100,000–300,000 – far less than the number of unfilled vacancies, and indicative of excess demand in the labour market which was bound to lead to excessive wage increases and thus to inflation. The central weakness in Sir Keith's argument lay in attaching great significance to the ratio between those he chose to define as *really* unemployed and the number of vacancies which employers happened to notify to employment exchanges as being unfilled; and, more generally, in its faith in the ability of one instrument – monetary policy – to achieve an economic outcome that would be generally regarded as satisfactory on all fronts.

[3] *The Times,* 21 October 1974. Joseph had said that 'our human stock is threatened' by high birth rates amongst 'the lowest socio-economic classes' and that 'if we do nothing, the nation moves towards degeneration'.

candidate for the leadership. But the ideas he had been propounding lived on. The right wing of the Conservative Party, with Sir Keith himself in the vanguard, re-grouped behind Margaret Thatcher, a supporter of Sir Keith who was best known to the outside world as the Secretary of State for Education from 1970–74 who had stopped schoolchildren from getting free milk. When the slightly eccentric new electoral machinery devised by Sir Alec Douglas-Home was set in motion, and eventually, on 4 February 1975, resulted in a ballot for the leadership, it was found that of the 276 Conservative MPs entitled to vote, sixteen had voted for Hugh Fraser, 119 for Heath and 130 for Margaret Thatcher. Since no candidate had secured the necessary overall majority, a second ballot had to be held; but it was apparent that Heath could not possibly win it and, with as good a grace as he could muster, he retired from the lists. A week later, against four new opponents, Mrs Thatcher obtained a clear overall majority.

The year 1975 was International Women's Year, and it was perhaps appropriate that it should begin with the first election of a woman to the leadership of one of Britain's main political parties. The event, nevertheless, came as a considerable surprise to even the closest observers. Among Cecil King and his well-informed friends, for example, who had spent such part of 1974 as they could spare from talking of the imminence of catastrophe and the need for a national government, in speculating about the next Conservative leader, her name had scarcely been mentioned (King, 1975). Seasoned political correspondents had for the most part been putting their money on William Whitelaw, the candidate most readily identifiable with the unifying, consensus approach to the nation's problems which Heath, however stiffly, had been trying to cultivate in his later days as Prime Minister. Both groups of observers seemed to have underestimated two things. One was the depth and the extent of the disillusionment felt by Conservative MPs with the record of the 1970–74 Government. The other was the importance attached by MPs to the ability of the party leader to score plenty of points off his opposite number in the House of Commons: to defeat him in argument, to expose his ignorance at question time, to embarrass him with an excoriating wit, and generally to humiliate him in front of his followers. To outside opinion it may seem alarming, even horrifying, that gladiatorial proficiency in these dialectical skills should play so large a part in determining who becomes party leader and consequently Prime Minister. But the House of Commons is – as the very seating arrangements demonstrate – a place of confrontation, a field of battle where you want your champion to defeat their champion. This has the consequence that the person most likely to get the job may not always be the person best fitted to perform it – a phenomenon unfortunately not confined to democratic politics, nor indeed to politics at all. But it does help to explain why Harold Wilson survived such a long time and Sir Alec Douglas-Home such a short time; and it does help to explain the election of Margaret Thatcher. Whatever the impression she had made on the general public, she was known by her colleagues in the House of Commons as a highly intelligent, very well-organized, exceedingly determined woman, who had all her political armoury, offensive and defensive, in excellent working order, and who had recently demonstrated, as Shadow Chancellor, a mastery of economic and taxation matters that was considerably more impressive than that of her immediate rivals. In this light, her election was not so surprising.

GETTING THROUGH THE REFERENDUM

With the ending of the Budget debate in April 1975, economic policy was tacitly put on ice for a month or two. For the Government's – and the Opposition's – next job was to get the country safely through the referendum, fixed for 5 June, on whether or not Britain should remain a member of the EEC.[1] In March a majority of the Cabinet – thinking, perhaps, that with the new cold winds blowing around the world this was no time to pull out of the EEC and go it alone – had decided that what were described as the new membership terms negotiated by James Callaghan were not, as the anti-Common Marketeers claimed, a charade, but an improvement on the deal negotiated by the Conservatives sufficiently significant to justify the Government advising the nation to say Yes to continued British membership. But since it was clear that a significant minority within the Cabinet, half the PLP, and a large majority of the party's active members in the country were going to say No, the Labour Party as a whole could not campaign in favour of the Government's line. So, for once, the principle of collective responsibility would be waived, and individual members of the Government would be free to campaign for or against, as their consciences directed. However, with the Prime Minister and most of the Cabinet, the overwhelming majority

[1] Wilson's strategy – or lack of strategy – on the EEC was discussed on pp. 154–7.

of the Conservative Party, and the whole of the Liberal Party in favour of staying in – and far more money being spent on publicity by the pros than the antis – the result of the referendum, when it came, was not altogether unexpected: 67.2 per cent of those who voted[1] said Yes; only 32.8 per cent said No.

One result of this two-to-one vote was obvious: after nearly fifteen years of alarms and excursions Britain, for better or for worse, was finally and permanently a member of the European Community. Another result, scarcely less obvious, was much commented upon by the centre and right-wing press, and acted upon by Harold Wilson. The Labour Left, egged on by Tony Benn and sustained by many union leaders, had campaigned hard for a No vote. The Left, it was implied – often explicitly claimed – spoke for the mass of the working people, in this as in a whole range of other matters. But the referendum result demonstrated that, on this issue at least, it did not speak for the mass of the working people. Its credibility, if not its self-confidence, was distinctly, if only transiently, damaged. And Wilson took the opportunity of Benn's loss of face to demote him from the Department of Industry, where his words and deeds had succeeded in reducing a large part of the nation's private industry to a state of near-hysteria, to the Department of Energy. Here, since negotiations with the oil companies over the terms of their participation in the North Sea was at first specifically excluded from his brief, it was hoped that he would not cause too much trouble.

BACK TO INCOMES POLICY

Economic policy-making may have been in a state of suspended animation during the month or two before the referendum in June 1975; economic events were less obliging. The balance of payments continued in heavy deficit, increasing the country's foreign debts at a rate of about £2 billion a year; unemployment rose steadily, but failed to prevent increasing numbers of workers – miners, civil servants, shipbuilding workers, power workers, railwaymen, printers – from getting wage increases of around 30 per cent. By the middle of June retail prices were 26 per cent higher than a year before, and the value of sterling had fallen by nearly 4 per cent during the previous six weeks. Much sober opinion saw the nation as teetering on the brink of a plunge into an uncontrollable hyperinflation.

[1] There was a turnout of 64 per cent, compared with 73 per cent in the October 1974 general election.

In spite of the urgency of the situation, and increasing concern on the part of both the TUC and CBI, nothing much happened until the Chancellor made a speech on 21 June, in which he said that by the end of July Britain would have to be able to show the rest of the world that it had a policy for bringing inflation under control, and for getting its rate down to single figures by the end of 1976. But he said nothing about how this might be done. Like King Lear, Mr Healey was proclaiming that he would do such things – what they were yet he knew not – but they would be the terrors of the earth. In common with similar pronouncements by earlier Chancellors, this had the opposite effect from that intended.[1] The pressure on sterling intensified and, despite substantial support by the Bank of England, its value rapidly declined by another 3½ per cent, to an all-time low of almost 29 per cent below the Smithsonian level. The crunch came on 30 June, when the pound fell by 1.3 per cent during a single trading session. Harold Wilson – discovered, Drake-like, or possibly Canute-like, eating strawberries and cream at the Royal Agricultural Show and assuring his listeners that the Government 'rejected panic solutions' – was summoned hastily back to London. The next day Healey repeated that the Government intended to bring the rate of inflation down to 10 per cent by the end of the next pay round, and to single figures by the end of 1976, and announced that to this end it would ensure that the increase in wages and salaries during the next round would not exceed 10 per cent. If possible, this would be done on a voluntary basis; if not, the Government would enact the necessary legislation to ensure that employers in both public and private sectors complied. The actual guidelines to be followed were published ten days later in a White Paper, and were very close to those proposed in the meantime by the TUC.[2] The central proposal – surrounded by a plethora of other proposals for the control of rents, dividends and the size of public sector wage bills – was for a

[1] The Machiavellian interpretation would be that it had precisely the effect intended. However the weight of the evidence available is that the Government was not being nearly so subtle – or so foolhardy – as deliberately to precipitate a massive run on sterling in the hope that this would bring home to people the seriousness of the crisis.

[2] Indeed part of the TUC policy document, which had been finalized on 9 July, was published in the White Paper as an annex. The only notable respect in which the TUC document – which was drafted under the influence of Jack Jones, General Secretary of the TGWU, who had for some time been calling for an incomes policy based on flat rate increases – differed from the White Paper was that it proposed that there should be no pay increase for those earning over £7,000 a year. The Government amended this figure to £8,500.

limit of £6 a week on pay increases over the period to 1 August 1976.

The £6 a week policy had three advantages. Because it applied not to rates but to earnings, it was simple and unequivocal: no employer or employee could be in any doubt about what they had to do to comply with it.[1] Secondly, it was – or could be represented by the Government as being – 'fair': at a time of national emergency, everyone was being treated equally. Thirdly, it would, if adhered to, bring about a drastic fall in the rate of inflation. Whether or not Healey's pledge to bring it down to single figures by the end of 1976 was actually achieved would depend in part on imponderables like the terms of trade and the growth of output; but overnight the pledge had become perfectly credible. But the proposal had one big disadvantage, which was the mirror-image of the advantages: by giving the same absolute amount to everyone, it would compress differentials, particularly if the effect was measured in terms of net income after tax, and particularly for those earning more than £8,500 a year. The real disposable income of most higher-paid wage and salary earners had already fallen over the previous few years, under the twin pressures of rising inflation and high marginal tax rates;[2] now the same people would be penalized afresh. To some extent such a redistribution of income was, of course, a deliberate objective of the Labour Government, and had been explicitly set out in both Labour's 1974 election manifestos. But it was not simply the board room bores or the pin-striped executives who were going to be discriminated against by the flat rate £6 a week limit: it was also the miners and the power station engineers, of whose militancy and industrial muscle nobody needed much reminder. The £6 limit might, with luck, be accepted for a year, provided that on other fronts – notably unemployment – the Government kept its flank reasonably well covered. But the compression of differentials and the creation of anomalies that would result from the £6 policy would make the 're-entry' problem in mid-1976 a tricky one.

In July 1975, however, all that lay in the future. The immediate task was to stop the bleeding, and this is what the £6 policy did. It did so, moreover – at least in a hair-splitting sense – without qualify-

[1] The only dispute of interpretation that in fact arose was over whether – as the Government contended – the £6 was a *ceiling* or whether – as the TUC claimed – it was an *entitlement.* The TUC interpretation proved more persuasive: most workers got the full £6 increase.

[2] A graphic demonstration of this was provided by a survey of 400,000 managerial jobs conducted by Hay–MSL, reported in the *Financial Times* on 15 September 1975.

ing as a 'statutory' incomes policy, that great *bête noir* of the unions and much of the Labour Party. Although the new policy did require some legislation to be rushed through Parliament,[1] this was mainly designed to relieve employers of the legal obligation to honour previously negotiated cost-of-living agreements; no legislation was enacted compelling employers to observe the £6 policy, and it was made clear that in no circumstances was there any question of *employees* being sent to jail, as had happened under the Conservatives.[2] The voluntary nature of the policy, however, was entirely cosmetic, and designed to save the faces of all those Labour Ministers, from Harold Wilson downwards, who had sworn never again to introduce a statutory policy. Ministers made it clear to all concerned that the Government had prepared legislation (all the more threatening because its content was never revealed) which they would introduce the moment any employer showed any signs of not co-operating with the £6 policy on a voluntary basis. So the Labour Government contrived to talk softly, while hinting that behind its back it carried a pretty big stick.

The £6 a week pay policy did not, by itself, represent a solution to the economic problems facing Britain in 1975; but it did represent a crucial element in such a solution. It would have been even more useful had it come much sooner. This, unfortunately, was scarcely possible. True to the Hyde syndrome, the Labour Party when in opposition had lent far too ready an ear to those who argued that inflation had nothing to do with wage increases, and had committed itself to abolishing Heath's statutory incomes policy and all that went with it. Under the social contract agreed between Labour and the unions inflation was to be dealt with by statutory price controls and voluntary wage restraint. Some leading Ministers in the new Labour Government were uneasy about this arrangement, but there was no way in which they could abrogate it. All they could do was wait for the psychological moment. This came in the middle of 1975, when many trade union leaders had become sufficiently alarmed by the rate of inflation to be receptive to the idea of a rigorous incomes policy – provided it was 'voluntary'. All the same, the delay of almost a year and a half before the introduction of an effective

[1] The Remuneration, Charges and Grants Bill was published on 16 July, and received the Royal Assent on 1 August.

[2] It was in fact under the Industrial Relations Act, and not the incomes policy legislation, that trade unionists had gone to jail (see pp. 128–9 above), but by mid-1975 memories of the precise circumstances had become somewhat blurred (see 'The pay crunch', *Sunday Times*, 6 July 1975).

incomes policy carried a heavy risk. It gave Britain an inflation rate two or three times as high as other OECD countries. Getting the rate back down to single figures seemed likely to be a long, hard struggle. In the meantime holders of sterling around the world might simply get fed up, and move their money out on a sufficient scale to send the sterling exchange rate spiralling downwards. By raising import prices, this would make it more difficult to reduce the inflation rate, and might lead to a situation – which would probably be welcomed by many of the Government's critics – in which economic policy was effectively being dictated by the IMF. This would be a sad ending to the social contract.

THE NEW INDUSTRIAL STRATEGY

Imperative though it was for the Labour Government to get on top of inflation, and essential though it was to have an incomes policy in order to do this, the counter-inflation policy was the negative rather than the positive element in a rational economic policy. The dramatic worsening in the terms of trade during 1973, culminating in the quadrupling of the oil price, emphasized the extent to which living standards in Britain were dependent on world forces over which she had no control and which might well, in the longer run, work to her disadvantage. If Britain was to survive and prosper in the last quarter of the twentieth century, she would more than ever need a highly efficient and dynamic manufacturing industry, capable of holding its own in increasingly competitive world markets against other countries, such as Germany and Japan, which also needed to import most of their food and raw materials.

The need for a strong manufacturing sector had been recognized by both Labour and Conservative governments. But no sustained success had been notched up in achieving it. The National Plan, which had put much emphasis on manufacturing investment, had been abandoned. The IRC, set up in order to arrange mergers in the manufacturing sector where this would increase efficiency, was abolished by the Conservatives. So was SET, designed to increase the flow of labour into manufacturing, and thus promote dynamic economies of scale. So were investment grants, introduced in place of investment allowances in order to simplify and streamline subsidies to manufacturing investment. It was hardly surprising that by 1973 the statistics for manufacturing industry should make gloomy reading. Investment was only 25 per cent higher than it had been in 1964, and considerably lower than it had been in 1969, 1970 and 1971 – and even in a relatively good year like 1971 it was calculated that investment per worker in Britain was less than half that in France, Japan and the U.S., and well below that in Germany and Italy.[1] Labour productivity had, it is true, grown at the fairly respectable rate of 3.8 per cent a year;[2] but this was still considerably less than the increase achieved in other countries, and was partly offset, as far as the expansion of total manufacturing output was concerned, by a 7 per cent fall in employment since 1964.

As the Labour Opposition grappled in the early 1970s with the problem of inadequate investment in manufacturing industry, some distinctly Hyde-like noises were to be heard emanating from the back rooms at Transport House. An official working party called for the nationalization of twenty-five of the 100 largest manufacturing firms, and there was talk of renationalizing without compensation firms which had been denationalized by the Conservatives. Seasoned observers of Labour politics may not have taken these proposals too seriously, but they received wide publicity, and did little to persuade private industry that an incoming Labour government would be sympathetic to their problems. This was the more true as in other parts of the field Labour was talking of 'a permanent system of price controls' which would 'have to concern itself deeply with profits, profit margins and productivity', thus preventing 'the erosion of real wages'. There was also talk of making the system of direct taxation 'very much more progressive'.[3] To socialists, all this was fairly commonplace. To businessmen in the private sector, it sounded like a further threat to their ability to make or keep profits, and provided a further excuse for not investing. A final blow seemed to be struck when Tony Benn, the Labour politician most closely identified in the public mind with the call for more nationalization and government intervention in industry, was made Secretary of State for Industry in the new Government.

Nevertheless, the radical proposals favoured by the Left had been much watered down by the time the Party's industrial strategy was outlined in its February 1974 election manifesto. It consisted of three strands. First, certain specific industries would be nationalized.

[1] HMG, 1974 (Aug.).
[2] *Economic Trends*, Annual Supplement, 1975, p. 81. This was, in fact, much the same as the rate projected in Labour's National Plan.
[3] TUC–Labour Party, 1973, pp. 4 and 6.

These included the ports (which Labour had been in the process of nationalizing when it lost office in 1970), shipbuilding and aircraft (which had both long been dependent on government assistance for their survival) and a few other bits and pieces. Secondly, instead of an elaborate new national plan, a series of planning agreements would be concluded between the Government and the main industrial firms. The firm would draw up its plans for future investment, output, exports and so on in consultation with the Government, making it aware of its problems and receiving where appropriate advice and assistance in return. The third strand in the strategy would be the establishment of a National Enterprise Board (NEB), which would in some ways resemble the former IRC, but have a wider field of operation and more money. The NEB would, among other things, take a shareholding – sometimes a 100 per cent shareholding – in firms or industries where this seemed essential in order to promote investment, exports, or other national objectives. However the form in which these last two proposals appeared in the manifesto was deliberately vague, leaving unanswered the two crucial questions: would planning agreements, and partial or complete takeover of firms by the NEB, be compulsory or voluntary? And would firms into which the NEB put money be required to make a commercial rate of return on the money, or would they be permitted to make losses or below-normal profits, on the grounds that this was in the national interest?

The answers to these questions were hammered out within the Government during the spring and summer of 1974. Broadly speaking the socialists, as represented by the Secretary of State for Industry, Tony Benn, wanted planning agreements and the acquisition of shares by the NEB to be compulsory, and below-normal profit rates to be permitted where this would help to steer investment into the less prosperous regions, or to prevent big redundancies. The social democrats, on the other hand, as represented by the Chancellor of the Exchequer, Denis Healey, wanted planning agreements and the acquisition of assets by the NEB to take place only with the consent of the private firms involved, and firms to be assisted financially only if they were likely to achieve a commercial rate of return on the capital. This battle was won by the Treasury, partly because of the nervousness felt by many ministers about the consequences for the exchange rate and the balance of payments of the kind of assault on the mixed economy – seen by many observers, particularly abroad, as irrelevant to the country's economic problems

– that Benn was calling for. Accordingly, the White Paper published in August made it clear that there would be no compulsion on firms to conclude planning agreements with the government; that all NEB shareholdings in companies, whether partial or total, would be acquired by agreement; and that – except for specific cases in which the Government would direct otherwise on social grounds – the NEB would be required to secure an adequate rate of return on those capital assets for which it was responsible.

If the NEB was to operate on commercial criteria and take a majority shareholding in private firms only with their consent, and if private firms were going to conclude planning agreements with the Government only if they chose to – presumably because they wanted government assistance or a market in the public sector for their goods – it was difficult to see what contribution these new arrangements were going to make. This may explain the Government's leisurely timetable for putting the ideas into practice: the Industry Bill, which embodied the proposals in the August 1974 White Paper, did not become law until November 1975, and the draft guidelines governing the operations of the NEB were not published until March 1976. By the middle of 1976 the NEB had not taken over a single firm in the private sector; it had merely had transferred to it the shares of a motley assortment of companies – Rolls-Royce (1971), British Leyland, Ferranti, Alfred Herbert and a few others – which Conservative and Labour governments had for one reason or another – usually to prevent collapse – previously taken into public ownership. Nor, by the middle of 1976, had a single planning agreement been concluded between the Government and a private firm. There were, however, rumours that the first planning agreement would shortly be negotiated – with British Leyland. The idea that the first planning agreement should be concluded not with some huge private firm over whose activities the government had no control, but a firm which had already been nationalized, provisionally promised £1,500 million of public money, and handed over to the NEB for detailed supervision, gave the whole concept of planning agreements a distinctly Ruritanian flavour.

If planning agreements and the NEB were not going to solve the problems of increasing manufacturing investment and establishing criteria for government assistance to individual sectors, what was? For a considerable time the Government operated on an *ad hoc* basis, under the powers conferred on it by the Conservatives' 1972 Industry Act. Money was made available to modernize a small number of specific industries,[1] and special assistance was also provided for certain investment projects in other industries. More controversial was the assistance made available by Mr Benn to some of the firms which applied to the Department of Industry in late 1974 and early 1975 for help to combat the effects of the deepening recession. In half a dozen of these cases,[2] Benn made government assistance available against the advice of the Industrial Development Advisory Board, which was charged under the 1972 Act with advising on whether or not projects assisted in this way appeared commercially viable. Many people regarded these actions – though technically within the Minister's powers – as flouting the spirit of the August 1974 White Paper, and they undoubtedly played a part in Benn's removal from the Department of Industry after the referendum in June 1975. Yet Benn's actions, if misguided, were understandable; and they all received Cabinet backing. From the Olympian heights of the editorial chairs of the serious newspapers, or with the birds-eye view of the macroeconomic commentators, it may have been clear that Benn was wasting public money and delaying much-needed changes in the nation's industrial structure. Seen from the vantage point of the Left, however, Benn was fighting to prevent people losing their jobs at a time of rising unemployment and – in three of the cases – giving a helping hand to groups of workers who were trying to put socialism into practice by taking over bankrupt or near-bankrupt firms and running them as workers' co-operatives. The actions in question did not in fact advance socialism, since backing hopeless ventures damaged the whole idea of workers' co-operatives; though they may have done something to advance Mr Benn in the eyes of the Left.

With the replacement of Benn in the summer of 1975 by Eric Varley – generally accounted a protégé of Harold Wilson – there was a change of direction in industrial policy. Instead of piecemeal and *ad hoc* intervention, an attempt would be made to establish a coherent set of criteria for government assistance to particular industries; and it was stressed more than before that the Government would proceed on the basis of agreement with the private sector and

[1] Initially, three industries were chosen: wool textiles, ferrous foundries and machine tools. Printing machinery and non-ferrous foundries were later added to the list.

[2] These were Aston Martin Lagonda (which in the end did not receive any government money); three 'workers' co-operatives' – Scottish News Enterprises, Norton Villiers Triumph-Meriden Co-operative, and Kirkby Manufacturing and Engineering Ltd; Alfred Herbert; and Bear Brand. Despite government assistance, most of these enterprises subsequently collapsed. Alfred Herbert was taken into public ownership.

not – with occasional exceptions – by compulsion. The first fruits of this new approach was a set of proposals for a long-term industrial strategy presented by the Government to a meeting of Neddy at Chequers in November. Instead of constructing a new National Plan, a more flexible approach would be adopted. The Government would select the most important sectors of industry, grouped in three different categories: those which were intrinsically likely to be successful, those which had the potential for success if appropriate action were taken, and those (like component suppliers) whose performance was of most importance to the rest of industry. Once these forty or so sectors – covering about two-thirds of manufacturing industry – were chosen, detailed tripartite discussions between government, industry and unions would be held within the Neddy framework to identify the actions needed to improve each industry's prospects, both short-term and long-term. The new industrial strategy was, in short, a development of the kind of consensus approach towards the improvement of the performance of the manufacturing sector which had characterized the work of Neddy under the Conservatives in the early 1960s and Labour's National Plan in the mid-1960s. It was a long way from the compulsory planning agreements and widespread takeovers by the NEB that the Left had called for, and continued to call for.[1] But if Britain was to remain a mixed economy it was probably the right way to proceed.

However, if the new industrial strategy was to work, two conditions had to be met, both of them running counter to the instincts of the Left. One was that industry should be allowed to earn a reasonable rate of profit on its operations; the other was that ailing firms or industrial sectors which did not look as though they could be made into successes should be allowed to go under, so that labour could be redeployed into the expanding sectors – even though this meant a temporary rise in unemployment. The first of these conditions was probably just about met by the slight relaxation of the Price Code conceded by the Government in the early summer of 1976 – though there were many in industry who vigorously denied it, arguing that controls on prices and profit margins were too tight to make new

[1] *Labour's Programme 1976*, a long document prepared by Transport House and endorsed by Labour's National Executive Committee in May 1976, called for the rapid conclusion of compulsory planning agreements with the top 100 manufacturing companies and for the NEB to acquire control of a leading company in each of the key sectors in industry and commerce.

investment attractive. The second condition, however, was breached in a spectacular way within a few weeks of the Chequers meeting.

In December the Government announced a £160 million rescue operation for Chrysler, the small and inefficient subsidiary of the smallest and least efficient of the three big American car firms. There was little apparent justification for this: the medium-term prospect was of severe over-capacity in the world's motor industries, and earlier in the year the Government had undertaken to put £1,500 million into a rival firm – British Leyland – of which it was now the major shareholder. But the Chrysler decision illustrated the agonizing nature of high-level political decisions. Had Chrysler been allowed to go to the wall, its extensive dealer network in Britain would almost certainly have been snapped up by the Japanese, and imports of foreign cars, already causing the Government considerable concern, would have risen even more. Discreet soundings seem to have been taken in Washington and with the EEC Commission in Brussels to see whether a blind eye would be turned to the imposition of temporary controls to avert these extra imports; the answer was no. Even closer to home were the immediate effects on employment of letting Chrysler collapse: some 17,000 men would probably lose their jobs directly, and many more indirectly. Moreover, 6,000 of those thrown out of work would be at the Scottish plant at Linwood, where there was little prospect of alternative employment; and a big rise in the number of Scottish unemployed. at a time when devolution was one of the main items on the parliamentary agenda, and the Scottish nationalist movement was already looking menacingly strong, could have started the U.K. on the slippery slope that led to full Scottish independence. On top of all this, the Secretary of State for Scotland might have resigned.

Whether the Chrysler case was going to be an isolated exception to the rule, or whether it was going to prove the first of many examples of the Government's inability – at any rate at a time of high unemployment – to stick to its strategy and let essentially unviable firms go under, remained to be seen. As 1976 got under way, increasing sums were being made available by the Government for training and retraining schemes, and in due course this might ease the problem, acting, with luck, as a springboard and not a mattress. But the best bet was that the problem of insulating the necessary long-term restructuring of the economy from the exigencies of day-to-day political pressures was still going to take a long time to solve.

PUBLIC AFFLUENCE AND PRIVATE SQUALOR?

During 1975 it became increasingly fashionable to argue either that public expenditure was 'out of control', or that its rapid growth over the past decade had been a prime cause of Britain's economic difficulties, or both. There was some substance in the first charge, though less than many commentators claimed; there was little substance in the second.

The most authoritative version of the charge that public expenditure was out of control came from Wynne Godley, Director of the Cambridge Department of Applied Economics, a leading member of the New Cambridge School, and a former Treasury forecaster who had specialized in forecasting public expenditure. Godley argued (Godley, 1975) that between 1970–71 and 1974–75 public expenditure had risen by £5 billion *more* than could be accounted for by announced policy changes. The Treasury challenged this argument, claiming that most of the £5 billion was the result of deliberate policy decisions taken by successive governments over the period. What was not contested was that over this period public expenditure had risen much more rapidly than the national income – from 51 per cent of GDP (at current prices) in 1970–71 to 58 per cent in 1974–75, and 60 per cent in 1975–76. This had certainly not been intended in 1970: the implication of the Conservative Government's first White Paper on public expenditure in January 1971 was that, even allowing for the relative price effect,[1] public expenditure would stay roughly unchanged as a proportion of the GDP.

Five separate reasons can be distinguished why public expenditure rose much faster over this period than originally planned; only the last one represented a real loss of control. The first was the series of boosts given to public expenditure in 1971 and 1972 by Mr Barber, in his attempts to stem the rise in unemployment (see pp. 140–1). The second lay in the food and housing subsidies which the Labour Government started to dole out upon taking office in March 1974 (see pp. 192–3), together with the increased grants necessary to cover the rising deficits of the nationalized industries, which were not permitted to raise their prices far enough or fast enough to offset their escalating costs. The third reason, though not representing deliberate policy decisions like the first two, was at least predictable: the rise in debt service which inevitably attended the rapidly rising

[1] See p. 222.

public sector borrowing requirement. The fourth reason did reflect a certain loss of control of public expenditure, though of a rather special and once-for-all kind: the massive reorganization of local government and of the National Health Service carried out by the Conservatives during 1972–74 had the effect of substantially increasing the number of people employed in the sectors concerned – partly as an inevitable result of the nature of the reforms, partly because of the wide scope they afforded to local empire-builders. It was only the fifth reason which represented a genuine loss of control. It was, however, a loss of control of a serious, if technical, kind.

Since the adoption of the recommendations of the Plowden Committee (HMG, 1961), successive governments had been planning public expenditure for five years ahead. On the basis of projections of the likely growth of the economy, and in the light of the Government's priorities, decisions were made about both the rise in total public expenditure over the next five years, and the allocation of this expenditure between departments.[1] To avoid the effects of inflation, all this was done at constant prices: it was real economic growth and the deployment of real resources, after all, that were at issue. However, because the output of the public sector is more labour intensive than the output of the private sector (a large part of public expenditure consisting of the pay of teachers, doctors, nurses, civil servants, local government officials and so on), there is less scope for increasing productivity in the public sector. In consequence, the price of public sector output rises faster – for any given *overall* inflation rate – than the price of private sector output. To allow for this 'relative price effect', the figures of public expenditure in 'volume' terms are adjusted upwards to arrive at a figure in 'cost' terms. One consequence of this is that even if public expenditure rises no faster than real GDP in volume terms, it will rise faster in cost terms. There is therefore a strong tendency, over time, for public expenditure to rise as a proportion of the national income; over the past decade or two, this effect has in fact been observed in all advanced industrial countries (OECD, 1972, table 17).

Although this system of controlling public expenditure worked reasonably well for a number of years, it contained certain flaws. One was that by working in volume terms and only subsequently translating the results into cost terms, the PESC system deprived the

[1] The detailed work was done by an inter-departmental committee of officials, known as the Public Expenditure Survey Committee (PESC), but the final decisions were of course made by ministers.

decision-making process of an element essential to rational choice in the economic sphere – the knowledge of how relative prices are changing over time. In other words, the system had no adequate feedback mechanism for ensuring that the overall allocation of resources took account of the increasing relative cost of public sector output. The second flaw in the system was that it gave agencies in the public sector – government departments and local authorities – no incentive to economize on the price they paid for their labour or materials. For they were entitled under the system to employ a certain *number* of people and buy a certain *amount* of inputs and, as wages and prices rose, they received from the Government more or less automatically whatever sums of money were necessary to cover the increased cost.[1] It seems plausible to argue that this virtual insulation from market pressures – at a time when rapidly rising unemployment may have been beginning to have a dampening effect on the size of wage settlements in the private sector – played a part in the huge wage increases conceded in 1974 and the first half of 1975 throughout the public sector, and in the consequent drastic rise in public expenditure at current prices. The third flaw is related to the second: at a time of rapid inflation particularly, it is difficult for the Treasury to tell how far the big money increase in the cost of fulfilling public sector programmes results from inflation, and how far it results from the volume of expenditure exceeding the amount allowed for. There is more than a suspicion that unauthorized increases in the standard of the service being provided (or, to put it more cynically, the quantity of inputs being purchased) was one of the factors behind the surge in public expenditure in the mid-1970s. It is certainly difficult to account fully for the huge increase in local authority expenditure in any other way.

In July 1975, in response to mounting criticism of the loss of control resulting from the PESC system of projecting public expenditure at constant prices (or in what was sometimes described as 'funny money'), the Treasury agreed to make greater use of cash limits as a control device; and it subsequently announced that in 1976–77 three-quarters of central government expenditure (other than social security payments) would be controlled in cash terms. It also undertook to apply cash limits to the local authorities' rate support grant, and to much local authority capital expenditure. Up to a point, this

[1] In this connection it is significant that between 1964 and 1975 the proportion of local authority expenditure financed by the central government's rate support grant rose from 50 per cent to 65 per cent.

greater use of cash ceilings is sensible: it limits government expenditure in actual money terms, and gives spending departments and local authorities a strong incentive to economize on costs and resist big wage claims. At the same time, if used too bluntly or insensitively, it threatens to lead to arbitrary and drastic changes – either up or down – in the volume or quality of services in the public sector simply as a result of failure to predict the rate of inflation correctly. This was precisely one of the risks the PESC system had been set up to avoid. There is little doubt that the Treasury can control public expenditure effectively if it really wants to – as was demonstrated by the very tight check imposed on public spending under Roy Jenkins in 1968–70. True, there was a marked loss of control in 1974 and 1975, but that was the consequence of a sudden and large increase in inflation impinging on a system of control which tried to abstract from inflation – a problem which has been recognized and, it would appear, put right. The danger in the second half of the 1970s may prove to be not one of public expenditure escalating out of control, but of its being held down too tightly, in the belief that this will solve the nation's economic problems.

This belief was certainly prevalent in 1976, and stemmed partly from the second charge being made against public expenditure at about this time: that its rapid growth had been the major cause of Britain's economic difficulties, by diverting labour into the public sector and away from manufacturing industry, and thus weakening the nation's capacity to produce the marketable goods that were needed for exports, productive investment, and consumers' expenditure.[1] This argument received a good deal of uncritical acceptance, because it was consistent with three familiar and well-documented phenomena: the low rate of investment, the slow growth of exports, and the big increase in employment in several parts of the public sector. It was also well received by those who are instinctively opposed to a high level of public expenditure.

On closer examination, however, the argument carried much less conviction. In the first place, the rising share of public expenditure in the GDP came mainly not from public consumption and investment, which make direct use of resources, but from transfer payments, which simply transfer resources from one person to another. Between 1964 and 1974, for example, when total public expenditure rose from 44 per cent of the GDP to 57 per cent, public consump-

[1] Bacon and Eltis, 1976.

tion and investment rose from 28 to 33 per cent, while transfer payments rose from 16 to 24 per cent. Much of this rise in transfer payments reflected demographic changes – notably the fact that over the period the number of old-age pensioners rose by about 1½ million. It is true that some of the rise in transfer payments took the form of increased subsidies on food, housing and the prices of the nationalized industries, and it can be argued that some of these subsidies reflected an inefficient allocation of resources; but this does not alter the fact that in so far as the rise in public expenditure took the form of higher transfer payments, it was not accompanied, except to the most trivial extent, by a rise in employment in the public sector of the kind with which Bacon and Eltis were concerned.

Employment in the public sector has, to be sure, risen substantially over the past decade, as the counterpart of the rise in the share of GDP accounted for by public consumption; though the rise – from 23½ per cent of the labour force in 1964 to 26 per cent in 1974[1] – has been smaller than many uninformed observers seem to imagine. Although a small part of this rise may have been the wasteful result of the reorganization of local government and the health service, most of it has reflected two inescapable facts: demographic change, and the inherently slow rise in public sector productivity which lies behind the relative price effect. The rise in the number of pensioners between 1964 and 1974, in addition to increasing the level of transfer payments, also increased the number of people employed in old people's homes and local authority welfare services. Similarly, the rise of more than 1½ million in the number of schoolchildren over the same period substantially increased the number of teachers required. This was necessary merely to maintain *existing* standards of education and health care. But if there was to be some *rise* in standards (and most would agree there should be some rise in standards over a decade in which real GDP rose by a quarter) then, in the nature of the services involved, this had to come from more staff rather than higher productivity.[2] In short, a fairly large rise in employment in the public sector was required over the period 1964–74 if existing standards of provision in key parts of the public sector were to be maintained, let alone improved.

[1] *British Labour Statistics Yearbooks*, 1974 and 1975.

[2] Because of technological progress, more and better cars and television sets can be made by the same number of men as time goes on; but more education and better welfare services by and large require more people to provide them.

This still leaves unanswered the question of whether the rise in employment in the public sector, however justifiable, caused a drop in the manufacturing labour force which weakened the nation's capacity to produce marketed goods for export, for investment and for import-saving consumption. The answer is almost certainly no. Much of the rise in employment in the public sector was among women – mainly married women – who had not worked in manufacturing and who would not have got jobs in manufacturing had they not found employment in the public sector.[1] In fact the main effect of a slower rise in employment in the public sector would have been a higher unemployment rate and – among married women – a lower participation rate in the labour force. This would have represented a much greater waste of resources than the high level of public expenditure which was so often a target for the charge of wastefulness. No evidence suggests that the output of manufacturing industry has been held back by a general shortage of labour, as opposed to shortages of particular kinds of skilled labour which it was the job of the training and re-training services to provide. Indeed the explanation of the slow growth of manufacturing output seems to lie as much on the demand side as on the supply side: output has grown slowly partly because the demand for exports and capital goods has grown slowly. Had demand grown faster as a result of less reliance on stop-go, a more intelligent exchange rate policy, and more drive and imagination on the part of management, manufacturing output would have risen faster. Judged by the low level of productivity characterizing much of British industry, there would have been plenty of scope for meeting this higher demand by increasing output per man; but some increase in the labour force would have been required as well. In those circumstances it would have been necessary to restrict the increase in employment in the public sector and – as SET tried to do (see pp. 65–8) – in the private service sector. Unfortunately, the circumstances never arose.

Finally, there is little evidence for the proposition, advanced by Bacon and Eltis among others, that in Britain a high level of public expenditure and the high level of taxation needed to finance it have presented workers with too high a level of public consumption and too low a level of private consumption, and that this has been a major factor behind inflationary wage demands. The level of both taxation and public expenditure in Britain, as a percentage of GNP, is

[1] See Glennerster, 1976, pp. 6–7, for a discussion of this and related points.

lower than in most other Western European countries.[1] Indeed Britain devotes a lower proportion of her GNP to social security, health and welfare provisions than any of the continental EEC countries.[2] There is nothing in this to suggest that Britain is devoting too much to the 'social wage' as opposed to the private wage. British workers may well be discontented with the rate at which their real private wages have been rising, but this reflects the slow growth rate of the whole economy. There is no reason to suppose that they would have welcomed higher levels of privately financed consumption at the expense of lower standards of provision of health, education or other public services, or of lower pensions or other social security benefits.

In a famous phrase coined in the 1950s, J. K. Galbraith wrote of the contrast between 'private affluence and public squalor'.[3] Much comment in the mid-1970s might have led an unwary observer to suppose that in Britain the roles had been reversed – a supposition which closer observation of the scene might have dispelled. It was true that in 1976 and 1977 the level of public expenditure would need to be kept under very tight control if resources were to flow into exports and investment on the scale that was required. But exactly the same was true of private consumption. Britain's economic problem was not that there were too few producers. It was that the producers were not producing enough, not exporting enough and not investing enough. The problem in 1976, in fact, was much the same as it had been for many years.

FUTURE UNCERTAIN

As Britain entered 1976, the economic situation had something of the quality of a nightmare. Unemployment was over 5 per cent – nearly a million and a quarter – and still rising. Prices were 24 per cent higher than a year before. The balance of payments in 1975 showed a current deficit of £1.7 billion. However, the sheer awfulness of the situation had a compensating advantage: it seemed to have engendered a certain realism, a wider recognition of the fact that Britain had for too long been living on borrowed time and

[1] Neild and Ward, 1976. The latest comparable figures relate to 1973. The position will have changed somewhat since then, but probably not enough to alter the basic conclusion.

[2] Glennerster, 1976, p. 6.

[3] Galbraith, 1958.

borrowed money, and a willingness to make the sacrifices necessary to put things right. So at any rate Harold Wilson claimed in a New Year message, and it was to be hoped that he was right; for sacrifices were going to be needed.

The Government had, above all, to do two things in 1976. One was to hold down public expenditure and private consumption enough to ensure that room would be left for the export boom promised by the revival of world trade, and the increase in investment of which the first signs were just beginning to appear. The other was to continue to bring down the rate of inflation by ensuring that the successful £6 a week pay policy, due to expire in July, was followed by a further round of pay restraint. To some extent these two requirements conflicted with each other: a standstill – or worse – in private living standards and the provision of public services was not the most favourable background for further trade union pledges on wage restraint. Somehow the Government had to strike a balance. This was what the public expenditure White Paper, published in February, and the Budget, introduced in April, attempted to do.

The public expenditure White Paper, after pointing out that in the past three years public expenditure had grown by nearly 20 per cent in volume, while output had risen by less than 2 per cent, went on to state that the present intention was 'broadly to stabilize the level of resources taken by expenditure programmes after 1976–77'. If anything, this understated the extent to which public expenditure was going to be restrained: because debt interest was expected to grow by 20 per cent between 1976–77 and 1978–79 (reflecting a continuing, though probably declining, PSBR), total expenditure on programmes (i.e. excluding debt interest) would fall by 1½ per cent over these two years.[1] This unprecedented reduction in public expenditure came under fire from within the Labour Party,[2] but the main criticism of the White Paper came from the Conservatives and the City, who argued that it was not enough to stabilize public expenditure *after* 1976–77: it ought to be stabilized, if not indeed cut back, immediately.[3] The Government had quite a strong case for resisting this argument. Even if immediate cuts could be made without considerable waste – a point on which past experience cast doubt – the effect during 1976 would probably be to increase

[1] In cost terms. In volume terms (i.e. before allowing for the relative price effect) the fall would be about 2 per cent.

[2] For a critical Fabian assessment, see Glennerster, 1976.

[3] Public expenditure was expected to rise by 2½ per cent between 1975–76 and 1976–77, though nearly all of this was accounted for by the rising burden of debt interest.

unemployment even further: there was plenty of slack to accommodate the rising demand for exports and stock-building in 1976; it would be in 1977 that public expenditure (and private consumption) would need to be held firmly in check. Nevertheless, the decision not to cut back expenditure in 1976–77 may have been an error of judgment. Britain was now very much at the mercy of her foreign creditors, and the rather leisurely timetable that the Government appeared to have set itself for reducing public expenditure, and the intense criticism of this in the City, had a bad effect on foreign opinion, and undoubtedly played a part in causing the drastic slide in the sterling exchange rate between March and June (see p. 230).

In his April Budget the Chancellor tackled the second of the Government's critical tasks – getting union agreement on a new round of wage restraint. In an otherwise fairly neutral Budget, he promised income tax concessions totalling almost £1 billion (in a full year) provided that the unions agreed to a 3 per cent limit on wage increases between August 1976 and August 1977.[1] In effect, Healey was saying that if workers tried to get larger wage increases he would ensure that the extra money would be neutralized by higher rates of tax. They would do equally well – and the inflation rate would come down much more – if they accepted smaller increases and paid less income tax. It was a gamble that deserved to pay off, and, in a slightly modified form, it did pay off. The TUC agreed to a formula, somewhat more flexible than the £6 a week formula, that would result in average increases of about 4½ per cent;[2] and this agreement was confirmed by a seventeen-to-one majority at a special TUC conference held in June. It was a remarkable achievement. The unions had agreed to a further year of pay restraint, in the knowledge that this would result in a fall in the living standards of virtually all their members. It was a tribute to the sense of responsibility of the unions, and a measure of the importance which the social contract – after an extremely shaky start – had now assumed.

Nevertheless, Britain was still very far from out of the wood. Foreign debt was still mounting rapidly: the cumulative balance of payments deficit for the three years 1973–75 had been over

[1] These concessions took the form of increases in personal and marriage allowances, and an increase in the threshold at which some of the higher rates of tax commenced. There were also some *unconditional* income tax concessions – notably on children's allowances – but these were largely balanced by increases in indirect taxes.

[2] There was a 5 per cent norm for the increase in a person's total earnings, with a lower limit of £2.50 a week and an upper limit of £4. It was reckoned this would result in average increases of about 4½ per cent (compared with around 10 per cent under the £6 limit).

£6 billion, and a further deficit of well over £1 billion seemed in prospect for 1976. In April the retail price index was still 19 per cent higher than a year before – an improvement on the record 27 per cent increase on a year before which had been registered in August 1975, but still a very high figure compared with other OECD countries. And the fact that the public sector borrowing requirement had been £10.5 billion in 1975–76, and seemed likely to be no smaller in 1976–77, caused concern in the City and elsewhere.[1] Some oil-producers, if they did not move funds out of London, at least became increasingly reluctant to move them in. Traders around the world started to hedge their bets by speeding up sterling payments and delaying foreign exchange receipts. Sterling started to slide, and the slide started to accelerate. The rate against the dollar, which had been over $2 at the beginning of March, fell to $1.70 by early June. The weighted depreciation in relation to the December 1971 Smithsonian agreement increased during the same period from 30 per cent to over 40 per cent.

There was no good economic reason for such a sudden and drastic fall in the external value of the pound,[2] particularly in view of the February public expenditure White Paper and the initial TUC endorsement of the 4½ per cent pay norm early in May. But in the short term, foreign exchange markets have little regard for underlying economic realities. To prevent the depreciation of the pound from getting completely out of hand, the Government hastily arranged a $5.3 billion package of short-term swap agreements with the central banks of the U.S. and a number of other countries: the immediate effect was to push the sterling-dollar rate back up above

[1] This out-turn was very close to what Healey had forecast in his March 1975 Budget – though the City had for long been titillating itself with what it regarded as scare stories of a PSBR of £12 billion or more. Much opinion in the City and abroad was so busy shaking its head and pursing its lips over the size of Britain's PSBR that it entirely failed to notice that in more successful countries the general government deficit (which covers central and local government, though not public corporations) was larger, as a percentage of GDP or GNP, than in Britain. In Germany, for example, it was 6 per cent in 1975, and in Japan 7 per cent, compared with a figure of 5 per cent for Britain (*Economic Trends*, May 1976, p. 85). Whatever else might be said about Britain's public sector deficit, it could hardly be regarded – as the City was inclined to regard it – as the sole source of the nation's troubles.

[2] This was particularly evident in the changed relationship between the pound and the dollar. As recently as March 1975 the exchange rate had been $2.40; thus the fall over the fifteen months to June 1976 was 30 per cent. Yet over this period American prices rose by 8 per cent compared with a rise in Britain of 25 per cent – a 17 per cent difference. The March 1975 and June 1976 rates could not both be right. Sterling was probably overvalued on the first occasion; but it was certainly undervalued on the second.

\$1.75. But even this implied a depreciation of sterling against the weighted average of other currencies of nearly 10 per cent since the beginning of the year. This would make British exports very competitive, and should add extra power to the export boom that already seemed to be under way.[1] But by raising the sterling cost of imports it would before long raise retail prices by 2 or 3 per cent, and put additional pressure on the 4½ per cent pay policy.[2] And although the short-term credits had stopped and reversed the fall in sterling for the time being, there was no guarantee that when they expired in December 1976 confidence in sterling would have been restored. If it had not been, the only recourse would be to the IMF – a body whose instincts lie much closer to monetarism than to Keynesian demand management. The conditions attached to an IMF loan, in terms of cuts in the PSBR and targets for the growth of the money supply, might well please the Conservatives and the City. But to many in the Labour Party, contemplating the very high unemployment figures, their acceptance could represent a humiliating surrender to a dangerously primitive and blinkered economic dogma.

The prospect that the Government's policies might soon be dictated by the IMF, and the more general feeling that the free trade policies which Britain had been pursuing for more than twenty years had left the country with a chronically sick balance of payments which was the immediate cause of potential IMF intervention, seemed to strengthen the case – long espoused by the Left of the Labour Party – for import controls. True, the traditional arguments for solving a balance of payments deficit by devaluing rather than by imposing controls on imports remained superficially persuasive. Unlike import controls, devaluation raised exports as well as reducing imports; it operated automatically, instead of requiring an elaborate administrative apparatus; it did not lead to retaliation; and it did not specifically protect inefficient industries.[3] But by the middle of 1976 these arguments, when closely scrutinized, were looking less convincing. The 40 per cent devaluation of sterling since December 1971 did not seem to have resulted in an increase in the volume of exports

[1] Between the third quarter of 1975 and the first quarter of 1976 the volume of exports rose at an annual rate of 20 per cent.

[2] Ironically, in view of the bitter opposition on the left of the Labour Party to Britain's membership of the EEC, and in particular to the Common Agricultural Policy (CAP), it was precisely the way in which the CAP now operated, by reference to imaginary exchange rates for agricultural produce (the 'green pound'), that prevented food prices in Britain from bearing the full brunt of the fall in the sterling exchange rate.

[3] See Corden *et al.*, 1975, for a new statement of this argument.

on the scale that might have been expected – and had certainly failed to stem the rising tide of manufactured imports. It seemed, in fact, as if the price elasticities of demand for both exports and imports might be considerably lower than was usually assumed, so that a very large devaluation would be needed to put the balance of payments right. But a very large devaluation would raise import prices, and thus reduce real incomes, on a scale which might set off an explosive new inflationary spiral. Import controls on manufactured goods, on the other hand, while risking some retaliation from other countries, would avoid a big rise in import prices, and permit the balance of payments deficit to be eliminated at a higher level of output, employment and real income than if the problem were left to be solved solely by the economy's response to changes in relative prices. Moreover, a convincing case can be made that a guarantee of some years of protection from foreign competition may be a necessary condition of rationalizing and raising the efficiency of some of Britain's industries.[1]

There was a certain piquancy in the calls during 1976 for the use of controls rather than of the price mechanism – particularly on the part of those Labour economists and politicians who had advocated devaluation a decade before. For the great long-time disbeliever in the price mechanism, the great believer in physical controls, was Harold Wilson, and early in 1976 he had gracefully – and unexpectedly – left the stage. He had reached the traditional civil service retiring age of sixty, and as a superb civil servant *manqué*, this was not without significance. He had been the longest serving peacetime Prime Minister since Gladstone, and as a master politician, this was not without significance either. As a personification of the Jekyll and Hyde syndrome, he carried a heavy responsibility for the nation's economic failures. But in very difficult times he had held both the Labour Party and the country together. When leaving Downing Street for the last time he may have thought, but did not say, 'Après moi, le déluge'.

[1] For a full statement of these arguments see CEPG, 1975 and 1976.

Chapter 7
SOME CONCLUDING REMARKS

In 1964 there was widespread dissatisfaction with Britain's economic performance. Unemployment had only recently come down from what was regarded as the intolerable level of 2½ per cent. Over the past decade GDP had grown at a rate of only 3 per cent – much more slowly than in other comparable countries. Inflation was eroding the value of the currency at an annual rate of 3 or 4 per cent. The balance of payments on current account was running a deficit of £400 million, or about 1.3 per cent of the GDP. And – according to the Labour Party at any rate – income and wealth were unjustly distributed. During the election campaign of October 1964, the major parties vied with each other in promising to make things much better in the future.

A true prophecy of the state of the economy in 1976 would not have been believed.[1] Unemployment in the early part of that year was over 5 per cent, and showed few signs of coming down. The growth rate since 1964, so far from attaining the 4 per cent Neddy target on which the policies of 1963 and 1964 had been based, had been only 2 per cent. Prices were more than 2½ times as high as in 1964 – an average inflation rate of 9 per cent a year, and one much faster at the end of the period than the beginning. The balance of payments deficit in 1975 had been £1.7 billion, representing nearly 2 per cent of the GDP. And although the upper income groups had been hard hit by the combination of inflation, lower profit margins and high marginal rates of taxation, there did not seem to have been any large or sustained improvement in the relative position of those in the bottom fifth of the income distribution.

[1] A bold attempt was made in 1965 to discuss the shape of the British economy in the mid-1970s (Beckerman and Associates, 1965). Although this was in no sense a forecast, the exercise was based on what was regarded as the reasonable assumption that between 1963 and 1975 the GNP would rise by 56 per cent. The actual rise was 31 per cent.

It was possible to find excuses and consolations for this sorry state of affairs. It was true, for example, that the terms of trade had deteriorated by 20 per cent since 1972. But the cumulative worsening over the twelve years since 1964 was only 15 per cent, which could account for only a fraction of the fact that real incomes in 1976 were so far below anything that would have seemed credible in 1964. Similarly, it was true that in 1976 Britain, despite its economic shortcomings, was still a reasonably tolerant, humane and cohesive society – something which the agitations set off by the Paris *événements* of May 1968, the steadily worsening situation in Ulster, and the political confrontations of the early 1970s had from time to time brought into question. Even so, the idea that one had to take comfort from this sort of reflection would have seemed very odd in 1964.

The hard facts were unavoidable. The performance of the economy since 1964 had been worse than most observers would have thought possible; and the situation in 1976 was so bad that it was reasonable to wonder whether the sacrifices that would be needed to get the economy back into internal and external balance could really be exacted by a government which had to rule by consent.

What had gone wrong? In 1976, as in other years, there was no shortage of explanations: everyone had at least one pet theory, and some people had several. The examination conducted in this book of the economic policy pursued during the period, and the forces which shaped it, suggests that much of what went wrong can be found in four sets of factors. For convenience they are here called *structural, technical, managemental* and *political.* Although they are all interlinked with each other, they can in broad terms be distinguished, and discussed separately.

STRUCTURAL FACTORS

The structural factors which have played a part in holding back Britain's economy have been not so much physical as psychological. There is, to be sure, the all too visible and tangible legacy of the industrial revolution: industries that are decaying, towns that are rotting, firms that are in the wrong places, factories and mills that are too small and too out of date, workers with obsolete skills. But all this would have mattered much less if these structural anachronisms and rigidities had not had their counterpart in the hearts and minds of men. No foreign observer ever fails to note how far British society is still riddled with class distinctions and class antagonisms, and permeated by the suspicious awareness of the difference between Us and Them. No doubt this explanation of the nation's ills is sometimes overdone: Britain's class divisions have practically become a tourist attraction. It can certainly be argued that class divisions are less marked, and much less destructive, than they were forty or even twenty years ago.

Nevertheless, there is something in the class explanation of Britain's economic weakness. More than most other comparable countries, Britain is still two nations – not least in the industrial arena. Far too many managers view their workers as the enemy – idle, shiftless, dishonest and irresponsible. Far too many workers see management as the enemy – privileged, inefficient and unaccountable. Managers fail to invest and modernize because 'confidence is lacking', and fail to involve workers in decision-making because decision-making is the prerogative of management, and none of the workers' business. Workers, for their part, refuse to yield an inch to the foe: they resist the introduction of new techniques, stop work for trivial reasons long before grievance procedures are exhausted, insist on manning levels appropriate to a bygone age, and refuse to change jobs in response to changing patterns of demand or technology. This, at any rate, is what it often looks like. The philosophy is the philosophy of the zero-sum game: if one side wins, the other loses, and nobody wants to be the side that loses. In fact, it is a positive-sum game: both sides stand to gain if they co-operate more effectively. Neither side can raise its living standards very far at the expense of the other; this can be done only by joining forces to defeat the recalcitrance of the physical universe and the threatening competition of better-organized foreigners. But, however easy it may be to discern all this from an ivory tower, it is a perspective that folk-memories and entrenched attitudes all too often obscure on the shop floor.

But it is not only in the persistence of class antagonisms that the trouble lies. Britain has been slow to adapt its values, its priorities, its policies, its educational institutions to the position in which it found itself after the war: no longer the centre of a great and economically beneficial empire, but a middle rank industrial country needing to compete with other highly efficient economies if it was to survive. Even as late in the day as the mid-1970s Britain did not seem to have come fully to terms with its new role. It was not difficult to see it – as many foreign observers did – as a lethargic country, clinging to old ways, reluctant to change, unwilling to face up to the implications of the revolutionary shifts taking place around it, and better at debating its problems than at doing anything to solve them.

It may be, of course, that contemporary Britain is not cut out for continual changes and a rapid rate of growth. In a world in which change is often regarded as synonymous with progress, and the new is often confused with the good, such a posture would have something to commend it. But the corollary of such a posture is that average living standards can rise only very slowly and – if intolerable poverty at the bottom of the income distribution is to be relieved – the living standards of the better-off cannot rise at all. Such a corollary has never been accepted. People want to have their cake and eat it too: they want ever-rising living standards, but they also want to stay in the same jobs in the same places and do the same old things in the same old way. Such contradictory demands, and the structural factors which lie behind them, constitute an unpromising background for the conduct of a successful economic policy.

TECHNICAL FACTORS

The technical factors which have had an adverse effect on economic performance are of two main kinds, both arising from lack of knowledge and both, up to a point, unavoidable. Forecasts are rarely highly accurate; and lack of knowledge about how the economy works means that policy measures sometimes have different effects from those intended. Although in practice it may be difficult to tell whether things have gone wrong because the forecast was bad, or because the policies adopted did not work in the way anticipated, in principle the distinction is clear.

On a number of occasions since the early 1960s the forecasts have gone wrong. One case was the failure to foresee the strength of the 1963–64 boom, and the consequent worsening in the balance of payments. Another was the consistent underestimation, over much of the period, of the upward trend of manufactured imports. Another was the failure to anticipate the full effects of the 1973–74 world commodity boom. There were also a number of cases where it was not so much the forecasts of exogenous variables that were at fault, as the inability of the forecasting models employed to relate one variable to another with any great accuracy. One example of this kind of technical failure was the unexpected extent to which the adverse demand-inflation effect of rapidly rising expenditure from

1972 onwards outweighed the favourable cost-inflation effect of rapidly rising output. Another was the way in which big increases in the money supply in 1972 and 1973 led to a rise in the price of existing assets – particularly land and property – rather than to the creation of new assets.

Although none of these errors was unimportant, it is hard to believe that, had they been avoided by a combination of better forecasts and more realistic economic models, policy decisions would have been substantially different. About two other examples, however, it is less easy to be sure. One was the overestimation of the growth of demand at the beginning of 1970. A more accurate forecast here would have led to a more expansionary Budget in 1970.[1] This might have resulted in the re-election of a Labour government in June 1970, with effects on subsequent history that can only be speculated about; but even in lieu of that, the recession of 1970–72 would have been less severe, and the measures taken by the Conservatives to get out of it less wildly expansionary. Some of the country's subsequent problems might have been distinctly smaller. The second example is the related phenomenon of the surge in public expenditure from 1972 onwards. Had the extent of this been properly anticipated, steps might have been taken earlier to cut back the growth of public expenditure to something more closely in line with the growth in output.

Nevertheless, it would probably be wrong to ascribe very much of the poor performance of the economy over the past ten or fifteen years to errors in forecasts or economic models. Unless one goes the whole hog with the monetarist or New Cambridge schools and abandons stabilization policy altogether – and this, as was argued on pp. 159–64 and 194–8, would probably result in an even more unacceptable outcome – one must accept that there will always be errors in the forecasts, and knowledge of how the economy works will always be less than complete. The more such technical sources of error can be eliminated, the better; but the real trick is to ensure that unavoidable errors of this kind are not compounded by avoidable errors of other kinds.

MANAGEMENTAL FACTORS

A third group of factors which has played a role in Britain's un-

[1] But there is some suspicion that the error was less technical than managemental; see p. 238.

impressive economic performance might be described as *managemental.*[1] In this category fall policies and decisions which reflect neither technical judgments on the one hand, nor party political pressures on the other. In practice it is often impossible to say just where technical judgments merge into managemental ones, or managemental judgments into political ones, but in principle the distinction seems useful.

It is tempting to think of technical judgments as being made by the economists and statisticians who are responsible for producing economic forecasts and advising on the effects of using particular economic instruments; managemental judgments as being made by the small number of senior civil servants who advise ministers about policy; and political judgments as being made by ministers. There is indeed some truth in this simple assignment of different functions to different groups in the machinery of government, particularly in the case of the clear distinction between technical and political functions: it is no good blaming politicians for errors in forecasts or for relying on figures which subsequently turn out to have been wrong; nor is it any good blaming economic forecasters for decisions which are taken on political grounds. The managemental function is more difficult to assign without ambiguity. On the borderline between managemental and technical factors there is not only the problem of technical judgments being made by the civil servants who are exercising the managemental function; there is also the fact that managemental judgments are bound to be heavily influenced by technical judgments, and by the economists who provide the forecasts and advise on the likely consequences of particular actions. An example of the first kind – where in a sense the technical function was usurped by the administrative civil servants – seems to have been the raising of the forecasts prepared at the beginning of 1970 (see footnote, p. 148). An example of the second kind – where a managemental decision was heavily influenced by the technical structure of the Treasury's forecasting model – was probably the 1972–73 strategy of giving a huge stimulus to the economy and expecting rapidly rising output to neutralize the inflationary effects of rapidly rising demand. Treasury economists and Treasury administrators are, however, all civil servants, and the overlap between technical and managemental judgments, and the question of who does what, is of

[1] This rare and somewhat unattractive word has been pressed into service to describe mistakes in managing the economy which stemmed from errors of judgment on the part of Ministers or the civil servants who advised them.

secondary interest compared with the overlap between the managemental and political functions, and the question of how far managemental judgments are made by ministers, and how far party political ones are made by civil servants.

There used to be a myth about the way British government worked, according to which ministers took office, told an impartial and acquiescent civil service what they wanted done, and let the civil servants get on with it. By this account, managemental judgments – and misjudgments – would be made by ministers. Subsequently, and particularly over the past decade or two, another myth has developed, much favoured by the Labour Left and, to a smaller extent, the Conservative Right. According to this, ministers take office, are told by a biased and domineering civil service what they ought to do and say, and get on with it. With this version, mistakes in managing the economy are the fault of the civil service. Just where, between these two diametrically opposed myths, the truth lies is difficult to say, partly because it lies in different places with different governments, different ministers, and different departments. The first myth can approximate to the truth when an able and determined minister, with the moral authority stemming from an overwhelming victory for his party in a general election, comes into a department where senior officials are weak or divided, or alternatively where the department's own instincts and inclinations coincide with those of the incoming minister. The second myth can be very close to reality when a department with pronounced views about how to solve the problems within its province is headed by a weak minister, particularly if the authority of the government as a whole is in question. Somewhere in between these two extremes lies the majority of cases.[1]

Any list of managemental misjudgments is bound to be subjective, and is likely to contain examples where technical and political factors were present in some degree. But there are certainly a number of instances since 1964 of bad managemental decisions having an adverse effect on the country's economic performance. One such instance was the failure of the Labour Government to devalue in 1964 or, failing that, in 1966. Although there was a political element

[1] The case where a strong minister with radical views comes into conflict with a strong permanent secretary determined to resist or emasculate them is probably fairly rare. The most famous and best documented case of the relations between a minister and his department (Crossman, 1975) appears to describe such a relationship, though the permanent secretary's version was somewhat different (Sharp, 1975).

in this – Harold Wilson's fear that Labour would be damagingly branded as the party of devaluation – it was essentially a managemental decision based on a misjudgment of the seriousness of the disequilibrium in the balance of payments, and of the role of Britain and sterling in the world economy. It was almost entirely a ministerial decision. While many government economists (particularly the temporary ones brought in by Labour) were in favour of devaluation, permanent officials – while in many cases probably against – recognized that it was an issue of such importance and of such possible political ramifications that they bent over backwards to maintain a neutral posture. The failure to devalue at the right time, as was argued in Chapter 3, was to have an adverse effect on the economy for many years.

If Labour's greatest managemental mistake lay in not devaluing earlier in a move to get securely-based, export-led growth, the Conservatives' greatest managemental mistake lay in giving far too great a stimulus to private consumption and public expenditure, in a way that practically guaranteed that the economy would be brought to a halt by a balance of payments crisis. Although the Barber boom was triggered off by strong ministerial concern with the implications for the party's image of high and rising unemployment that the Government seemed to be doing nothing about, it seems to have been supported, in general terms, by the civil service and the Treasury economic establishment. They correctly perceived the recession of 1971–72 to be the result of the failure of the Government to apply orthodox Keynesian remedies to a situation of sluggish demand. But the hope that a sufficient expansion of domestic demand would soon stimulate productive investment and – helped by a floating exchange rate – lead to an adequate growth of exports proved much too optimistic. A similar managemental miscalculation had been made on a smaller scale in 1963–64, when Mr Maudling tried his dash for growth. There was little excuse for its being made again.

Another adverse managemental factor lay in the failure to realize how rapidly public expenditure was rising, and a failure to bring its growth under more effective control. This miscalculation was first made under the Conservatives, but continued under Labour during 1974 and 1975. To some extent, as was indicated earlier, this was a technical failure, in that the Treasury was slow to grasp the implications of controlling public expenditure at constant prices at a time of rapid inflation. To some extent, too, it resulted from the fact that the scale and nature of public expenditure is one of the main sources of disagreement between the two main political parties. Nevertheless, the fact that between 1972 and 1976 public expenditure rose very much faster than the GNP must be regarded as to a very large extent a failure of economic management which in various ways had damaging consequences for the performance of the economy as a whole.

POLITICAL FACTORS

The final reason for Britain's poor economic performance since 1964 lies in the way the political system has been working. Both Labour and Conservative parties, while in opposition, have succumbed to the temptation to condemn a large proportion of the government's policies and have promised to reverse many of these policies when they themselves took office. The result has been a fatal lack of continuity. Incoming governments have spent their first year or two abolishing or drastically modifying the measures – often quite sensible – of their predecessors, and pressing ahead with the measures – often unrealistic or irrelevant – which they have formulated in opposition. After a year or two they have come to closer terms with reality, and changed course, but by that time much harm has been done, and the benefits that would have accrued from continuing the policies they inherited have been lost.

The most important victim of this Jekyll and Hyde syndrome has been incomes policy. This is a crucial new policy instrument. If one rejects the monetarist thesis that a complex modern society, with powerful trade unions capable of crippling the economy almost overnight if their demands are not met, can be satisfactorily run simply be regulating the money supply, then an incomes policy is essential if reasonably full employment is to be combined with a tolerable degree of price stability. But an incomes policy, usually widely welcomed when first introduced because it offers relief from mounting inflation, always becomes unpopular before long, as those affected come to focus more on the restraints it imposes on them than on the benefits they receive from the restraints it imposes on others. Such a policy can only succeed in the long run if it is consistently supported by both the main parties, and not regularly repudiated by the one in opposition in the hope of gleaning electoral dividends. Conservative attacks made inevitable Labour's abandonment of its incomes policy in 1969, and led to the 1969–70 wage explosion; and Labour attacks on the belatedly-adopted incomes policy of the Heath administration made inevitable the round of 30 per cent wage increases in 1974–75 which gave Britain an inflation rate from which full recovery is proving exceedingly difficult. If the Opposition had in each case refrained from making party capital out of the Government's incomes policy, the rate of inflation during the 1970s would probably have been considerably lower, and the general performance of the economy considerably better. It was a welcome change that Conservative attacks on Labour's 1975–76 incomes policy were, at any rate at first, muted and oblique – indeed from the Heath wing of the party the policy received some support; but as 1976 wore on, Opposition speakers increasingly ignored its advantages and emphasized its disadvantages.

Incomes policy, however, is a necessary rather than a sufficient condition of a satisfactory economic performance. What really matters is the efficiency with which resources are utilized, and the extent to which productive potential is increased by investment and the introduction of new technologies. Here Britain's record has been dismal, and here, too, political factors have been partly to blame. Quite apart from the adverse effects on investment of the stop-go cycle – partly a product of technical and managemental errors, but also the result of the pre-election boom required by party political considerations – have been the effects of the chopping and changing of governmental attitudes, and assistance, to industry. Labour replaced investment allowances by investment grants; the Conservatives changed back to investment allowances. Labour introduced SET; the Conservatives abolished it. Labour introduced REP, to make more use of idle resources in the regions; the Conservatives made no attempt to maintain its effective value. Labour set up the IRC; the Conservatives did away with it. This process shows no signs of coming to an end: in 1976 Michael Heseltine, the Conservative Opposition's chief spokesman on industry matters, pledged that the next Tory government would repeal Labour's 1975 Industry Act and abolish the NEB.[1] Nor were the nationalized industries immune: put on a realistic footing by Labour's White Paper (HMG, 1967 (ii)), they were subjected in the early Conservative years to haphazard interference with their financial targets, and futile attempts to hive off their profitable activities. Similarly, the Conservatives agreed a long-term policy for the steel industry in the early 1970s; in the mid-1970s Labour drastically amended it. And so on.

[1] Reported in *The Times*, 10 July 1976.

The story is much the same in other parts of the field. By the end of the 1960s, for example, the Conservatives were talking as though there was scope for massive cuts in public expenditure without anybody getting hurt very much – conveniently ignoring the social, demographic and environmental realities which had caused irresistible demands for rising public expenditure. When they took office in 1970 they found that unless the whole fabric of the welfare state was to be destroyed – the political implications of which they were not willing to face – the scope for cuts was very limited. Such cuts as they did make were either pure sleight-of-hand (like the replacement of investment grants by investment allowances) or (like the cuts in the subsidies for school milk and meals) petty and divisive. Labour, by contrast, tends to lose sight in opposition of the hard facts of public finance which it has painfully learnt in office, and to talk as though large increases in public expenditure can be painlessly met out of the fruits of faster growth. Hence its insistence, in 1974 and 1975, on increasing public expenditure in the form of subsidies of all kinds, even though public expenditure was already rocketing as a result of Mr Barber's recklessly expansionary measures of 1971–72. Not for nearly two years did the Labour Government get a real grip on public expenditure, with the White Paper of February 1976.

At the heart of the Jekyll and Hyde problem lies the role of the Opposition. The existence of an Opposition free to criticize the Government as it chooses is widely regarded as the acid test of a modern democracy.[1] It is clear that the democratic system will be something of a sham if the Opposition opposes in only a formal and ritualistic way, in practice rubberstamping whatever the Government does. This will deny legitimacy to genuine opposition, compelling it to take extra-parliamentary or illegal forms. The system of parliamentary democracy will be jeopardized: the stage will be set for revolution or totalitarian repression. It is presumably considerations of this kind which underlie the doctrine that 'it is the duty of the Opposition to oppose'. First formulated in the eighteenth century by George Tierney,[2] this doctrine became widely accepted in the nineteenth century,[3] and still enjoys wide currency today. It was an article of faith with the late Richard Crossman, and was recently

[1] Ionescu and de Madariaga, 1972, p. 9.

[2] 'The duty of an Opposition is very simple – it is to oppose everything and propose nothing.' (Quoted in Hanham, 1971.)

[3] Hanham, 1971, p. 137.

propounded by Reginald Maudling, Shadow Foreign Secretary and former Chancellor of the Exchequer.[1]

In the nineteenth century this doctrine may have been harmless enough: the Government's role in the economy was a limited one, and so correspondingly was the impact of abrupt changes in government policy. Nowadays, with extensive government intervention in the economy, things are different. Modern democracy may not work properly if parliamentary opposition is of no more than a token kind; but neither will it work properly if the Opposition automatically and vociferously opposes everything the Government does. In a world of limited resources and virtually unlimited wants, any government must make many hard and unpopular decisions. If the Opposition regularly tries to cash in on this unpopularity for electoral reasons, by condemning such decisions, however justified and necessary, and promising to reverse them, a different kind of threat is posed to the democratic system. The electorate will be encouraged to believe that there is an easy way out, that hard choices can be avoided, and that all their problems stem from the mistakes of a confused and incompetent government. The result will be precisely what has so frequently been witnessed since 1964: the Government is deflected from the path of responsible action by the need to protect its flank against Opposition attacks in an attempt to ward off electoral disaster; and when the Opposition in due course becomes the Government, it is committed by its conduct and promises in opposition to reversing many of its predecessor's policies, however sensible, and pushing through new measures of its own, however silly and irrelevant. The resulting poor performance of the economy can itself become a potential threat to a democratic system of government.

This is not at all the same thing as saying that *all* the early policies pursued by incoming governments since 1964 have been misguided, and that it has taken a year or two for common sense to break through. The two main political parties, as was argued in Chapter 2, have different values and philosophies, and are largely supported by different groups within the community. It is not only inevitable, but right, that many policies should be changed or modified when one party replaces the other in government, and sometimes the problem is not that the changes are too easily made, but that they meet too much resistance from the civil service and the Establishment gener-

[1] 'An Opposition is bound to do all it can to frustrate the Government in domestic affairs.' (*The Times*, 21 January 1976.)

ally. Active Labour supporters, for example, who work for the return of a Labour government so that it may change society, argue that the first year or two is the time when it fights to put its principles into practice, and the later period is when it surrenders to the forces of reaction, worn down and outmanouevred by the civil service. This view is not without some validity, particularly where it is a question of Labour's egalitarian policies for income distribution and the social services. But it is not a compelling case as far as the main consensus objectives of economic policy since 1964 are concerned. Here, the Jekyll and Hyde analogy seems the more accurate one.

No easy solution to the Jekyll and Hyde problem suggests itself. One possibility might be to make public funds available to the Opposition so that it can avail itself of more advice and research. But although this might improve the briefing of shadow ministers for debates in the House of Commons, it would be unlikely to change the fundamental situation very much. Policy in opposition tends to get made by the zealots in each party, who are always the quickest to denounce what the other party is doing, and always the keenest to introduce sweeping changes. Their influence might not be much diminished – it might even be enhanced – by state financing of the Opposition. A much more radical solution – increasingly advocated nowadays – would be electoral reform, designed essentially to provide the Liberals with a number of seats in the House of Commons more closely commensurate with the number of votes they get in general elections. The idea is that if the Liberals had 100 seats, either a Labour or a Conservative government would require their formal or informal support, and would only obtain this by jettisoning the more extreme elements in their programme. Although this solution has its attractions, it suffers from a fatal drawback. Nobody can predict what would happen in practice. The balance of power might turn out to be held not by the centre, but by a collection of extremists – the National Front, the Workers' Revolutionary Party, or simply those bent on total devolution for this or that bit of the United Kingdom. There is something in the argument that the present electoral system has served the nation well for 150 years, while the Jekyll and Hyde problem has only existed in acute form for fifteen years, and that dropping the former would be a very drastic way of trying to cure the latter.

The answer must lie, in the last resort, with the politicians themselves, and with those whose actions and words influence the climate of opinion within which the politicians operate. Whatever the differences of emphasis, the main objectives of economic policy are sufficiently common to the two main parties to permit a broadly consensus approach. Such an approach is essential if continuity is to be ensured. It can, of course, be argued that Britain's economic problems cannot be solved by such a consensus approach: that the mixed economy suffers from fatal contradictions, and that the economic conditions which people demand – full employment, higher living standards, stable prices – can only be provided if there is a radical change in the organization of society. The Left regard as essential a drastic move towards far greater state control of the economy; the Right regard as essential a drastic move towards a free market economy. Such claims cannot be disproved; indeed they may even be correct. But one thing that is conclusively demonstrated by the history of the last decade or so is the impossibility of achieving drastic change – in either direction – by democratic procedures: the resistance is too strong. The Conservatives' Industrial Relations Act, for example, was mild compared with the curbs that would have to be imposed on the unions if a free market economy were to be re-established; and the fate of the Industrial Relations Act was described in Chapter 5. Similarly, the Labour Left's plan to take a controlling interest in twenty-five of the 100 largest manufacturing companies early in the life of the 1974 Labour Government – a large but far from final step on the road to socialism – came nowhere near commanding a majority even in the Labour Cabinet, let alone in the nation as a whole.

It would seem, then, that if the system is to remain democratic, drastic change must be ruled out, at least for the present. And if drastic change is ruled out, the only answer is to make the present system work better. Changes there must assuredly be, but they must command sufficient agreement to stand a good chance of not being reversed when a new government takes over. The Opposition must, at all costs, be at liberty to disagree with the Government, and to use its influence to improve and modify government policies. But it must resist the temptation to turn liberty into licence. By the same token, there is a responsibility on the Government not to pursue policies which are so divisive that the Opposition feels bound to pledge itself to reverse them when it takes office.

The economic problems that Britain faces in the late 1970s are formidable indeed. Full employment must be restored. Inflation must be brought under control. A large balance of payments deficit must be eliminated, as must an enormous budget deficit. The economy must be got back onto a respectable growth path. There must be more investment and innovation, more training and retraining, more job mobility, more willingness to change old ways, more co-operation between management and men. Inequities in the distribution of wealth and income must be reduced – not least the haphazard inequities that have developed in recent years in the wake of rampant inflation and rough-and-ready incomes policies. All this will require intelligent, tough, sustained policies which have the backing of both major parties, and which accordingly are not constantly criticized by the Opposition and drastically changed each time a new government takes office.

Nor is this a requirement only for the rest of the 1970s. Peering into the future one can discern, however dimly, a world in which the problems of resource depletion and the disposal of the by-products of industrial civilization loom increasingly large; in which the Malthusian nightmare of the planet's population being controlled by famine and plague becomes ever more real; in which the huge imbalances between the wealth and living standards of the world's have and have-not nations threaten the most explosive possibilities; in which material living standards in countries like Britain must cease to rise and perhaps start to fall. In such a world Britain will no longer be able to afford the luxury of making or breaking economic policies for the sake of party politics or the whims of particular politicians. There will be plenty of things for the parties to disagree about, without their disagreements paralysing the operation of the economy. It is high time the political parties sorted out the difference between the things which, as a nation, we can afford to disagree about, and the things which we cannot.

SOURCES AND REFERENCES

ABRAMS, Mark, 1960. *Must Labour Lose* (Penguin Books)

ALEXANDER, Andrew and WATKINS, Alan, 1970. *The Making of the Prime Minister 1970* (Macdonald Unit 75)

ARMSTRONG, Sir William, 1968. *Some Practical Problems in Demand Management* (Stamp Memorial Lecture – University of London)

ARTIS, Michael, 1972. 'Fiscal Policy for Stabilization' *in* Beckerman (editor) 1972

ASH, J. C. K. and SMYTH, D. J., 1974. *Forecasting the U.K. Economy* (Heinemann)

ATKINSON, A. B., 1972. *Unequal Shares* (Allen Lane The Penguin Press)

BACON, Robert and ELTIS, Walter, 1976. *Britain's Economic Problem: Too Few Producers* (Macmillan)

BALACS, P. D., 1972. 'Economic Data and Economic Policy', *Lloyds Bank Review,* April 1972

BALOGH, Thomas, 1970. *Labour and Inflation* (Fabian Tract 403)

BALOGH, Thomas, 1974. Letter to *The Times,* 28 January 1974

BANK OF ENGLAND, 1971 (i). *Competition and credit control*

BANK OF ENGLAND, 1971 (ii). *Reserve Ratios and Special Deposits*

BAUCHET, Pierre, 1964. *Economic Planning – the French Experience* (Heinemann)

BECKERMAN, Wilfred, 1962. 'Projecting Europe's Growth', *Economic Journal,* December 1962

BECKERMAN, Wilfred and Associates, 1965. *The British Economy in 1975* (Cambridge University Press)

BECKERMAN, Wilfred (editor), 1972. *The Labour Government's Economic Record: 1964–1970* (Duckworth)

BEHREND, Hilde, 1972. 'Public acceptability and a workable incomes policy' *in* Blackaby (editor), 1972

BISPHAM, J. A., 1975. 'The New Cambridge and Monetarist Criticisms of Conventional Economic Policy-Making', *National Institute Economic Review,* November 1975

BLACKABY, Frank (editor), 1972. *An Incomes Policy for Britain* (Heinemann)

BLONDEL, Jean, 1963, 1974. *Voters, Parties and Leaders* (Penguin Books)

BRANDON, Henry, 1966. *In the Red: the Struggle for Sterling 1964–66* (Deutsch)

BRAY, Jeremy, 1970. 'The Road to Faster Growth', *The Economist,* May 1970

BRAY, Jeremy, 1971. 'Dynamic Equations for Economic Forecasting', *Journal of the Royal Statistical Society,* Series A, 1971

BREAK, G. F., 1957. 'Income Taxes and Incentives to Work', *American Economic Review,* September 1957

BRECHLING, Frank and WOLFE, J. N., 1965. 'The End of Stop-Go', *Lloyds Bank Review,* January 1965

BRISTOW, J. A., 1968. 'Taxation and Income Stabilisation', *Economic Journal,* June 1968

BRITTAN, Samuel, 1967. *Inquest on Planning in Britain* (PEP Vol. 33 no. 499)

BRITTAN, Samuel, 1968. *Left or Right: The Bogus Dilemma* (Secker and Warburg)

BRITTAN, Samuel, 1969, 1971. *Steering the Economy* (Secker and Warburg). (Page references in text are to 1971 Pelican edition)

BRITTAN, Samuel, 1975. *Second Thoughts on Full Employment Policy* (Centre for Policy Studies)

BROWN, A. J., 1967. 'The Green Paper on the Development Areas', *National Institute Economic Review,* May 1967

BROWN, A. J., 1968. 'Regional Problems and Regional Policy', *National Institute Economic Review,* November 1968

BROWN, George, 1971. *In my Way* (Victor Gollancz)

BUCHAN, Alasdair, 1972. *The Right to Work* (Calder and Boyars)

BUTLER, D. E. and ROSE, Richard, 1960. *The British General Election of 1959* (Macmillan)

BUTLER, D. E. and KING, Anthony, 1965. *The British General Election of 1964* (Macmillan)

BUTLER, D. E. and KING, Anthony, 1966. *The British General Election of 1966* (Macmillan)

BUTLER, D. E. and STOKES, Donald, 1969. *Political Change in Britain: Forces shaping Electoral Choice* (Macmillan)

BUTLER, D. E. and PINTO-DUSCHINSKY, Michael, 1971. *The British General Election of 1970* (Macmillan)

BUTLER, D. E. and KAVANAGH, Dennis, 1974. *The British General Election of February 1974* (Macmillan)

CAIRNCROSS, Alec (editor), 1970. *The Managed Economy* (Blackwell)

CAIRNCROSS, Frances and McRAE, Hamish, 1975. *The Second Great Crash* (Methuen)

CASTLE, Barbara, 1971 (i). 'Understanding Mr. Carr – Round I', *New Statesman,* 5 February 1971

CASTLE, Barbara, 1971 (ii). 'Freedom under Licence', *New Statesman,* 26 February 1971

CAVES, Richard E. and Associates, 1968. *Britain's Economic Prospects* (The Brookings Institution, George Allen and Unwin)

CEPG, 1975. *Economic Policy Review No. 1,* February 1975 (Cambridge Department of Applied Economics)

CEPG, 1976. *Economic Policy Review No. 2,* March 1976 (Cambridge Department of Applied Economics)

CLEGG, Hugh, 1971. *How to Run an Incomes Policy and Why We Made Such a Mess of the Last One* (Heinemann)

COLE, H. S. D. and others, 1973. *Thinking About the Future* (Chatto and Windus)

CONSERVATIVE POLITICAL CENTRE, 1968. *Fair Deal at Work*

CORDEN, W. M., LITTLE, I. M. D. and SCOTT, M., FG., 1975. *Import Controls versus Devaluation and Britain's Economic Prospects* (Trade Policy Research Centre, Guest Paper No. 2)

CORNER, D. C., 1969. 'Recent Trends in Retail Distribution', *National Westminster Bank Review,* May 1969

CRIPPS, Francis, GODLEY, Wynne and FETHERSTON, Martin, 1974. Evidence to the Expenditure Committee, Ninth Report, *Public Expenditure, Inflation and the Balance of Payments,* Session 1974 (HMSO, HC 328, 30 July 1974)

CROSLAND, Anthony, 1956. *The Future of Socialism* (Jonathan Cape)

CROSLAND, Anthony, 1960. *Can Labour Win?* (Fabian Tract 324)

CROSLAND, Anthony, 1971. *A Social Democratic Britain* (Fabian Tract 404)

CROSLAND, Anthony, 1974. *Socialism Now* (Jonathan Cape)

CROSSMAN, Richard, 1960. *Labour in the Affluent Society* (Fabian Tract 325)

CROSSMAN, Richard, 1975. *The Diaries of a Cabinet Minister Volume One 1964–66* (Hamish Hamilton and Jonathan Cape)

CURWEN, P. J. and FOWLER, A. H., 1976. *Economic Policy* (Macmillan)

DAHL, Robert A. (editor), 1966. *Political Oppositions in Western Democracies* (Yale University Press)

DENISON, Edward F., 1967. *Why Growth Rates Differ* (The Brookings Institution)

DEPARTMENT OF EMPLOYMENT, 1971. *Prices and Earnings in 1951–69: an Econometric Assessment* (HMSO)

DIAMOND, Lord (Chairman), 1975. *Report No. 1 of the Royal Commission on the Distribution of Income and Wealth,* Cmnd. 6171 (HMSO)

DONOVAN, Lord (Chairman), 1968. *Report of the Royal Commission on Trade Unions and Employer's Associations* (1965–1968), Cmnd. 3623 (HMSO)

DOW, J. C. R., 1964. *The Management of the British Economy 1945–60* (Cambridge University Press)

ENSOR, R. C. K., 1936. *England 1870–1914* (Oxford University Press)

FAY, Stephen and YOUNG, Hugo, 1976. 'The Fall of Heath', *The Sunday Times,* 22 and 29 February and 7 March 1976

FIELDS, D. B. and STANBURY, W. T., 1971. 'Income Taxes and Incentives to Work: Some Additional Empirical Evidence', *American Economic Review,* June 1971

FIGGURES, Sir Frank, 1974. *Problems of Managing an Incomes Policy* (Manchester Statistical Society)

FISK, Robert, 1975. *The Point of No Return* (André Deutsch)

FLEMING, J. Marcus, 1968. 'Targets and Instruments', *IMF Staff Papers,* 1968

FLEMMING, John *et al.,* 1976. *Catch '76?* (IEA)

FRIEDMAN, Milton, 1959. 'Monetary Theory and Policy', reprinted in Ball and Doyle (editors), *Inflation* (Penguin Books)

FRIEDMAN, Milton, 1968. 'Monetary Policy', *American Economic Review,* March 1968

GALBRAITH, J. K., 1958. *The Affluent Society* (Hamish Hamilton)

GLENNERSTER, Howard (editor), 1976. *Labour's Social Priorities* (Fabian Research Series 327)

GLYN, Andrew and SUTCLIFFE, Bob, 1972. *British Capitalism, Workers and the Profit Squeeze* (Penguin Books)

GODLEY, Wynne and CRIPPS, Francis, 1973. Article in *The Times,* 8 January 1973

GODLEY, Wynne, 1975. Evidence to the Public Expenditure Sub-committee of the Select Committee on Expenditure, 3 November 1975

GORDON WALKER, Patrick, 1972. *The Cabinet* (Fontana)

GRAHAM, Andrew, 1972. 'Industrial Policy' *in* Beckerman (editor) 1972

GRANT, R. M. and SHAW, G. K. (editors), 1975. *Current Issues in Economic Policy* (Philip Allan)

HACKETT, John and Anne-Marie, 1963. *Economic Planning in France* (Allen and Unwin)

HAGUE, D. C., OAKESHOTT, W. E. F. and STRAIN, A. A., 1974. *Devaluation and Pricing Decisions* (Allen and Unwin)

HANHAM, H. J., 1971. 'Opposition Techniques in British Politics' *in* Rodney Barker (editor) *Studies in Opposition,* 1971 (Macmillan)

HANSEN, Bent, 1969. *Fiscal Policy in Seven Countries 1955–65* (OECD)

HARDIE, Jeremy, 1972. 'Regional Policy' *in* Beckerman (editor), 1972

HARRIS, Ralph and SEWILL, Brendon, 1975. *British Economic Policy 1970–74: Two Views* (IEA)

HC, 1972. *Seventh Report from the Expenditure Committee,* Session 1971–72, HC 450 (HMSO)

HC, 1973. *Fifth Report from the Expenditure Committee,* Session 1972–73, HC 149, 15 February 1973 (HMSO)

HC, 1975. *The Financing of Public Expenditure:* Observations by the Treasury on the First Report of the Expenditure Committee, Session 1975–76, HC 178 (HMSO)

HEATH, C. G., 1971. *A Guide to the Industrial Relations Act 1971* (Sweet and Maxwell)

HECLO, Hugh and WILDAVSKY, Aaron, 1974. *The Private Government of Public Money* (Macmillan)

HEFFER, Eric, 1973. *The Class Struggle in Parliament* (Victor Gollancz)

HEMMING, M. F. W., 1963. 'The Regional Problem', *National Institute Economic Review,* August 1963

HENDERSON, P. D., 1954. 'Retrospect and Prospect: The Economic Survey 1954', *Bulletin of the Oxford Institute of Statistics,* 1954

HENDERSON, P. D. (editor), 1966. *Economic Growth in Britain* (Weidenfeld and Nicolson)

HEY, John D., 1975. 'Macroeconomic policy: formulation and implementation' *in* Grant and Shaw (editors), *Current Issues in Economic Policy* (Philip Allan)

HILL, T. P., 1964. 'Growth and Investment According to International Comparisons', *Economic Journal,* June 1964

HILTON, Kenneth and HEATHFIELD, David F. (editors), 1970. *The Econometric Study of the U.K.: Proceedings of the 1969 Southampton Conference on Short-Run Econometric Models of the U.K. Economy* (Macmillan)

HINDESS, Barry, 1971. *The Decline of Working Class Politics* (MacGibbon and Kee)

HIRSCH, Fred and HIGHAM, David, 1974. 'Floating Rates – Expectations and Experience', *Three Banks Review,* June 1974

HMG, 1944 (May). *Employment Policy,* Cmd. 6527 (HMSO)

HMG, 1961. *Control of Public Expenditure* (The Plowden Report), Cmnd. 1432 (HMSO)

HMG, 1964 (i). *Report of the Committee on Turnover Taxation* (Richardson Committee), Cmnd. 2300 (HMSO)

HMG, 1964 (ii). *The Economic Situation* (HMSO)

HMG, 1965 (April). *Prices and Incomes Policy,* Cmnd. 2639 (HMSO)

HMG, 1965 (Sept.). *The National Plan,* Cmnd. 2764 (HMSO)

HMG, 1966 (July). *Prices and Incomes Standstill,* Cmnd. 3073 (HMSO)

HMG, 1966 (Nov.). *Prices and Incomes Standstill: Period of Severe Restraint,* Cmnd. 3150 (HMSO)

HMG, 1967 (i). *Prices and Incomes Policy After 30 June 1967,* Cmnd. 3235 (HMSO)

HMG, 1967 (ii). *Nationalised Industries: A Review of Economic and Financial Objectives,* Cmnd. 3437 (HMSO)

HMG, 1969 (i). *In Place of Strife,* Cmnd. 3888 (HMSO)

HMG, 1969 (ii). *Productivity, Prices and Incomes Policy,* Cmnd. 4237 (HMSO)

HMG, 1970 (i). *The Reorganization of Central Government,* Cmnd. 4506 (HMSO)

HMG, 1970 (ii). *New Policies for Public Spending,* Cmnd. 4515 (HMSO)

HMG, 1971 (Jan.). *Public Expenditure 1969–70 to 1974–75,* Cmnd. 4578 (HMSO)

HMG, 1971 (Nov.). *Public Expenditure to 1975–76,* Cmnd. 4829 (HMSO)

HMG, 1972 (Dec.). *Public Expenditure to 1976–77,* Cmnd. 5178 (HMSO)

HMG, 1973 (Jan.). *The Programme for Controlling Inflation: The Second Stage,* Cmnd. 5205 (HMSO)

HMG, 1973 (Oct.). *Consultative Document on the Price and Pay Code,* Cmnd. 5444 (HMSO)

HMG, 1974 (Aug.). *The Regeneration of British Industry,* Cmnd. 5710 (HMSO)

HMG, 1975 (i). *Public Expenditure to 1978–79,* Cmnd. 5879 (HMSO)

HMG, 1975 (ii). *The Attack on Inflation,* Cmnd. 6151 (HMSO)

HMG, 1976. *Public Expenditure to 1979–80,* Cmnd. 6393 (HMSO)

HOBSBAWM, E. J., 1968. *Industry and Empire* (Weidenfeld and Nicolson)

HOWARD, Anthony and WEST, Richard, 1965. *The Making of the Prime Minister* (Jonathan Cape)

HUDSON INSTITUTE, 1974. *The United Kingdom in 1980* (Associated Business Programmes Ltd.)

HUGHES, Emrys, 1962. *Macmillan: Portrait of a Politician* (Allen and Unwin)

HUGHES, James J., 1972. 'The Role of Manpower Retraining Programmes: A Critical Look at Retraining in the United Kingdom', *British Journal of Industrial Relations,* 1972

HUTTON, J. P. and HARTLEY, K., 1966. 'The Selective Employment Tax and the Labour Market', *British Journal of Industrial Relations,* 1966

IEA, 1967. *Planning in Britain: the Experience of the 1960s* (Research Monograph 11)

IEA, 1972. *Inflation: Economy and Society* (IEA Readings 8)

IONESCU, Ghita and DE MADARIAGA, Isabel, 1972. *Opposition* (Penguin Books)

JACKSON, Dudley, TURNER, H. A. and WILKINSON, Frank, 1972. *Do Trade Unions Cause Inflation?* (Cambridge University Press, Occasional Paper 36)

JAY, Peter, 1976 (i). *A General Hypothesis of Employment, Inflation and Politics* (IEA)

JAY, Peter, 1976 (ii). Article in *The Times,* 15 April 1976

JENKINS, Peter, 1970. *The Battle of Downing Street* (Charles Knight and Co.)

JOHNSTON, J. and HENDERSON, Margaret, 1967. 'Assessing the effects of the import surcharge', *Manchester School of Economic and Social Studies,* May 1967

JONES, Aubrey, 1970. 'The Price of Prosperity' (*The Observer,* 1 November 1970)

JONES, Aubrey, 1973. *The New Inflation* (Penguin Books)

KAHN, Lord and POSNER, Michael, 1974 (i). 'Cambridge Economics and the Balance of Payments', *The Times,* 17 and 18 April 1974

KAHN, Lord and POSNER, Michael, 1974 (ii). Evidence to the Expenditure Committee, Ninth Report, *Public Expenditure, Inflation and the Balance of Payments,* Session 1974 (HMSO, HC 328, 30 July 1974)

KAHN-FREUND, Otto and HEPPLE, Bob, 1972. *Laws Against Strikes* (Fabian Research Series 305)

KALDOR, Nicholas, 1966. *Causes of the Slow Rate of Economic Growth of the United Kingdom* (Inaugural Lecture, Cambridge University Press)

KALDOR, Nicholas, 1971. 'Conflicts in National Economic Objectives', *Economic Journal,* March 1971

KENNEDY, M. C., 1969. 'How Well Does the National Institute Forecast?', *National Institute Economic Review,* November 1969

KENNEDY, M. C., 1973. 'Employment Policy: What Went Wrong?' *in* ROBINSON, Joan (editor), 1973, *After Keynes* (Blackwell)

KERR, *et al.,* 1966. *Beyond the Freeze: a Socialist Policy for Economic Growth*

KEYNES, J. M., 1936. *The General Theory of Employment, Interest and Money* (Macmillan)

KING, Cecil, 1972. *The Cecil King Diary 1965–1970* (Jonathan Cape)

KING, Cecil, 1975. *The Cecil King Diary 1970–1974* (Jonathan Cape)

KNAPP, J. and LOMAX, K., 1964. 'Britain's Growth Performance: the Enigma of the '50's' *Lloyds Bank Review,* October 1964

LABOUR PARTY, 1963. Report of the Sixty-second Annual Conference, 1963 (Transport House)

LABOUR PARTY, 1973. *Labour's Programme 1973* (Transport House)

LABOUR PARTY, 1976. *Labour's Programme 1976* (Transport House)

LAIDLER, David, 1973. 'Monetarist Policy, Prescriptions and their Background', *Manchester School of Economic and Social Studies,* March 1973

LAMFALUSSY, Alexandre, 1961. *Investment and Growth in Mature Economies* (Macmillan)

LAPPING, Brian, 1970. *The Labour Government 1964–70* (Penguin)

LCES, 1972. *The British Economy: Key Statistics 1900–1970*

LINDBECK, Assar, 1975. *Swedish Economic Policy* (Macmillan)

LIPSEY, R. G. and LANCASTER, K. J., 1956. 'The General Theory of Second Best', *Review of Economic Studies,* Vol. XXIV, 1956, No. 1

LIPSEY, R. G. and PARKIN, J. M., 1970. 'Incomes Policy: a Reappraisal', *Economica,* May 1970

LITTLE, I. M. D., 1964. Review of Dow, 1964, *Economic Journal,* December 1964

LUNDBERG, Erik, 1968. *Instability and Economic Growth* (Yale University Press)

McCRONE, Gavin, 1969. *Regional Policy in Britain* (Allen and Unwin)

McKENZIE, Robert T., 1958. *British Political Parties* (Heinemann)

MACLEOD, Iain, 1964. Review in *Spectator,* 17 January 1964

MACMILLAN, Harold, 1972. *Pointing the Way, 1959–61* (Macmillan)

MACMILLAN, Harold, 1973. Talk with Robert McKenzie, *The Listener,* 11 October 1973

MACPHERSON, H., 1971. Political Commentary, *Spectator,* 7 August 1971

MADDISON, Angus, 1964. *Economic Growth in the West* (Allen and Unwin)

MAJOR, R. L., and SURREY, M., 1970. 'Errors in National Institute Forecasts of the Balance of Payments', *National Institute Economic Review,* May 1970

MATTHEWS, R. C. O., 1968. 'Why Has Britain had Full Employment Since the War?', *Economic Journal,* September 1968

MEADOWS, D. L. *et al.,* 1972. *The Limits to Growth* (Earth Island Ltd. London)

MITCHELL, Joan, 1966. *Groundwork for Economic Planning* (Secker and Warburg)

MITCHELL, Joan, 1972. *The National Board for Prices and Incomes* (Secker and Warburg)

MOORE, B. and RHODES, J., 1973. 'Evaluating the Effects of British Regional Economic Policy', *Economic Journal,* March 1973

MUELLBAUER, J., 1974. 'Prices and Inequality: The United Kingdom Experience', *Economic Journal,* March 1974

NAIRN, Tom, 1973. *The Left Against Europe?* (Penguin Books)

NEDC, 1963 (i). *Growth of the U.K. Economy 1961–1966* (HMSO)

NEDC, 1963 (ii). *Conditions Favourable to Faster Growth* (HMSO)

NEDC, 1964. *The Growth of the Economy* (HMSO)

NEILD, Robert, 1964. 'Replacement Policy', *National Institute Economic Review,* November 1964

NEILD, Robert, 1974. Letter to *The Times,* 26 February 1974

NEILD, Robert and WARD, Terry, 1976. *The Budgetary Situation: An Appraisal* (Cambridge Department of Applied Economics) (summarized in *The Times,* 12 July 1976)

NIESR, 1972. 'The Effects of the Devaluation of 1967 on the Current Balance of Payments', *Economic Journal,* March 1972 (Supplement)

NOBAY, A. R., 1973. 'The Bank of England, Monetary Policy and Monetary Theory in the United Kingdom, 1951–71', *Manchester School of Economic and Social Studies,* March 1973

OECD. *Annual Economic Surveys of the United Kingdom*

OECD, 1966. *National Accounts Statistics, 1955–1964*

OECD, 1970 (i). *The Outlook for Economic Growth*

OECD, 1970 (ii). *The Growth of Output, 1960–80*

OECD, 1972. *Expenditure Trends in OECD Countries, 1960–1980*

OPIE, Roger, 1972. 'Economic Planning and Growth' *in* Beckerman (editor) 1972

PAIGE, D. C., 1961. 'Economic Growth – the Last 100 Years', *National Institute Economic Review,* July 1961

PAISH, F. W. and HENNESSY, J., 1964. *Policy for Incomes* (IEA)

PARKIN, Michael and SUMNER, Michael T. (editors), 1972. *Incomes Policy and Inflation* (Manchester University Press)

PAY BOARD, 1974 (Jan.). *Problems of Pay Relativities,* Cmnd. 5535 (HMSO)

PAY BOARD, 1974 (March). *Relative Pay of Mineworkers,* Cmnd. 5567 (HMSO)

PEP, 1960. *Growth in the British Economy* (Allen and Unwin)

PEP, 1968. *Economic Planning and Policies in Britain, France and Germany*

PEPPER, Gordon and THOMAS, Robert, 1972. 'Money and Economic Activity in the UK', *The Banker,* May 1972

PHELPS, E. S., 1967. 'Phillips Curves, Expectations of Inflation and Optimal Unemployment Over Time', *Economica,* August 1967

PHELPS, E. S., 1972. *Inflation Policy and Unemployment Theory: The Cost Benefit Approach to Monetary Planning* (Macmillan)

PHELPS BROWN, E. H., 1971 (i). 'Effects of the Industrial Relations Bill', *The Banker,* April 1971

PHELPS BROWN, E. H., 1971 (ii). *Collective Bargaining Reconsidered* (Stamp Memorial Lecture – University of London)

PHILLIPS, A. W., 1958. 'The Relationship between Unemployment and the Rate of Change of Money Wage Rates in the UK, 1861–1957', *Economica,* vol. 25, November 1958

PRICES AND INCOMES BOARD, 1968. *Third General Report,* Cmnd. 3715 (HMSO)

PRYKE, Richard, 1967. *Though Cowards Flinch: An Alternative Economic Policy* (MacGibbon and Kee)

READING, Brian, 1969. *In Place of Growth* (Conservative Political Centre)

REDDAWAY, W. B., 1968. *The Effects of U.K. Direct Investment Overseas: Final Report* (Cambridge University Press)

REDDAWAY, W. B., 1970. *Effects of the Selective Employment Tax. First Report – The Distributive Trades* (HMSO)

REDDAWAY, W. B., 1971. 'The Productivity Effects of Selective Employment Tax: A Reply by W. B. Reddaway', *National Institute Economic Review,* August 1971

RHODES JAMES, Robert, 1972. *Ambitions and Realities: British Politics 1964–1970* (Weidenfeld and Nicolson)

ROBINSON, Derek, 1972. 'Labour Market Policies' *in* Beckerman (editor) 1972

ROBINSON, Joan (editor), 1973. *After Keynes* (Blackwell)

ROSE, Richard, 1974. *The Problem of Party Government* (Macmillan)

ROWTHORN, R. E., 1975. 'What Remains of Kaldor's Law?', *Economic Journal,* March 1975

SARGENT, J. R., 1963. *Out of Stagnation* (Fabian Tract No. 343)

SEMPLE, M., 1975. 'The effect of changes in household composition on the distribution of income 1961–73', *Economic Trends*, December 1975

SHARP, Dame Evelyn, 1975. Interview in *The Sunday Times*, 5 October 1975

SHEPHERD, J. R., EVANS, H. D. and RILEY, C. J., 1974. *The Treasury Short Term Forecasting Model* (HMSO)

SIMPSON, R. C. and WOOD, J., 1973. *Industrial Relations and the 1971 Act* (Pitman)

SINGH, A. and WHITTINGTON, G., 1968. 'Growth, Profitability and Valuation', Cambridge Department of Applied Economics *Occasional Papers No. 7*

STAFFORD, G. B., 1970. 'Full Employment Since the War – Comment', *Economic Journal*, March 1970

STEWART, Michael, 1967 (2nd ed. 1972). *Keynes and After* (Pelican)

STEWART, Michael, 1972. 'The Distribution of Income' *in* Beckerman (editor) 1972

SURREY, M. J. C., 1971. *The Analysis and Forecasting of the British Economy* (Cambridge University Press)

TAYLOR, A. J. P., 1965. *English History 1914–1945* (Oxford University Press)

THEIL, Henri, 1964. *Optimal Decision Rules for Government and Industry* (North Holland Publishing Company)

THOMAS, Hugh (editor), 1968. *Crisis in the Civil Service* (Anthony Blond)

TINBERGEN, Jan, 1952. *On the Theory of Economic Policy* (North Holland Publishing Company)

TOBIN, James, 1964. 'Economic Growth as an Objective of Policy', *American Economic Review*, May 1964

TOWNSEND, Peter and BOSANQUET, Nicholas (editors) 1972. *Labour and Inequality* (Fabian Society)

TUC – LABOUR PARTY LIAISON COMMITTEE, 1973. *Economic Policy and the Cost of Living*, 28 February (Transport House)

VERDOORN, P. J., 1949. 'Fattori che regolano lo sviluppo della produttivita del lavoro', *L'Industria*, 1949

WALLIS, K. F., 1971. 'Wages, prices and incomes policy: some comments', *Economica*, August 1971

WHITLEY, J. D. and WORSWICK, G. D. N., 1971 (i). 'The Productivity Effects of Selective Employment Tax', *National Institute Economic Review*, May 1971

WHITLEY, J. D. and WORSWICK, G. D. N., 1971 (ii). 'The Productivity Effects of Selective Employment Tax. A Rejoinder', *National Institute Economic Review*, November 1971

WIGHAM, Eric, 1975. 'How the two-party system is thwarting progress in industrial relations', *The Times,* 6 May 1975

WILLIAMS, Marcia, 1972. *Inside Number 10* (Weidenfeld and Nicolson)

WILSON, Harold, 1971. *The Labour Government 1964–70, A Personal Record* (Weidenfeld and Nicolson and Michael Joseph). (Page references in text are to Pelican edition, 1974)

WILSON, Thomas, 1966. 'Instability and the Rate of Growth', *Lloyds Bank Review,* July 1966

WOOTTON, Barbara, 1974. *Incomes Policy: an Inquest and a Proposal* (Davis-Poynter)

WORSWICK, G. D. N. and ADY, P. H. (editors), 1952. *The British Economy 1945–50* (Oxford University Press)

WORSWICK, G. D. N. and ADY, P. H. (editors), 1962. *The British Economy in the 1950's* (Oxford University Press)

WORSWICK, G. D. N. and BLACKABY, F. T. (editors), 1974. *The Medium Term: Models of the British Economy* (Heinemann)

WORSWICK, G. D. N., 1974. Memoranda submitted to the Expenditure Committee, Ninth Report, *Public Expenditure, Inflation and the Balance of Payments,* Session 1974 (HMSO, HC 328, 30 July 1974)

WYATT, Woodrow, 1973. *Turn Again Westminster* (André Deutsch)

YOUNG, Stephen (with LOWE, A. V.), 1974. *Intervention in the Mixed Economy* (Croom Helm)

YOUNG, Wayland, 1963. *The Profumo Affair: Aspects of Conservatism* (Penguin Books)

ABBREVIATIONS

ASLEF Associated Society of Locomotive Engineers and Firemen
BIS Bank for International Settlements
CAP Common Agricultural Policy
CBI Confederation of British Industry
CEPG Cambridge Economic Policy Group
CPRS Central Policy Review Staff
CSO Central Statistical Office
DCE Domestic Credit Expansion
DEA Department of Economic Affairs
DE(P) Department of Employment (and Productivity)
DHSS Department of Health and Social Security
EDC Economic Development Council
EEC European Economic Community
EFTA European Free Trade Area
FBI Federation of British Industry
FIS Family Income Supplement
GAB General Arrangements to Borrow
GATT General Agreement on Tariffs and Trade
GDP Gross Domestic Product
GNP Gross National Product
HC House of Commons
HMG Her Majesty's Government
HP Hire Purchase
IBRD International Bank for Reconstruction and Development
IEA Institute of Economic Affairs
IMF International Monetary Fund
IRC Industrial Reorganization Corporation
LCES London and Cambridge Economic Service
NAFTA North Atlantic Free Trade Area
NBPI National Board for Prices and Incomes (Prices and Incomes Board)
NCB National Coal Board
NEB National Enterprise Board
NEDC National Economic Development Council
NEDO National Economic Development Office
NIER National Institute Economic Review
NIESR National Institute of Economic and Social Research
NIRC National Industrial Relations Court
NUM National Union of Mineworkers

NUR	National Union of Railwaymen
NUS	National Union of Seamen
OECD	Organization for Economic Co-operation and Development
OEEC	Organization for European Economic Co-operation
OPEC	Organization of Petroleum Exporting Countries
ORC	Opinion Research Centre
PESC	Public Expenditure Survey Committee
PIB	Prices and Incomes Board (National Board for Prices and Incomes)
PLP	Parliamentary Labour Party
PSBR	Public Sector Borrowing Requirement
REP	Regional Employment Premium
RPI	Retail Price Index
SET	Selective Employment Tax
TGWU	Transport and General Workers' Union
TUC	Trades Union Congress
UN	United Nations
VAT	Value Added Tax

STATISTICAL APPENDIX

For ease of reference, this appendix gives some of the most important economic series since 1960. Where the figures are in index number form, 1964 has been taken as 100. The main source is *Economic Trends*, June 1976, though for some of the earlier years use has been made of *Economic Trends, Annual Supplement 1975* and of LCES, *The British Economy: Key Statistics 1900–1970*.

	Real GDP[1]	Consumption[2]	Total Investment[3]	Manufacturing Investment[4]	Public Consumption[5]
1960	87.6	88.8	76.8	92.0	90.7
1961	89.9	90.8	84.4	109.3	94.0
1962	91.0	92.8	84.5	100.9	96.9
1963	94.5	96.8	85.6	88.5	98.5
1964	100.0	100.0	100.0	100.0	100.0
1965	102.9	101.5	104.7	110.6	102.7
1966	104.7	103.4	107.3	113.6	105.6
1967	106.9	105.4	116.3	111.3	111.5
1968	111.2	108.0	121.7	118.6	111.9
1969	113.2	108.4	121.9	126.7	110.1
1970	115.2	111.1	124.4	136.5	111.8
1971	117.2	114.4	126.6	127.5	115.1
1972	119.8	121.2	129.3	111.3	119.4
1973	126.2	126.7	132.7	119.4	124.3
1974	126.4	125.4	130.0	133.7	128.0
1975	124.2	125.0	129.4	115.9	132.2

(1) Gross domestic product at factor cost, 1970 prices, average estimate.
(2) Consumers' expenditure at 1970 market prices.
(3) Gross domestic fixed capital formation at 1970 market prices.
(4) Gross fixed investment in manufacturing industry at 1970 prices.
(5) Public authorities' current expenditure at 1970 market prices.

	Volume of exports[6]	Volume of imports[6]	Average earnings[7]	*Per cent change on previous year*	Prices[8]	*Per cent change on previous year*	Per cent unemployment[9]	Balance of payments current account £m.[10]
1960	87.4	84.7	(83)		88.1		1.5	−265
1961	90.3	83.8	(87)	*+5*	91.1	*+3.4*	1.4	− 4
1962	92.2	86.5	(90)	*+3*	95.0	*+4.3*	1.9	+112
1963	96.6	89.8	93.2	*+4*	96.9	*+2.0*	2.4	+114
1964	100.0	100.0	100.0	*+7.3*	100.0	*+3.2*	1.5	−355
1965	105.2	100.0	107.3	*+7.3*	104.8	*+4.8*	1.3	− 27
1966	109.3	101.9	114.5	*+6.7*	108.9	*+3.9*	1.4	+101
1967	107.9	110.3	118.6	*+3.6*	111.7	*+2.5*	2.2	−298
1968	121.1	121.3	127.8	*+7.8*	116.9	*+4.7*	2.3	−270
1969	132.3	121.9	138.0	*+8.0*	123.2	*+5.4*	2.3	+460
1970	136.8	129.0	154.6	*+12.1*	131.1	*+6.4*	2.5	+735
1971	146.0	134.5	172.0	*+11.3*	143.4	*+9.4*	3.3	+1,058
1972	145.8	150.1	194.3	*+13.0*	153.6	*+7.1*	3.6	+131
1973	166.6	172.8	220.4	*+13.4*	167.8	*+9.2*	2.6	−842
1974	178.0	174.5	259.1	*+17.5*	194.6	*+16.1*	2.5	−3,611
1975	170.9	162.1	328.3	*+26.7*	241.7	*+24.2*	3.9	−1,700

(6) On a balance of payments basis.

(7) Wages and salaries combined, all industries and services, Great Britain. January 1964 = 100. No comparable series exists before 1963; the figures in brackets are weekly wage rates of manual workers.

(8) Retail price index, all items; average for year.

(9) Percentage rate of unemployment, Great Britain, excluding school-leavers and adult students; average for year.

(10) These are the figures given in *Economic Trends*, June 1976, which in some cases represent substantial revisions of earlier estimates (see p. 146). Figures in the text differ from these figures when attention is being focused on the effect on policy of the figures believed at the time.

INDEX